Fantasy Literature
and Christianity

CRITICAL EXPLORATIONS IN SCIENCE FICTION AND FANTASY
(a series edited by Donald E. Palumbo and C.W. Sullivan III)
Earlier Works: www.mcfarlandpub.com
Recent Works: 37 *Lois McMaster Bujold: Essays* (ed. Janet Brennan Croft, 2013)
38 *Girls Transforming: Invisibility and Age-Shifting in Children's Fantasy Fiction Since the 1970s* (Sanna Lehtonen, 2013)
39 Doctor Who *in Time and Space: Essays* (ed. Gillian I. Leitch, 2013)
40 *The Worlds of* Farscape: *Essays* (ed. Sherry Ginn, 2013)
41 *Orbiting Ray Bradbury's Mars* (ed. Gloria McMillan, 2013)
42 *The Heritage of Heinlein* (Thomas D. Clareson and Joe Sanders, 2014)
43 *The Past That Might Have Been, the Future That May Come* (Lauren J. Lacey, 2014)
44 *Environments in Science Fiction: Essays* (ed. Susan M. Bernardo, 2014)
45 *Discworld and the Disciplines: Critical Approaches to the Terry Pratchett Works* (ed. Anne Hiebert Alton, William C. Spruiell, 2014)
46 *Nature and the Numinous in Mythopoeic Fantasy Literature* (Christopher Straw Brawley, 2014)
47 *J.R.R. Tolkien, Robert E. Howard and the Birth of Modern Fantasy* (Deke Parsons, 2014)
48 *The Monomyth in American Science Fiction Films* (Donald E. Palumbo, 2014)
49 *The Fantastic in Holocaust Literature and Film* (ed. Judith B. Kerman, John Edgar Browning, 2014)
50 Star Wars *in the Public Square* (Derek R. Sweet, 2016)
51 *An Asimov Companion* (Donald E. Palumbo, 2016)
52 *Michael Moorcock* (Mark Scroggins, 2016)
53 *The Last Midnight: Essays* (ed. Leisa A. Clark, Amanda Firestone, Mary F. Pharr, 2016)
54 *The Science Fiction Mythmakers: Religion, Science and Philosophy in Wells, Clarke, Dick and Herbert* (Jennifer Simkins, 2016)
55 *Gender and the Quest in British Science Fiction Television* (Tom Powers, 2016)
56 *Saving the World Through Science Fiction: James Gunn* (Michael R. Page, 2017)
57 *Wells Meets Deleuze* (Michael Starr, 2017)
58 *Science Fiction and Futurism: Their Terms and Ideas* (Ace G. Pilkington, 2017)
59 *Science Fiction in Classic Rock: Musical Explorations of Space, Technology and the Imagination, 1967–1982* (Robert McParland, 2017)
60 *Patricia A. McKillip and the Art of Fantasy World-Building* (Audrey Isabel Taylor, 2017)
61 *The Fabulous Journeys of* Alice *and* Pinocchio: *Exploring Their Parallel Worlds* (Laura Tosi with Peter Hunt, 2018)
62 *A* Dune *Companion: Characters, Places and Terms in Frank Herbert's Original Six Novels* (Donald E. Palumbo, 2018)
63 *Fantasy Literature and Christianity: A Study of the Mistborn, Coldfire, Fionavar Tapestry and Chronicles of Thomas Covenant Series* (Weronika Łaszkiewicz, 2018)
64 *The British Comic Invasion: Alan Moore, Warren Ellis, Grant Morrison and the Evolution of the American Style* (Jochen Ecke, 2019)
65 *The Archive Incarnate: The Embodiment and Transmission of Knowledge in Science Fiction* (Joseph Hurtgen, 2018)

Fantasy Literature and Christianity

A Study of the Mistborn, Coldfire, Fionavar Tapestry and Chronicles of Thomas Covenant Series

WERONIKA ŁASZKIEWICZ

CRITICAL EXPLORATIONS IN
SCIENCE FICTION AND FANTASY, 63

Series Editors Donald E. Palumbo *and* C.W. Sullivan III

McFarland & Company, Inc., Publishers
Jefferson, North Carolina

LIBRARY OF CONGRESS CATALOGUING-IN-PUBLICATION DATA

Names: Łaszkiewicz, Weronika, 1986– author.
Title: Fantasy literature and Christianity : a study of the Mistborn, Coldfire, Fionavar Tapestry and Chronicles of Thomas Covenant series / Weronika Łaszkiewicz.
Description: Jefferson, North Carolina : McFarland & Company, Inc., Publishers, 2018 | Series: Critical explorations in science fiction and fantasy ; 63 | Includes bibliographical references and index.
Identifiers: LCCN 2018042622 | ISBN 9781476671703 (softcover : acid free paper) ∞
Subjects: LCSH: Fantasy fiction, American—History and criticism. | Fantasy fiction, Canadian—History and criticism. | Christianity in literature. | Religion in literature.
Classification: LCC PS374.F27 L37 2018 | DDC 813/.0876609—dc23
LC record available at https://lccn.loc.gov/2018042622

BRITISH LIBRARY CATALOGUING DATA ARE AVAILABLE

ISBN (print) 978-1-4766-7170-3
ISBN (ebook) 8-1-4766-3483-8

© 2018 Weronika Łaszkiewicz. All rights reserved

No part of this book may be reproduced or transmitted in any form or by any means, electronic or mechanical, including photocopying or recording, or by any information storage and retrieval system, without permission in writing from the publisher.

Front cover image © 2018 iStock

Printed in the United States of America

McFarland & Company, Inc., Publishers
Box 611, Jefferson, North Carolina 28640
www.mcfarlandpub.com

To my grandmother, Mieczysława,
and
to my husband, Mariusz
—for their endless support

Acknowledgments

The following work is based on my Ph.D. dissertation, which was written under the supervision of Professor Zbigniew Maszewski and defended at the University of Białystok (Poland) in 2016. I would like to sincerely thank Professor Maszewski for his continuous support, patience, and invaluable advice. I would also like to thank Professor Andrzej Wicher and Professor Paweł Frelik, whose reviews of my dissertation allowed me to further improve my work. Thanks, as well, to the two anonymous readers who provided feedback on the first book draft. Last, but not least, I would like to thank my institution, the University of Białystok, for the funds thanks to which I was able to continue my research and complete this book.

It should be noted that some of the ideas developed in this book were first approached and tested in the following of my articles: "Finding God(s) in Fantasylands: Religious Ideas in Fantasy Literature" (*Crossroads. A Journal of English Studies*, 1/2013), "Phenomenology of Religion and the Study of Modern Fantasy Literature" (*Acta Neophilologica*, XVI (1), 2014), "Reinterpretacja chrześcijańskiego motywu ofiary i odrodzenia w cyklu *Fionavarski Gobelin* Guya Gavriela Kaya i *Trylogii Zimnego Ognia* Celii S. Friedman" (*Motywy religijne we współczesnej fantastyce* ["The Reinterpretation of the Christian Motif of Sacrifice and Rebirth in Guy Gavriel Kay's *Fionavar Tapestry* and Celia S. Friedman's *Coldfire Trilogy*." In *Religious Motifs in Contemporary Fantastic Literature*], eds. Mariusz M. Leś and Piotr Stasiewicz, Białystok: Wydawnictwo Uniwersytetu w Białymstoku, 2014), and "Benevolent and Malevolent Creatures in Guy Gavriel Kay's *Fionavar Tapestry*" (*Imaginary Creatures in Medieval and Modern Fantasy Literature*, ed. Łukasz Neubauer, Kraków: Libron, 2016).

Table of Contents

Acknowledgments	vi
Preface	1
Introduction	3

1 Religion in Modern Fantasy Literature—A Cross-Disciplinary Approach

Definitions and Classifications of Modern Fantasy Literature	9
The Influence of Myths on the Religious Aspects of Modern Fantasy	24
Phenomenology of Religion and the Study of Fantasy Literature	32
Christianity in Fantasy Literature—Recent Studies	42

2 The Christian Foundation of Stephen R. Donaldson's *The Chronicles of Thomas Covenant*

Introduction to The Chronicles	57
Images of the Numinous	61
The Numinous and Institutionalized Religion	65
Other Faces of the Numinous	69
Secondary Mythology, Instruments of Power, Sacred Places and Events	73
Biblical References in the Figure of Thomas Covenant, the Unbeliever	79
Christianity and Donaldson's Fictional Gods	82
Christian Undertones in the Selected Themes of The Chronicles	86
Christian Symbols and Language in The Chronicles	91

The Chronicles *and Christian Ethics*	96
Criticism of Institutional Religion	101
Stephen Donaldson and the Religious Dimensions of The Chronicles	103

3 Christianity as a Constituent of Religious Pluralism in Guy Gavriel Kay's *Fionavar Tapestry*

Introduction to The Fionavar Tapestry	107
Images of the Numinous	108
Other Faces of the Numinous	114
Religious Practices and Institutions in the World of Fionavar	117
The Protagonists' Experiences of the Numinous	120
Diversity in the Structures of Fionavar's Secondary Religions	123
Christianity and the Fionavarian Numinous	127
Biblical Motifs and Christian Ethics in The Fionavar Tapestry	129
Guy Gavriel Kay and the Religious Dimensions of The Fionavar Tapestry	133

4 The Fantastic (De-)Evolution of Christianity in Celia S. Friedman's *The Coldfire Trilogy*

Introduction to The Coldfire Trilogy	136
Images of the Numinous	138
The Church on Erna and other Religious Institutions	140
The Church on Erna and Christianity	145
Biblical References and Christian Morality in the Portrayal of the Protagonists	150
Coldfire *and the Motif of (Self-)Sacrifice*	155
Divine Grace and Salvation Through Faith	158
Celia S. Friedman and the Religious Dimensions of The Coldfire Trilogy	161

5 The Alternative Vision of Salvation Through Christ in Brandon Sanderson's *Mistborn* Series

Introduction to the Mistborn *Series*	164
Images of the Numinous	166
Religious Institutions and the Process of Religious Reformation	
Deification	175
Religious Pluralism in the Wax and Wayne *Series*	176

Christian Elements in the Portrayal of the Fictional Numinous   181
The Christ Figure and the Fictional Church   184
Christianity and Ascension to Godhood   188
Brandon Sanderson and the Religious Dimensions of the Mistborn Series   191

Conclusion   194
Chapter Notes   199
Works Cited   205
Index   211

Preface

The aim of this work is to investigate the representations of Christianity in American and Canadian fantasy novels and, in that way, contribute to the ongoing debate on the multifaceted relationship between Christianity and the fantasy genre. Since the majority of the available publications on fantasy and Christianity deal with the works of J.K. Rowling, J.R.R. Tolkien, C.S. Lewis, and Philip Pullman, to acknowledge other voices this volume analyzes a selection of works by North American fantasists: Stephen R. Donaldson's *Chronicles of Thomas Covenant*, Guy Gavriel Kay's *Fionavar Tapestry*, Celia S. Friedman's *Coldfire Trilogy*, and Brandon Sanderson's *Mistborn* series. The secondary religions appearing in these series are examined with the use of theories and methods offered by the phenomenology of religion—a discipline which is concerned with the study of existing religions, yet its approach can be modified to serve as a tool of literary criticism. A phenomenological approach facilitates a thorough investigation of fictional religions, which can be then followed by objective evaluation of the extent to which these fictional religions rework or are informed by biblical tradition, Christian theology, and Christian morality (or any other religious tradition).

This work is divided into five chapters. Chapter 1 discusses some theoretical aspects of fantasy literature, introduces the methodology of the study, and investigates a selection of critical works which have examined both the Christian aspects of contemporary fantasy fiction and the presence of the fantastic within the Bible. Chapters from 2 to 5 explore fantastic gods and religions appearing in the selected series, and evaluate their correlations with Christianity. The conclusion summarizes the ways in which the chosen novels address the topics of Christianity and religion, and offers some final remarks on the complex relationship between the fantasy genre and Christianity.

Introduction

In a way, everything started because of J.K. Rowling's *Harry Potter* series. Before Rowling's young wizard became an internationally recognized persona and children of all ages turned into voracious readers who impatiently awaited another installment of his adventures, the religious dimensions of modern fantasy literature had not been much of an issue. Of course, the topic was raised by academia, and occasionally a scholarly publication dealing with some religious or spiritual aspects of a given series would appear. But it was only after the commercial success of *Harry Potter* that readers and viewers of various backgrounds started to question the religious aspects of fantasy literature. The controversy surrounding *Harry Potter* soon evolved into an international debate which encompassed other prominent titles: C.S. Lewis's *The Chronicles of Narnia*, J.R.R. Tolkien's *The Lord of the Rings*, and Philip Pullman's *His Dark Materials*. Today, readers can choose from a variety of scholarly and popular publications dealing with the religious dimensions of the aforesaid titles. This does not mean, however, that the topic has been sufficiently researched.

First of all, the majority of the available publications deal with the works of Rowling, Tolkien, Lewis, and Pullman, who are either regarded as masters of the genre or whose popularity has been greatly enhanced by the success of the movies based on their works. Because other fantasists have received markedly less scholarly attention, there are still several aspects of the relationship between fantasy literature and religion that require investigation. Secondly, some of the available publications (particularly the non-academic ones) seem strongly affected by the authors' personal beliefs and feelings. Consequently, they run the risk of becoming either a devotional reading or a harsh critique of a chosen series. While in the case of the former, fragments of a fantasy novel might be exaggeratedly interpreted so that they will fit the proposed analysis (e.g., the stages of a hero's adventures are read in the context of some—apparently similar—episodes from the Bible), in the case of the latter, authors might become too serious in their condemnation of what is essentially a work of imagination (and argue, for instance, that fantasy literature is altogether inappropriate for Christian readers because of its portrayals of magic). Thirdly, some publications start with an unshaken conviction that a given fantasy novel is or is not entirely grounded in a particular religion (e.g., Christianity), and what follows is an analysis which almost unanimously supports the author's claim. As a result, such works do not explore in detail the imaginary gods and religions that appear in the chosen narrative or explore them without consistent methodology (especially in the case of non-academic publications).

The following work has been created with the intention of contributing to the discourse on the relationship between modern fantasy literature and religion—and Christianity in particular. The scope of the study was narrowed down to Christianity and to American and Canadian fantasy fiction for several reasons. Christian authorities (be they Catholic, Protestant, Anglican or other) have been particularly strongly involved in the debate on the religious and moral aspects of fantasy fiction, and the majority of the available publications on Tolkien, Lewis, Rowling, and Pullman analyze their novels from a Christian perspective. Thus, the following book will become a part of the ongoing and still very lively debate on the representations of Christianity within modern fantasy.

As far as the issue of nationality is concerned, the fantasists whose works have so far dominated the discourse on the religious aspects of fantasy—Tolkien, Lewis, Rowling, Pullman—are all British; hence there is a demand for a critical work which would provide a cross-sectional research on fantasists from a different literary tradition. Thus, the following book focuses on a selection of works by North American writers (listed chronologically): Stephen R. Donaldson's *Chronicles of Thomas Covenant*, Guy Gavriel Kay's *Fionavar Tapestry*, Celia S. Friedman's *Coldfire Trilogy*, and Brandon Sanderson's *Mistborn* series. These works have been chosen for analysis because, first of all, they present complex secondary (i.e., fantastic) religions which significantly affect the state of their imaginary worlds and the actions of their heroes. Two other criteria for such a choice were the subgenre of fantasy literature and date of publication. All of the chosen works represent the subgenre of high/epic fantasy in which the plot is set entirely or primarily in a full-fledged secondary realm. Though other subgenres of fantasy fiction also incorporate references to Christianity or deal with issues related to faith, the following study focuses mainly on the analysis of those purely fantastic deities and religions invented by the writers, in order to examine how Christianity is incorporated into a fantastic world and creatively reconstructed.

As far as the date of publication is concerned, the chosen series represent a spectrum of several decades: Donaldson's *Chronicles of Thomas Covenant* were published between the years 1977 and 2013, Kay's *Fionavar Tapestry*—1984–1986, Friedman's *Coldfire Trilogy*—1991–1995, and Sanderson's *Mistborn*—2006–2016. Works published earlier than the 1980s (with the exception of the first part of Donaldson's *Chronicles*) were not chosen, because of the state of the development of high/epic fantasy in the United States and Canada. In the U.S., the beginning of the second half of the 20th century was dominated by Tolkien's influence over the evolving genre and only after some time were American fantasists able to learn from Tolkien's success and create their own original fantasies. It is Ursula K. Le Guin's *Earthsea* cycle (1968–2001) that is often considered the first example of an original American epic fantasy after Tolkien. A limit in the timeline should therefore ensure that the American novels selected for this study display a greater variety of ideas and solutions, also in terms of their representations of Christianity, than some earlier works heavily influenced by Tolkien's conception of Middle-earth. In the case of Canada, the 1980s were a period of rapid development of Canadian fantasy literature; prior to Kay's *Fionavar Tapestry* there were hardly any other (if any at all) high/epic Canadian fantasy novels available. Though *The Fionavar Tapestry* is similar to Tolkien's *The Lord of the Rings* in many respects, Kay has his own ideas as far as imaginary religions are concerned, and approaches the topic of religion in an entirely different way than Tolkien. Another reason behind the proposed selection was the fact that in the 1980s and 1990s some fantasists consciously decided to interweave their imaginary worlds with Christianity in order to avoid the appropriation and exploitation of stories preserved by other cultures (Attebery 2014, 141). All in all, by analyzing a group of novels which spans almost four decades, the book accounts for the continuing presence of Christianity in American and Canadian fantasy literature.

This book consists of five chapters. Chapter 1 discusses the theoretical aspects of fantasy literature and introduces the methodology of the study. Part one indicates which definitions and categories of fantasy as a modern genre are applied in this study, and provides a brief summary of the genre's development in the United States and Canada. Part two focuses on the relationship between fantasy and myth, which conditions the genre's incorporation of mythological and religious motifs and patterns. This section refers to the scholarly works of Brian Attebery (the genre's exploitation of myth), Bogdan Trocha (the genre's degradation of myth), Joseph Campbell (the pattern of the monomyth), and Marek Oziewicz (the concept of a new mythology for a unified humanity). It also indicates how the category of myth can be applied to the Bible, in order to suggest that the research conducted by Attebery and other scholars pertains also to the genre's reconstruction of the biblical tradition. Part three discusses the key concepts of the phenomenology of religion as described in the works of Rudolf Otto, Gerardus van der Leeuw, and Mircea

Eliade, which serves as the axis for the proposed analysis. Though the phenomenology of religion is a discipline concerned with the study of existing religions, its approach can be modified to serve as a tool of literary criticism, as has been demonstrated by the research of Bogdan Trocha, Jolanta Łaba, and Chris Brawley, which is discussed further in Chapter 1. The final part of Chapter 1 focuses on a range of critical works which have dealt with some Christian aspects of fantasy fiction or explored the presence of the fantastic within the Bible. Though the former concentrate mostly on the works of Tolkien, Lewis, Rowling, and Pullman, many of their remarks pertain to the relationship between the fantasy genre and Christianity in general.

Following the rules of the phenomenological analysis, Chapters 2 through 5 focus on the works of individual writers in order to assess how the medium of fantasy fiction allows them to explore, question, or endorse Christianity. While these chapters can be read separately (e.g., readers interested in Sanderson alone need not read about the other writers to fully comprehend the analysis), Chapter 1 is recommended to all readers, because it contains an introduction to the phenomenological method.

Chapter 2 examines Stephen R. Donaldson's *Chronicles of Thomas Covenant*—a series of ten volumes in which Thomas Covenant, a modern American man afflicted with leprosy, is transported to a magical realm which he has to save from destruction. Covenant's rambling adventures allow Donaldson to showcase various aspects of his complex imaginary world, including fantastic gods and religions. Chapter 3 focuses on Guy Gavriel Kay's *Fionavar Tapestry* which features a group of modern Torontonians transported to the Kingdom of Brennin where they become involved in a cosmic conflict between gods. Kay's imaginary land abounds in gods, goddesses, and fantastic religions, which readers explore together with the protagonists. Chapter 4 analyzes Celia S. Friedman's *Coldfire Trilogy* which, set on a distant planet colonized by humans, follows the adventures of two men who struggle to save their world from an evil demon. Since one of the protagonists is a priest of the Church of the Unification of Human Faith and the other its ex–Prophet, the trilogy constantly revolves around the heroes' perception of faith and their relationship with the fictional religious institution. Chapter 5 deals with Brandon Sanderson's *Mistborn* series which is set in a theocratic empire tyrannized by the divine Lord Ruler whom the protagonists, a group of social outcasts, intend to overthrow. Unfortunately, their coup d'état liberates a malevolent deity who becomes an even greater threat to their world. Chapter 5 is followed by a conclusion, which summarizes the variety of ways in which the chosen works address Christianity, and provides some final remarks on the nature of the relationship between fantasy fiction, Christianity, and postmodern readers.

Two issues which are not addressed in this work are the internal divisions within Christianity and allegories. The main reference texts for the proposed analysis are the Old and the New Testament, complemented by some critical works on the biblical tradition and the relationship between religion and literature. Though my analysis does occasionally define some motifs or ideas as characteristic for the Catholic, Protestant, or Mormon Church, it does not explore the differences between various branches of Christianity because that would require in-depth theological study and could eventually raise questions about the status of various Christian denominations. Rather than delve into the meanders of Christian diversity and lose sight of the chosen subject, this work is written with the spirit of Global Christianity in mind, which promotes an inclusive approach to the heterogeneity of the Christian world. As David Chidester points out in *Christianity: A Global History* (2000), Christianity has become a global phenomenon whose variants can display "distinctive local features" (vii), which makes it difficult to provide a definition that is not restrictive. Likewise, in *The Next Christendom: The Coming of Global Christianity* (2011) Philip Jenkins states:

> Ever since the movement began two thousand years ago, the range of groups describing themselves as followers of Jesus has always been very diverse, and we should acknowledge and accept that broad range of self-conceptions. For the purposes of this book, a Christian is someone who describes him- or herself as Christian, who believes that Jesus is not merely a prophet or an exalted moral teacher, but in some unique sense the Son of God and the Messiah. Beyond that, we should not inquire into detailed doctrine, whether a person adheres to the Bible alone, accepts the Trinity, or has a literal belief in Jesus's bodily resurrection [111].

Similar premises have been adopted in the case of this work, because they allow to avoid the risky (and unnecessary here) task of passing judgment on Christian identity and membership. Since Christianity is not, and perhaps has never been, a monolithic entity, Jenkins, too, advises caution to anyone who wants to deliver any categorical definitions; the growing number of Christians in Africa and Latin America and the decline of Western/Catholic Christianity suggest that in the not that distant future "the phrase 'white Christian' may sound like a curious oxymoron" (Jenkins 3). It is difficult to talk about Christian identity even within North America alone, because North America, too, has had its share of doctrinal diversity. Consequently, in *American Christianities: A History of Dominance and Diversity* (2011) Catherine A. Brekus and W. Clark Gilpin opt for a similar solution as Jenkins: "Whatever else it involves, Christianity is a religion of redemption; it envisions a humanity that has 'fallen' from its proper place in the cosmos and must be saved from this fate by Jesus Christ and the redemptive community that extends his person and work through history—the church" (10). Though some scholars of religion might argue that such approaches are too broad and simplistic, in my work I would rather risk this than being judgmental and restrictive.

As for the notion of allegory, the chosen novels are not investigated in terms of their being allegorical reconstructions of Christianity. As Matthew Dickerson and David O'Hara explain in reference to C.S. Lewis's *The Chronicles of Narnia*, when readers focus on the series' allegorical aspect, they might disregard or miss its other connotations and possible ways of interpretation (59). Thus, rather than search for self-explanatory Christian allegories, the following study focuses on exploring the ways in which American and Canadian fantasists address and creatively reconstruct Christian tradition.

Modern fantasy is a powerful medium of expression because it allows fantasists to freely explore imaginary worlds and reconstruct old traditions in ways that are unattainable to mainstream literature. Readers of fantasy are, in turn, invited to question ideas which they have taken for granted and, in the case of religion, to reevaluate both their religious convictions and perception of faith. The fact that so many individuals and authorities have strongly defended or opposed the moral/religious messages conveyed by Tolkien's *The Lord of the Rings*, Rowling's *Harry Potter*, and Pullman's *His Dark Materials* proves that fantasy literature does have a significant influence over people's opinions and beliefs, and is therefore a force that should be reckoned with. This does not mean, however, that the genre, with its questioning and reconstructing of old traditions, stands in opposition to or is an adversary of Christianity or any other religion. In the preface to *Faith Journey Through Fantasy Lands* (2003), a volume which deals with *Harry Potter*, *Star Wars*, and *The Lord of the Rings*, Russell W. Dalton writes:

> This book advocates an approach that neither condemns these stories nor accepts them as gospel. Instead, it places these stories in a dialogue with the Christian faith, so that we can explore them and at the same time stay connected to our own faith traditions. This book explores today's fantasy stories as a way for Christians to reflect on their own faith journeys [ix].

If what Dalton says is true, as I believe it is, then accomplished fantasy novels can provoke readers to reassess their attitude to religion and, perhaps, to reestablish their connection with the sacred. That is why it is vital to conduct further research on the topic of Christianity and fantasy fiction, and objectively evaluate both the components of fantastic religions and the position of these religions within their respective imaginary worlds. Only such evaluations will allow us to fully comprehend the spiritual message hidden in a particular narrative.

1

Religion in Modern Fantasy Literature— A Cross-Disciplinary Approach

Definitions and Classifications of Modern Fantasy Literature

In *Fantasy: The Liberation of Imagination* (2002), Richard Mathews describes his research on the fantasy genre in the following way:

> Because of the oceanic scope of the subject and the nature of its revolutionary form, I have found my task to be like trying to grasp water. My hands sometimes come up wet or even dripping, but they are empty nonetheless. Beyond them I can see the oceans and unceasing waves, the rivers and white water, the transformations in the water cycle as dews evaporate and reform into mists [xii].

Mathews's metaphorical recapitulation of the scope of his research emphasizes the plurality and fluidity of forms adopted by the modern fantasy genre. Such a multitude of forms and lack of clear-cut boundaries are, on the one hand, very thought-provoking and offer scholars a greater degree of freedom in their exploration of the genre. On the other hand, the range of possibilities might discourage some researchers, because regardless of the scope of their work, they will always see numerous related, but still uninvestigated topics.

Another immediate result of fantasy's plurality is the number of its definitions which, among others, attempt to differentiate between three issues: fantasy as a synonym of human imagination in general, the notion of "the fantastic" identified in various texts not classified as part of the fantasy genre, and the fantasy genre *per se*. The first category denotes humankind's innate ability to fantasize and create stories; as such, this ability should not be treated as the domain of children or adults who wish to compensate for what they lack in real life. On the contrary, it is an extraordinary potential hidden in the human mind, which conditions the creation of any story, not exclusively fantasy fiction.

As far as the two other categories are concerned, a precise distinction between elements of "the fantastic" identified in various texts and the fantasy genre proper is crucial for understanding the genre's emergence in the middle of the 19th century and its subsequent development in the 20th century. The assumption that, since the times of antiquity, elements of the fantastic have continuously reappeared in various types of literature which cannot, by any stretch, be considered the fantasy genre proper, underlies the chronology of the genre's development provided by many scholars, including Mathews. Mathews's selection of works which contributed to the shaping of modern fantasy begins with *The Epic of Gilgamesh* (ca. 2000 BCE) and incorporates various texts from different countries, periods, and traditions, including Homer's *The Odyssey*, Valmiki's *Ramayana*, the Germanic *Nibelungenlied*, Dante Alighieri's *Divine Comedy*, the Welsh *Mabinogion*, Edmund Spenser's *The Faerie Queene*, John Milton's *Paradise Lost*, the Finnish *Kalevala*, Charles Dickens's *The Christmas Carol*, Carlo Collodi's *Pinocchio*, Carl Gustav Jung's *Psychology of the Unconscious*, Robert E. Howard's *Hour of the Dragon*, J.R.R. Tolkien's *The Hobbit*, Andre Norton's *Witch World*, Gabriel García Márquez's *One Hundred Years of Solitude*, and John Crowley's *Little, Big* (Mathews xv–xx), thus forming quite an eclectic compilation.

The issue of differentiating between the fantastic and the fantasy genre has been aptly resolved by Brian Attebery in *Strategies of Fantasy* (1992), in which the author delineates a distinction between fantasy as a literary mode, as a literary formula, and as a literary genre. According to Attebery, fantasy as a literary mode is "a vast subject, taking in all literary manifestations of the imagination's ability to soar above the merely possible" (1992, 2) and "a basic operation of narrative" (1992, 4). Such explanation not only corresponds to the definition of fantasy as the universal human ability to formulate stories, but also accounts for the presence of fantastic elements in world literature since *The Epic of Gilgamesh*. In fact, Attebery claims that, with the exception of a period from the middle of the 19th century to the middle of the 20th century, most literature incorporated elements of the fantastic (1992, 4). This claim can be understood on two levels. Firstly, various texts today not classified as fantasy fiction have frequently made use of fantastic elements, such as supernatural beings, magic items, otherworldly figures, etc., for diverse purposes. This point is aptly addressed by W.R. Irwin who states:

> Elements of the fantastic may be introduced, singly or in combination, into almost any form of imaginative literature from heroic epic to farce. It can have a place anywhere in the range from the remotest chivalric romance to immediately contemporaneous satire, from the sheerly entertaining to the purely didactic. […] Thus the fantastic is just as evident in the folk tale and the popular ballad as in the postrealistic fiction [8].

Secondly, Attebery's claim pertains to the ambiguous relationship between fantasy and realism/mimesis. Fantasy literature's supposed lack of realism (conditioned by the appearance of magic and the supernatural) has long been one of the main arguments against recognizing the genre's literary quality. Yet Attebery argues that fantasy and mimesis are not necessarily contradictory terms that must exclude one another. On the contrary, they coexist, because "there are no purely mimetic or fantastic works of fiction. Mimesis without fantasy would be nothing more but reporting one's perceptions of actual events. Fantasy without mimesis would be a purely artificial invention, without recognizable objects or actions" (1992, 3). In this sense, fantasy and mimesis can be perceived as indispensable components of any narrative, and they remain in a state of correlation, not contradiction.

Following Attebery's argument, opposite to the concept of fantasy as a literary mode is the concept of fantasy as a formula, embodied by mass-produced commercial fantasy fiction constructed on easily predictable themes and recurring patterns. Though, as Attebery contends, formulaic fantasy is able to provide a range of entertaining and amusing works (1992, 9), this generally intellectually non-demanding sort of fiction often offers very little in terms of literary quality. Between the notions of fantasy as a mode and as a formula rests the third definition of fantasy—as a separate genre which developed because the mode of the fantastic was gradually regulated by certain restrictions (Attebery 1992, 10). These restrictions include the setting and mood of *Märchen*, as well as patterns, structures, and vocabulary introduced by such writers as William Morris, George MacDonald, Lord Dunsany, and J.R.R. Tolkien (Attebery 1992, 10). Attebery argues that the concept of the fantasy genre is "a useful way of designating stories that are more alike than required by the mode, and yet less uniform than dictated by the formula" (1992, 11). All in all, Attebery's three definitions of fantasy—as a literary mode which employs fantastic elements in narratives not categorized as modern fantasy, as a set of predictable patterns in formulaic fantasy books, and as the modern genre whose development was heavily influenced by J.R.R. Tolkien—allow us to understand how these three notions are interrelated yet not synonymous. They explain why scholars of fantasy trace the beginning of the genre from the times of antiquity, and they also clarify why the "fantasy" of *The Odyssey* and of Andre Norton's *Witch World* are not of the same category.

This, however, does not resolve all problems, because the task of defining the fantasy genre proper is still further complicated by its contemporary multitude of forms. Ever since William Morris and George MacDonald published their first works in the middle of the 19th century (thus initiating the development of modern fantasy), the genre has generated numerous subcategories which differ in narrative patterns and approaches to fantasy (and the publishing market with its many methods of advertising books has also added to the confusion surrounding the genre's terminology). This multitude of forms has inspired various scholarly classifications of the genre's internal structure, e.g., John H. Timmerman's deconstruction of fantasy fiction into six generic traits, Lisa Tuttle's list of subgenres based on their diverse heroes, themes, and moods, and Farah Mendlesohn's division of fantasy fiction informed by the ways in which fantastic elements and events are introduced into the fictional worlds.[1] Since this book deals with a specific subgenre of fantasy fiction—high/epic fantasy—let us briefly focus on this category alone.

Lying at the heart of the genre, high/epic fantasy has acquired several definitions which emphasize its different aspects. In fact, even the name itself can differ depending on the source consulted, though the modification of the name does not seem to entail any radical changes in the definition itself. For instance, *The Encyclopedia of Fantasy* (1997) describes high fantasy novels as "[f]antasies set in Otherworlds, specifically Secondary Worlds, [...] which deal with matters affecting the destiny of those worlds" (Clute and Grant 466). All elements mentioned in this brief definition appear also in that of "epic fantasy" which is, however, listed as a separate entry (Clute and Grant 319). Perhaps recognizing this redundancy of terms, in *Writing Fantasy and Science Fiction* (2005) Lisa Tuttle combines the two categories in question and writes about high/epic fantasy, which she defines as being longer than heroic fantasy (which typically operates with the pattern of a traditional quest-adventure like, e.g., the *Conan* series by Robert E. Howard) and having a greater range of prominent characters (10–13). However, in Brian Stableford's *Historical Dictionary of Fantasy Literature*, also published in 2005, epic fantasy and high fantasy are again separated. The former Stableford describes as characterized by vast and complex secondary worlds developed in multivolume series (130–131), whereas the latter is defined mostly by statements specifying what is not considered high fantasy (198). Stableford ends the definition of high fantasy by declaring: "The term never thrived, partly because it was difficult to establish dividing lines between high fantasy and some of these other subgenres, and partly because of the difficulty of accommodating portal fantasies to the scheme" (198). Yet the results produced by Internet search engines prove that the name is very much in use as far as fans and readers of fantasy fiction are concerned.

For the sake of this work, high/epic fantasy is defined as a category of fantasy fiction, which typically revolves around a hero or group of heroes inhabiting or temporarily visiting a full-fledged secondary reality, i.e., an imaginary world, equipped with fantastic countries, languages, cultures, maps, creatures, and religions. The heroes of high/epic fantasy are usually involved in a cosmic battle against an evil force, with the safety and future of the imaginary realm at stake. The plot might consist of several minor quests and adventures, which ultimately lead the heroes to their final goal. A prototypical example is therefore J.R.R. Tolkien's *The Lord of the Rings*.

It should be noted that some classifications of fantasy fiction include also the categories of religious fantasy and Christian fantasy. However, their definitions are even more ambiguous than those of high/epic fantasy. For instance, *The Encyclopedia of Fantasy* provides an entry only on Christian fantasy, which the authors describe as a literary category connected to allegory and religious propaganda, and encompassing Dante's *Divine Comedy*, Milton's *Paradise Lost*, and John Bunyan's *The Pilgrim's Progress*, as well as the works of G.K. Chesterton and C.S. Lewis (191). Tuttle's division includes neither religious nor Christian fantasy, whereas Stableford's *Dictionary* describes both. While his definition of Christian fantasy is similar to the one appearing in *The Encyclopedia*, he then describes religious fantasy as "an awkward category," because "religions embody items of belief that seem obviously fantastic to nonbelievers but are accepted as matters of faith by adherents" (345). In his rather brief entry on religious fantasy, Stableford mentions its inspirational and satirical aspects, and suggests that such texts may serve as a means of exploring religion; the category is exemplified by the works of C.S. Lewis and by G.P. Taylor's *Shadowmancer*. Yet another approach to Christian and religious fantasy is provided in *The Cambridge Companion to Fantasy Literature* (2012) edited by Edward James and Farah Mendlesohn. Recognizing the prominence of religious themes in modern fantasy fiction, Graham Sleight writes about the "fantasy of religion." Sleight defines a work from this subcategory as "a text that depicts or makes use of commonly understood religious tropes, but which recasts them in the context of additional fantastic narrative elements" (248). Some of these works, e.g., John Crowley's "Novelty" and James Morrow's *Only Begotten Daughter*, attempt to reconstruct Christianity by introducing unexpected twists into the biblical story and by describing their consequences. Some other works, e.g., G.K. Chesterton's *The Man Who Was Thursday* and Gene Wolfe's *The Book of the New Sun*, which retell the traditional biblical story in a fantastic setting, may offer some religious insights (Sleight 250). Sleight also acknowledges works that deal with other religions and traditions, for instance, Neil Gaiman's *American Gods* and *Anansi Boys*, which reconstruct elements from various world mythologies.

These and other attempts at defining religious/Christian fantasy again point to the genre's internal diversity and its lack of clear-cut boundaries. The topic of religious and Christian fantasy is discussed in more detail at the end of this chapter, together with an analysis of relevant scholarly publications (e.g., Colin Manlove's *Christian Fantasy*). At this point, suffice it to say that the high/epic fantasy series chosen for analysis in this book are also examples of religious/Christian fantasy, because all of them include complex secondary religions informed by Christian doctrines and biblical tradition, engage their heroes in quests strongly related to religion, and—by offering reconstructions of religious material—invite readers to pose questions about faith and religious commitment. While none of the chosen series could be described as pure allegory or religious propaganda, they do occasionally lean toward praising or criticizing certain aspects of religious/Christian practices and beliefs. Their praise and criticism are also discussed in the following chapters.

To complete this section on the definitions and classifications of the fantasy genre, it is worth pointing out that the genre's popularity is constantly growing, of course partly due to the growing popularity of movies, TV dramas, and games inspired by or set in fantastic worlds. It is truly remarkable that such a diversity and plurality of forms developed in less than two hundred years. Like Richard Mathews, most scholars who examine the development of modern fantasy focus—to implement Attebery's terminology—on a transition from fantasy as a literary mode to fantasy as a genre. Thus, they begin their study with ancient epics, move through medieval and Renaissance literature to the period of Enlightenment when fantasy was mostly abandoned in favor of the novel of Realism, then focus on its return during Romanticism, and finally reach the year 1856 in which William Morris published his first work and which is, therefore, frequently considered the beginning of modern fantasy in the English-speaking world. In Britain, the works of Morris, and also those of George MacDonald, became a wealthy repository of themes, motifs, and conventions for subsequent writers. Both Morris and MacDonald were very prolific writers. Though they frequently drew from different sources—Morris extensively borrowed from myths and medieval romances, while MacDonald focused on addressing Christian values—both produced texts which diverged from the novel of Realism and presented complex secondary worlds. The variety of their strategies and narrative structures eventually became the foundation for the present variety of modern fantasy, e.g., Morris's *The Earthly Paradise* (1868–1870) and *The Story of Sigurd the Volsung* (1877) are successful retellings of myths, his juxtaposition of the medieval and modern world in *A Dream of John Ball* (1888) is a predecessor of what Tuttle defines as time-slip fantasy, and his prose romance *The Wood Beyond the World* (1894) is a precursor of high/epic fantasy; MacDonald's highly acclaimed *Lilith* (1895) can be considered an example of Mendlesohn's portal-quest fantasy.

Among other works which further contributed to the genre's development in Britain were Lewis Carroll's *Alice in Wonderland* (1865) with its secondary reality full of amazing creatures and bizarre encounters, H. Rider Haggard's *King Solomon's Mines* (1885) featuring a hero's adventures in an unexplored region of Africa, which established the tradition of the "lost world" subgenre, Bram Stoker's *Dracula* (1897) which is a milestone in literature about vampires, Lord Dunsany's *The Gods of Pagana* (1905) with its pantheon of imaginary deities, and T.H. White's *The Sword in the Stone* (1938) which retells King Arthur's boyhood. Subsequent publications, most notably Tolkien's *The Hobbit* (1938) and *The Lord of the Rings* (1954–1955), and Lewis's *The Chronicles of Narnia* (1950–1956), became prototypical examples of modern fantasy and dictated the rules of the genre's development for many years. While Tolkien's works were strongly inspired by those of Morris and MacDonald, he, in turn, had a great impact on the shaping of both American and Canadian fantasy.

Similar to the development of British fantasy fiction, the emergence of the fantasy genre in the United States was preceded by a transitional period during which fantasy functioned mostly as a literary mode. Between the 17th and 19th century, fantastic elements appeared in texts representing various literary categories in which they served diverse purposes. From the religious writings of the Puritans fraught with the menace of demons and witches, to the modernist stories of Henry James filled with some undefined ghostly presence, American authors used motifs which balanced on the border of the rational and the imaginary, which hinted at the existence of something supernatural, or which explicitly pertained to the realm of fairy tales and fantasy. It was the continuing presence of these motifs that opened new dimensions within American literature and eventually produced a background on which the American fantasy genre could emerge and crystallize into its present form. While the works of Morris and MacDonald signaled a breakthrough in British fantasy, L. Frank Baum's *The Wonderful Wizard of Oz* (1900)—with its intricate and marvelous parallel reality which is not rationalized as the protagonist's dream or madness—marked the beginning of American fantasy. As Attebery writes, "Baum proved, without doubt, that an American writer could write fantasy from American materials [...]. Even with his weaknesses, he is our Grimm and our Andersen, the man who introduced Americans to their own dreams" (1980, 107–108). *The Wonderful Wizard of Oz* was followed by several works which transported their heroes and readers to fairy realms, utopian civilizations, and lost worlds, as in, e.g., Eva Katharine Gibson's *Zauberlinda the Wise Witch* (1901), Jack London's *Before Adam* (1906) and *The Star Rover* (1915), Charlotte Perkins Gilman's *Herland* (1915), and Edgar Rice Burroughs's *A Princess of Mars* (1917). Though Gibson's work was heavily inspired by Baum's Oz and the works of London, Gilman, and Burroughs had rather little in common with modern fantasy fiction, their overall divergence from mainstream realism also contributed to the development of the American fantasy genre. Of particular significance was Burroughs's work, since the pattern established by him in *A Princess of Mars*—the adventures of a male hero who excels at fighting and wins the girl at the end of the story—became a prominent formula underlying, most notably, the works of Robert E. Howard. The barbarian warrior Conan, the most recognizable among Howard's heroes, made his first appearance in "The Phoenix on the Sword" (1932) published in *Weird Tales*, one of the many so-called pulp magazines which featured stories that were a mixture of fantasy, horror, mythology, and romance. The name of the magazine is connected with the subgenre called "weird fiction." Works categorized as weird fiction were published in the United States between the end of the 19th century and the 1930s; they were a blend of fantasy, horror, science, and the macabre. Paul Kincaid describes them as "a decidedly American form which owes an obvious debt to Poe's more outré mannerisms" (in James and Mendlesohn 44). Other notable works of weird fiction were Robert W. Chambers's collection of stories *The King in Yellow* (1895), A. Merritt's *The Moon Pool* (1919), and H.P. Lovecraft's "The Call of Cthulhu" (1928). Apart from *Weird Tales*, some of the most popular pulp magazines, which attracted writers of both fantasy and science fiction, were *The All-Story* (1906), *Astounding Stories* (1930), and *Strange Tales* (1931). Pulp magazines gradually lost popularity and ceased publishing during the 1940s and '50s, yet they left a significant heritage. Some of their stories were expanded and developed into multivolume series, which marked the beginning of a new trend in American fantasy fiction and later established one of its most recognizable subgenres: sword and sorcery. Because the storyline of sword and sorcery fantasy typically focused on a male warrior's quests and battles, it ran the risk of becoming formulaic and highly predictable. Nonetheless, since these tales were usually exclusively set in fantastic realms, secondary worlds ceased to be a feature of children's fairy stories (like Baum's Oz), and gradually became a valid component of texts aimed at adult readers.

Yet sword and sorcery fantasy was not the only type of fiction diverging from realism that was offered to American readers in the first half of the 20th century. James Branch Cabell published texts which either remain on the subtle border between the real world and a fantasy realm (*The Cream of the Jest*, 1917) or delve into an imaginary realm, but opt for a different sort of hero than the warrior male of sword and sorcery, as they interweave fantasy and legends with witty satire and philosophical disputes (*Biography of the Life of Manuel*, 1919–1929). James Thorne Smith also combined fantasy with reality, yet instead of inventing separate imaginary realms to which his heroes might be magically transported, he allows fantasy to manifest its presence in American towns and to affect the lives of average American citizens, which is the cause of many awkward, but amusing events (*Topper*, 1926; *The Stray Lamb*, 1929; *The Night Life of the Gods*, 1931). H.P. Lovecraft also inserts the supernatural into the ordinary world, but his fiction is grounded in the experience of "cosmic horror," i.e., the puny human mind cannot comprehend the nature of the monstrous deities from outer-spaces whom Lovecraft's heroes are constantly forced to encounter. Lovecraft's unmistakable style generated several imitators, and his Cthulhu Mythos (a term coined by August Derleth) became a prominent part of contemporary popular culture. Ray Bradbury found literary inspiration both in Lovecraft's terror, as well as in Burroughs's space adventures. While some of Bradbury's science fiction texts (*The Martian Chronicles*, 1950) are reminiscent of Burroughs's series about John Carter's adventures on Mars, his other works contain elements of fear and horror, which are, however, attached not to ancient deities that threaten humankind, but to everyday objects and events appearing in the lives of ordinary Americans (*Dandelion Wine*, 1957; *Something Wicked This Way Comes*, 1962). Alongside Howard's barbarian warriors, Lovecraft's ancient deities, and Bradbury's magical realism, James Thurber published fables and fantastic tales strongly inspired by fairytales and Baum's marvelous Oz (*Fables for Our Time and Famous Poems Illustrated*, 1940; *The White Deer*, 1945; *The 13 Clocks*, 1950).

Taking all of these works into consideration, the first half of the 20th century accommodated various types of fiction which either remained on the fluid border between fantasy and realism or explored downright fantastic realms. Yet, as Paul Kincaid explains, this multitude of conventions, styles, and subject matter could hardly be recognized as a separate genre, even less as a genre worthy of literary criticism (in James and Mendlesohn 48). By and large, Kincaid seems rather critical of the development of fantasy as an American genre between the years 1820 and 1950:

> Any attempt to identify a distinctively American characteristic in the fantasy of this period is doomed to fail. Many used the American landscape; a typical hero would represent the pragmatic, can-do attitude in which the country prided itself; fantasy would equally often chaff against the puritanical restrictions that are just as much a part of the American character; but none of these traits are invariably to be found, even in the work of just one author [in James and Mendlesohn 49].

Though Kincaid criticizes the inconsistency of the traits reappearing in early American fantasy, this inconsistency should be regarded rather as something positive, not negative. After all, the unspoken aim of the evolving genre was not to perfectly mirror the land or the nation, but to establish fantasy as an accepted form of literature, imbued with elements characteristic of the New World. Thus, there was no need for every fantastic story to begin in Kansas, no need for every hero to be pragmatic and bold, no need to explain everything with dreams, illusions or the character's madness. Such practices helped American readers place fantasy within the boundaries of their familiar world and accept it as yet another variety of adult literature. They were not meant to limit authors or turn their works into formulaic structures. Though many recurring motifs and patterns were generated, there was still enough creative space left for Howard to invent Conan, for Lovecraft to conceive Cthulhu, and for Cabell to envision the land of Poictesme.[2]

A major change in the development of the American fantasy genre occurred after Americans were introduced to Tolkien's Middle-earth. Attebery convincingly explains why *The Lord of the Rings* was so influential:

> It seemed on the one hand to sum up the whole Western tradition of the marvelous, with its echoes of Homer, Dante, and Wagner and its outright borrowings from the *Kalevala*, the Scandinavian Eddas, *Beowulf*, the *Mabinogion*, George MacDonald, and William Morris. On the other hand, the trilogy was an integrated story with a perception and a point of view that many readers found appropriate to the contemporary world [1980, 154].

After the publication of *The Lord of the Rings*, fantasists—particularly those writing high/epic fantasy—had to deal with Tolkien's legacy in one way or another. Among the most notable American writers in the second half of the 20th century were Andre Norton, Madeleine L'Engle, Lloyd Alexander, Peter S. Beagle, Ursula K. Le Guin, Terry Brooks, Roger Zelazny, Stephen R. Donaldson, Piers Anthony, Glen Cook, and David and Leigh Eddings. Their efforts and imagination produced an incredible gamut of works which secured the position of the fantasy genre within the literary tradition of the United States.

Many of the abovementioned authors tried their hand at writing high/epic fantasy. In fact, though high/epic fantasy runs the risk of being formulaic and Tolkien-dependent, it has proven to be the most popular and enduring subgenre in American fantasy of the late 20th and the beginning of the 21st century. What is more, several American high/epic fantasy novels have become popular worldwide, thus imprinting on the condition of the fantasy genre in general. Among the most acclaimed authors are Patricia McKillip with her *Riddle-Master* trilogy (1976–79), Raymond E. Feist with *The Riftwar Cycle* (1982–2013), Tad Williams with *Memory, Sorrow, and Thorn* (1988–94), Robert Jordan with *The Wheel of Time* (started in 1990 and finished in 2013 by Brandon Sanderson after Jordan's death), Terry Goodkind with *Sword of Truth* (1994–2014), George R.R. Martin with *A Song of Ice and Fire* (1996–present), and Christopher Paolini with *The Inheritance Cycle* (2002–2011). The popularity of these works has been greatly enhanced by television and cinema: the first volume of Paolini's *Inheritance Cycle*, *Eragon*, was adapted into a movie in 2006; Goodkind's *Sword of Truth* was turned into a TV series entitled *The Legend of the Seeker* (2008–2010); Martin's *A Song of Ice and Fire* is the basis for the immensely popular TV series entitled *Game of Thrones*, which premiered in 2011 and is still running; and the first season of *The Shannara Chronicles*, based on Terry Brooks's high/epic series, was aired in 2016. Given the success of these adaptations, as well as the success of Peter Jackson's screen versions of *The Hobbit* and *The Lord of the Rings*, it is not unlikely that other movies and TV series based on high/epic fantasies will follow.

The other subgenre which has recently dominated the American market of fantasy fiction is supernatural (paranormal) romance which combines a romantic storyline with elements of fantasy, horror, and the occult. This subgenre is targeted mostly at teenagers and young adults, and particularly at female readers. It is characterized by a modern-world setting which contains (though often hidden) areas of magic and the occult inhabited by an array of supernatural creatures, as well as strong-willed female protagonists who are falling in love with a supernatural male and combating evil forces, or doing both at the same time. The subgenre has flourished thanks to Stephenie Meyer's *Twilight* saga (2005–2008) and its subsequent movie adaptations. The idea of a romance between a mortal girl and a vampire has had a great influence on the tastes of readers all over the world. As a result, *Twilight*'s popularity has led to an increasing interest in the subgenres of supernatural romance and urban fantasy. Though many of these works lack literary quality, it should be acknowledged that they have successfully adapted the American landscape (including townscapes and cityscapes) and the lives of American citizens as the background for supernatural drama. In fact, the ease with which everyday America has been transformed into a scene for paranormal adventures, as well as the immense popularity of both high/epic fantasy and supernatural romance (and urban fantasy) among American readers of all ages, prove that fantasy has been successfully assimilated by American tastes and minds. Thus, it seems that what Ursula K. Le Guin wrote in her essay "Why Are Americans Afraid of Dragons?" (1974)—that given their Puritan work ethic and aim at success, Americans intensely disapprove of fantasy (34)—is no longer true in the 21st century.

As far as Canadian fantasy is concerned, the study of its historical development is complicated by factors which do not appear in the case of American fantasy. Firstly, to thoroughly analyze the Canadian transition from fantasy as a literary mode to fantasy as a genre, one would need to take into consideration both the English- and French-language texts that constitute Canadian literature. Only such investigation of Canada's bilingual heritage can account for the different manifestations of the fantastic in Canadian literature and for the varied purposes which these manifestations served in particular texts. Secondly, there is the problem of the genre's maturity. In comparison to British and American fantasy, Canadian fantasy literature is a relatively recent phenomenon, since its emergence can be traced back to the year 1984 and the publication of Guy Gavriel Kay's *The Summer Tree* (the first volume of *The Fionavar Tapestry*). Arguably, Kay's work—like *The Wonderful Wizard of Oz* in the United States—marked the beginning of a successful transition from fantasy as a literary mode to fantasy as a genre, and opened the Canadian market for fantasy literature. In *Canadian Fantasy and Science-Fiction Writers*, a volume published in 2002, Douglas Ivison writes: "Twenty, even ten, years ago it would have been impossible to assemble this book, for it has only been in the 1990s that Canadian science fiction and fantasy has reached the point where it could be identified as such" (xvii). Ivison's words confirm that Canadian fantasy literature—which he groups together with science fiction under the general name of speculative fiction, i.e., a broad literary category which encompasses texts operating with elements of fantasy, science fiction, and the supernatural—is a genre still relatively fresh and in-the-making. Thus, while critics can comment on the style of individual Canadian fantasists, they might find it difficult to talk about the characteristic features of Canadian fantasy in general, because the genre is barely more than three decades old. In fact, in *The Canadian Fantastic in Focus* (2015), Allan Weiss states that since David Ketterer's *Canadian Science Fiction and Fantasy* (1992) no attempt has been made at an extensive study of "Canadian fantastic," and that even Ketterer's work "is more a catalogue of what was published than an attempt at a broader synthesis" (3).

The third factor that complicates the study of Canadian fantasy is the question of the writers' nationality. Ivison's reference guide provides entries on thirty-eight authors (the oldest one born in 1833), yet the Canadian nationality of some is "disputable," because Ivison includes/excludes authors who have migrated to and from Canada. Ivison argues, for instance, that "American-born William Gibson is included by virtue of the fact that he has lived in Canada for his entire writing career, while a Canadian-born writer such as Gordon S. Dickson, who spent his entire adult life in the United States, is not" (xvii); he adds that his choice is grounded in "logistical reasons" (xvii). Though such a selection of writers makes the boundaries of Canadian fantasy somewhat obscure, Ivison is not alone in his method of categorization, because similar criteria of inclusion/exclusion have been applied to mainstream Canadian literature. In *A History of Canadian Literature* (2003), W.H. New writes: "'Canadian literature' is not bounded by citizenship (there were writers before there was a 'Canada,' and there have been immigrants and long-term visitors since, for whom Canada has been home). It is not restricted to Canadian settings" (4). In his work, New accounts for exiles and expatriates whose literary work is nonetheless connected with Canada, and distinguishes them from Canadian-born writers whose work displays little or no connection with their mother country (4). Taking these and other factors into consideration, he concludes that "definitions of a single Canadian identity are suspect. It is the cultural plurality inside the country that most fundamentally shapes the way Canadians define their political character, draw the dimensions of their literature, and voice their commitment to causes, institutions and individuality" (4).

Apart from the argument that the boundaries of Canadian literature are, in general, rather fluid, Ivison's inclusion of American-born writers in his reference guide might be justified by the historical connection between Canadian fantasists and the American market for fantasy fiction. According to Ivison, starting from the 1930s, many Canadian writers published mostly in American pulp magazines, and in the 1950s and 1960s "there was still no real SF scene in Canada" (xxi). Even Phyllis Gotlieb—who called herself "a Canadian poet and an American science fiction writer" (in Ketterer 1)—published her stories in American magazines. David Ketterer adds that in the 1970s, Canada still had neither a distinct tradition in science fiction writing nor a fantasy writer matching Gotlieb's achievement in the field of science fiction (1). One of the reasons behind the stagnation of Canadian fantasy might have been the writers' inability to find their own voice in the genre. Ketterer states that Canadian writers were originally not much into speculative fiction, because, on the one hand, it seemed an American product and, on the other, the English models of fantasy, e.g., *Alice in Wonderland* and *The Lord of the Rings*, "might have proved similarly offputting" (4).³

Arguably, the connection between Canadian and American fantasy literature can be extended even beyond the group of writers who are acknowledged in both countries and beyond the American pulp magazines in which authors of either nationality published extensively. Certain similarities appear also in the context of the Canadian and American transition from fantasy as a literary mode to fantasy as a genre. In *The Backwoods of Canada* (1836), Catharine Parr Traill describes her experience of settling in Canada and voices her opinion about the country's lack of the supernatural:

> As to ghosts or spirits they appear totally banished from Canada. This is too matter-of-fact a country for such supernaturals to visit. Here there are no historical associations, no legendary tales of those that came before us. Fancy would starve for lack of marvellous food to keep her alive in the backwoods. We have neither fay nor fairy, ghost nor bogle, satyr nor wood-nymph; our very forests disdain to shelter dryad or hamadryad [108].

Traill's comment about Canada being "too matter-of-fact" for the supernatural and marvelous preceded a similar statement made by Nathaniel Hawthorne about the United States. In *The Marble Faun* (1860), Hawthorne writes:

> No author, without a trial, can conceive of the difficulty of writing a romance about a country where there is no shadow, no antiquity, no mystery, no picturesque and gloomy wrong, nor anything but a commonplace prosperity, in broad and simple daylight, as is happily the case with my dear native land ["Preface," n.p.].

Thus, both Traill and Hawthorne express a similar dissatisfaction with their countries' apparent lack of marvels and mysterious shadows. While Hawthorne's pessimistic view was countered by writers who explored various dimensions of the fantastic (the menace of the supernatural, the motif of time travel, the vision of a utopian society, etc.), Traill's judgment was contested by both English- and French-Canadian authors who experimented with various fantastic motifs and diverged from mainstream realism. Their texts expedited the Canadian transition from fantasy as a literary mode to fantasy as a genre. As far as English-language texts are concerned, the transition was facilitated by James de Mille (*A Strange Manuscript Found in a Copper Cylinder*, 1888), Sir Charles D.G. Roberts (*In the Morning of Time*, 1922), Stephen Leacock (*Literary Lapses*, 1910; *Nonsense Novels*, 1911; *The Iron Man and the Tin Woman with Other Such Futurities*, 1929), Howard O'Hagan (*Tay John*, 1939), Gwendolyn MacEwen (*Julian the Magician*, 1963; *King of Egypt, King of Dreams*, 1971), and Timothy Findley (*Not Wanted on the Voyage*, 1984). As for French-language publications, Canadian fantasy is indebted to Philippe Ignace François Aubert de Gaspé (*L'Influence d'un livre*, 1837), Jules-Paul Tardivel (*Pour la patrie*, 1895), Georges Bugnet (*Siraf*, 1934), and Anne Hébert (*Les Enfants du sabbat*, 1975; *Héloïse*, 1980). When all of these English- and French-Canadian texts are taken into consideration, it becomes clear that from de Mille to Hébert, Canadian writers used the fantastic for diverse purposes: to generate utopias and lost worlds, to speculate about science and politics, to revisit history and fantasize about the future, and to question various aspects of the contemporary world, including religion. Thus, Canadian fantasy literature proper was preceded by a variety of texts which contributed to the genre's current multitude of forms and themes.

The 1980s was a period of rapid development of both Canadian fantasy and science fiction for several reasons. First of all, Kay's fantasy trilogy *The Fionavar Tapestry* (1984–1986) and William Gibson's science fiction novel *Neuromancer* (1984) achieved global recognition. Secondly, the growth of fan communities significantly strengthened the development of both genres (Weiss 7). Thirdly, publication of anthologies such as John Robert Colombo's *Other Canadas* (1979) and *Tesseracts* (first published by Judith Merril in 1985) made the genres available to a wider audience. Finally, some mainstream Canadian writers also began to use fantastic motifs in their fiction: for instance, in *The Handmaid's Tale* (1985), Margaret Atwood creates a dystopian society in which women are deprived of freedom and civil rights. The 1990s can be summarized as a period of further development and consolidation. Many Canadian authors became famous worldwide and their works began to achieve academic recognition. In 1992 Ketterer published his seminal work *Canadian Science Fiction and Fantasy*, probably the first in-depth study on the subject. It was because of these combined efforts of the writers, readers, and critics of Canadian fantasy and science fiction that in 2002, Ivison could write in the introduction to his reference guide:

> Whom to include in a volume such as this one, of course, is always a dilemma. That such a dilemma would have been nearly unimaginable only one or two decades ago is an exciting sign of the rapid development of Canadian SF from the occasional isolated story or novel, or sometimes writer, to a community and a tradition [xxvi].[4]

Among the most popular contemporary Canadian fantasists are R. Scott Bakker, Dave Duncan, Steven Erikson, Nalo Hopkinson, Tanya Huff, K.V. Johansen, and Charles de Lint, whose works represent a range of subgenres. Bakker has gained recognition as the author of *The Second Apocalypse* (2004–present)—a vast epic series which follows the unfolding of a Holy War in a world that is threatened by the return of a being known as No-God. Bakker's imaginary world of Eärwa is a complex creation consisting of various cultures, and his heroes display a psychological depth which many formulaic heroes of fantasy fiction lack. Duncan is one of Canada's most prolific writers of high/epic fantasy novels, in which he combines standard motifs and tropes (e.g., an orphaned stable-boy wins the princess) with reversals of the genre's clichés (e.g., one of his protagonists befriends a savage orc). Since his debut in 1986, he has published around a dozen series and standalone novels, many of which are set in his imaginary world of Pandemia. Erikson has become a global bestselling author thanks to his multivolume epic fantasy series *Malazan Book of the Fallen* (1999–2011) which describes centuries of war and political intrigue within the fictional Malazan Empire. Erikson has been praised for his extensive world-building which produced a realm steeped in fictional history and permeated by the sense of a past long gone, as well as for his detailed characterization, witty dialogues, and playful approach to standard formulas of fantasy fiction. In contrast to Bakker's, Duncan's, and Erikson's grand fantasy narratives which span several volumes, Hopkinson's fiction (*Brown Girl in the Ring*, 1998; *Midnight Robber*, 2000) explores an entirely different dimension of fantasy, inspired by her Afro-Jamaican roots and her position as a female writer of color. Hopkinson is a writer who uses fantasy fiction not to create extravagant fantastic adventures, but to explore themes of female empowerment, social injustice, connection between the past and present, and the struggle for happiness. The fantastic elements of her novels are rooted in African and Afro-Caribbean culture and folklore. Huff, another prominent female fantasist, is mostly known for her urban fantasy fiction which is characterized by a modern-day setting (typically a Canadian city) disrupted by the intrusion of magic and the supernatural, strong female protagonists who deal with the intrusion, and a romantic storyline which pairs off the female with a supernatural male (*Blood Books*, 1991–1997; *The Keeper's Chronicles*, 1998–2003). Huff has been praised for her gripping storytelling, her ability to interweave elements of science with magic, and her empowered female characters who are often a rarity in formulaic fantasy. Johansen is both an established author and scholar of fantasy literature. Apart from writing high/epic novels for both young and adult readers, she has published several articles and three books dealing with children's literature and fantasy fiction. Finally, de Lint, who has written dozens of novels and short stories since the beginning of his career in 1984, is regarded as one of the Canadian masters of fantasy. His works are categorized as a blend of urban fantasy, magical realism, and mythic fiction. They are often set in a fictional North American city called Newford, in which the real world and the supernatural meld, clash, or somehow coexist. They are also strongly inspired by Native American and European folklore, whose elements de Lint creatively reworks (e.g., in *Moonheart*, 1984; *Yarrow*, 1986; *The Wild Wood*, 1994; *Forests of the Heart*, 2000).

Given that Canadian fantasy literature proper began to emerge in the 1980s, it is a truly remarkable achievement that in such a short period of time it has developed into such a multitude of forms and generated so many internationally acclaimed authors. What is more, regardless of their early dependence on the American publishing market and external influences, Canadian fantasists have managed to discover their own individual voice and use the genre to address topics important for Canadian society and culture. According to Ivison, Canadian speculative fiction "is often concerned with isolation and survival; is less optimist about the virtues of technology; is often set against a northern, wilderness backdrop; is more interested in characterization; and is more concerned with literary quality than is American SF" (xxv). Given the Canadian experience of a vast, but sparsely populated wilderness and the country's different route to independence in comparison to the rebellious colonies of the United States, Ivison is right to single out isolation, survival, and wilderness as characteristic elements of Canadian fiction. Nonetheless, his claims that Canadian speculative fiction pays more attention to characterization and the quality of the prose are perhaps an exaggeration based on the fact that the American market for fantasy fiction has had more time to generate scores of writers who, alongside fantasists truly concerned about the literary quality of their texts, produce formulaic and derivative narratives modeled on books that have become bestsellers, in hopes of sharing their financial success. Inarguably, Canadian fantasy fiction does possess certain distinctive features which set it apart from American novels written in the same genre. Nonetheless, the diversity and originality of North American fantasy literature can be fully accounted for and appreciated only if both Canadian and American fantasists are given equal attention.

The Influence of Myths on the Religious Aspects of Modern Fantasy

Inarguably, the complex relationship between fantasy fiction and mythology has had a significant impact on the religious aspects of the genre. The nature of this relationship can be better grasped if we investigate two related issues: the genre's connection with ancient narratives and its reconstruction of mythological material. As far as the first issue is concerned, by establishing the genre's connection with texts of antiquity, scholars have indicated, first of all, that the modern genre did not appear out of nowhere, but was the product of complex transformations within world literature. Secondly, the connection between modern fantasy and antiquity is significant because ancient heroic epics and myths form a body of narratives which use various fantastic elements in order to represent religious concepts, address matters that transgress the boundaries of everyday existence, and create a link between humankind and the sacred. By means of fantastic personae and events, these narratives, which constituted a substantial part of ancient knowledge and beliefs, tried to answer questions about the nature of divinity, the origin of human life, and the point of death (Rabkin 7). The fantasy genre can, therefore, be perceived as a modern heir to that mythological tradition in which the fantastic was used to question the nature of the material and the spiritual world. Thirdly, myths and ancient heroic epics left a rich heritage of symbols, motifs, and patterns that the modern genre could incorporate, among them archetypes of questing heroes searching for magical artifacts and immortality, themes of comic struggles between men and gods, and images of ferocious monsters and grand battles. In time, these elements have become hallmarks of modern fantasy.

Contemporary fantasists consciously draw their inspiration from various mythological traditions and reconstruct ancient tales in their own narratives. Since they often do not (or cannot) erase the religious connotations of the motifs and symbols that they borrow, their inspiration from mythology and heroic epics is one of the reasons why modern fantasy fiction embraces a range of religious elements and ideas. Therefore, to fully evaluate the secondary religions and fictional gods appearing in the selected American and Canadian fantasy series, we need to identify not only their Christian components, but their mythological borrowings as well. Hence the necessity to investigate the multifaceted relationship between myth and the fantasy genre. The studies conducted by Bogdan Trocha, Brian Attebery, Joseph Campbell, and Marek Oziewicz are particularly helpful in this respect, because they highlight various aspects of the relationship in question.

In *Degradacja mitu w literaturze fantasy* [*The Degradation of Myth in Fantasy Literature*] (2009), Bogdan Trocha evaluates the extent to which fantasy fiction reworks mythological borrowings, particularly in the context of fictional religions. Trocha uses Rudolf Otto's concept of the numinous (Latin *numinosum*), Gerardus van der Leeuw's analysis of power and magic, and Mircea Eliade's distinction between the sacred (Lat. *sacrum*) and profane (Lat. *profanum*) in order to catalog and evaluate various elements that continuously reappear in fantasy fiction, but which originate from mythological sources. His research demonstrates how greatly fantasy literature and its fictional religions are indebted to mythological imagery.

First of all, by applying Otto's category of the numinous to the deities appearing in the secondary worlds of fantasy, Trocha is able to assess their attributes and position within the fictional universes, and analyze the inhabitants' attitudes to their gods. He then examines different components of fictional religions such as religious practices, figures responsible for addressing and manipulating otherworldly forces, artifacts endowed with power, journeys to the land of the dead, and all sorts of magic permeating the natural world (84–111). This investigation of the relationship between humanity and the divine is followed by a study of how the fictional numinous may manifest itself in imaginary worlds. Here the author refers to the categories of religious phenomena distinguished by Mircea Eliade, which illustrate how in different areas of the world people have related divinity to various parts of the natural environment, how they have adjusted their behavior according to their religious beliefs, and how all of that has affected their general understanding of such notions as life, death, and time. Trocha investigates the worlds of fantasy fiction in a similar manner, and explains how their inhabitants might associate the divine with the elements (earth, air, fire, water), parts of the natural world (minerals, metals, trees, plants, and animals), and fragments of the landscape (mines, caves, forests, or mountains). His research also accounts for various examples of secondary mythologies and beliefs, which condition the characters' understanding of their world as well as their choices and deeds (112–145).

Trocha does not simply catalog the range of mythological borrowings appearing within fantasy literature, but, more importantly, he analyzes the consequences of their presence in the genre. He claims that even though modern people live in a de-sacralized world in which the sphere of the sacred is dispersed, they may still preserve remnants of the sacred (in case a complete return to a life in *sacrum* is not possible). Preservation is possible when fragments of myths are assimilated by other structures, including fantasy literature. Such assimilation, however, has dual consequences. Because the preserved mythological elements can still interact with human consciousness, the demythologized modern world can be partially re-mythologized, and the sphere of the sacred can be retrieved. At the same time, incorporation into the structures of fantasy fiction contributes to further degradation, or at least distortion, of mythological elements, since they are isolated from their primary narratives (Trocha 8–14, 48–83). According to Trocha, this process of borrowing—or appropriation—is developed in several ways. The features of the mythological borrowing which the fantasist deems irrelevant for their work can be eliminated (the borrowing is shortened) or reduced (the borrowing is simplified and narrowed down to a few desired features). These features can also be condensed (so that the item introduced into the narrative consists of layers of borrowings) or transposed (features associated with one entity are bestowed onto another). Nevertheless, even such fragmentary borrowings can be useful to the writer's conception of an imaginary world, and then more or less skillfully woven into the narrative which further embellishes them with additional elements— the scholar employs the term "mythopoeic speculation" to define such literary reconstructions of mythological material (Trocha 197–213).[5]

Trocha was not the first scholar to notice the dual relationship between fantasy fiction and myths. In "Exploding the Monomyth: Myth and Fantasy in a Postmodern World" (2007), Brian Attebery suggests that in their pursuit of ideas which can complement their novels, fantasists commit the crime of cultural exploitation, because they remove mythological symbols, figures, and patterns from their original cultural background and from the society which preserved them (214–216). Nevertheless, even though fantasy literature, as Attebery argues, occasionally "shamefully exploits mythic traditions" (Attebery 209), it also allows modern people to preserve the remnants of their heritage.

While discussing the relationship between myth and modern fantasy, Attebery is particularly critical of the monomyth which Joseph Campbell identifies in mythological narratives and which can also be identified in some fantasy narratives. In his research, Campbell juxtaposes myths and beliefs of different traditions in order to indicate their shared themes and archetypes— the monomyth, i.e., the pattern of a hero's journey (developed in *The Hero with a Thousand Faces*, 1949)—as well as to uncover the existence of general truths disguised under mythological symbols. Campbell divides the monomyth into three main stages: departure (separation), initiation, and return, with each containing individual steps. In the stage of departure, the hero receives a call to adventure, meets a herald and/or a guide, leaves his/her community, and crosses the threshold between the realms of known and unknown (2004, 45–88). The stage of initiation involves several tasks and challenges which the hero must face and complete (often with some supernatural help), before s/he will be able to obtain the goal of the quest. This stage also provides the hero with experiences—e.g., of false death—that grant him/her greater wisdom about human existence, but also widen the gap between him/her and the original community (2004, 89–178). When the final goal is achieved, the hero has to return to his/her society to bring aid and share the gained wisdom. Campbell points out that at this stage the hero's spiritual transformation might be so advanced that s/he does not wish to return to the original society, or that even after returning to the community, the hero feels alienated from others by his/her otherworldly experiences. To acquire aid for the community is only one of the two goals of the monomyth; the other, more significant one, is the spiritual transformation that the hero undergoes during the quest, which allows him/her to ascend to a higher level of consciousness and existence.

Campbell's approach to myths through the prism of monomyth—and not only to myths since he claims that "there's a universally valid hero deed represented in the story of Jesus" (1991, 170)—has been criticized for exaggerating the similarities between various tales and failing to account for their differences. This line of accusation can be transferred onto the relationship between fantasy fiction and the monomyth. Myth-inspired fantasy, particularly high/epic fantasy, does emulate certain stages of the hero's journey. Examples have been identified within Tolkien's *The Lord of the Rings*, Robert Jordan's *The Wheel of Time*, or Ursula K. Le Guin's *Earthsea* cycle, in which the heroes are ripped away from a monotonous, but stable life, faced with several challenges, and offered spiritual development at the end of their quests. Attebery argues, and rightly so, that too much emphasis on the monomyth "encourages writers to mine various cultures for their fantastic motifs and to turn those motifs into formulaic fantasies," which is not something particularly desirable, neither from the standpoint of fantasy fiction nor of the cultures in question (2007, 209).

Campbell's other observations about the nature of myths can be applied to the structures of fantasy literature perhaps more successfully than the monomyth, and confirm the genre's position as heir to mythological tradition. Campbell outlined four major functions of myth (1991, 38–39): mystical, i.e., presenting the wonders and mysteries of the world; cosmological, i.e., providing explanation about the origins and nature of the world and the universe; sociological, i.e., establishing practices and beliefs that enhance social order; and pedagogical, i.e., showing the way to live a good life. It can be argued that, in its own ways, fantasy literature also functions within these four categories. Fantasy literature is mystical, because similarly to myths, which allow people to behold the wonders of their universe, it resorts to fantastic imagery in order to teach readers something about the beauty of their world. Fantasy literature is cosmological, because its secondary religions intend to explain the origins and nature of the (secondary) world and human life. It is sociological, because it teaches about rules and values which allow a person to properly function within a healthy society. Finally, it is pedagogical, because it promotes positive features of character and provides role models of appropriate behavior. All four functions are linked, if not directly with human religiousness, then with human spirituality. By offering visions of other worlds with their own gods, beliefs, and moral standards, fantasy—like myth—prompts readers to introspection and evaluation of both their perception of the world and their place in it. Finally, the genre's position as a successor to the traditions and functions ascribed to myth finds indirect support also in Campbell's remarks about the reconstruction of mythological material by new media of expression. Campbell argues that "unless the symbols, the metaphors, are kept alive by constant recreation through arts, the life just slips away from them" (1991, 73), and that "[t]he artist is the one who communicates myth for today" (1991, 122).[6]

Inarguably, fantasy fiction cannot replace myths because it preserves only their fragments and because myths are linked to ceremonies and rituals, which are the actual enactments of religious knowledge and beliefs. Nonetheless, Marek Oziewicz argues that fantasy literature can significantly alter modern people's mindset. In *One Earth, One People* (2008), Oziewicz discusses mythopoeic fantasy, i.e., a subgenre embedded in myth-making and operating with symbols and archetypes (84), established by the novels of Tolkien and C.S. Lewis, whose critical texts provide a theoretical background for understanding various aspects of mythopoeic fantasy: its secondary worlds immersed in morality, its incorporation of mythological patterns, and its relevance for human ethical and psychological dilemmas (66). Oziewicz believes that the emergence of mythopoeic fantasy in the 20th century is connected with the process of globalization, which has drastically affected the quality of people's lives. He argues that "the rise of fantasy in its mythopoeic variety must be linked with the disintegration of Western culture's common ground and with the onset of new challenges," such as nuclear and economic threats, which generate universal anxiety about the future (5). Mythopoeic fantasy, which addresses various issues related to morality and religion, might help people reflect on their heritage and spirituality, reshape their mindset, and instruct them on how to address their problems. Oziewicz also postulates that mythopoeic fantasy novels, e.g., the works of Ursula K. Le Guin, Lloyd Alexander, Madeleine L'Engle, and Orson Scott Card, whom he calls "modern myth-makers concerned with the well-being of our world" (117), explore "the components of a new mythology for a unified humanity" (7). This new mythology should highlight such issues as mutual respect and harmony between people of various races, denominations, and backgrounds, as well as the integration of past heritage with possibilities of the future (116–117). Thus, Oziewicz is not particularly concerned with the problems of appropriation and distortion emphasized by Attebery and Trocha. Instead, he highlights mythopoeic fantasy's (potentially) beneficial and restorative influence on human psychology and interrelations.

The novels of Donaldson, Kay, Friedman, and Sanderson chosen for this study can also be perceived as part of this grand process. First, the category of "mythopoeic fantasy" overlaps that of "high/epic fantasy."[7] Second, Oziewicz mentions religion as one of the issues addressed by the subgenre in question. Third, by presenting prominent fantastic religions inspired by existing systems of belief, Donaldson, Kay, Friedman, and Sanderson invite their readers to question and evaluate their own perception of and attitude toward religion. Such deliberation may results in one's reconnection with the sacred, and eventually lead to the restoration of the sacred in the modern world, which can also be a significant factor in the shaping of "the unified humanity" postulated by Oziewicz.

Trocha's, Attebery's, and Oziewicz's remarks on the relationship between fantasy and myth pertain not only to the ways in which the genre reconstructs Germanic or Celtic tales, but also to the ways in which it reworks the biblical tradition, since the category of "myth" can be applied to Christianity as well. Contrary to modern beliefs, myths should not be defined as fictitious ancient tales of gods and monsters, but as sacred stories which particular cultures use to preserve their religious knowledge. In *The Battle for God* (2001), Karen Armstrong explains that in antiquity people operated with two complementary modes of thinking and cognition: *mythos* and *logos* (xv–xviii). *Mythos*, rooted in the unconscious, was concerned with perennial questions about existence and meaning, whereas the rational *logos* focused on more pragmatic issues and scientific progress. Both modes offered a better understanding of humanity's existence and its relationship with the rest of the universe, yet in different spheres: the spiritual (psychological) and the empirical (physical). The stories related by *mythos* did not require tangible evidence: "To ask whether the Exodus from Egypt took place exactly as recounted in the Bible or to demand historical and scientific evidence to prove that it is factually true is to mistake the nature and purpose of this story. It is to confuse *mythos* with *logos*" (Armstrong 2001, xvi). As Armstrong points out, in the past people acknowledged the necessity of both modes of thinking, because these served distinct purposes: "A scientist could make things work more efficiently and discover wonderful new facts about the physical universe, but he could not explain the meaning of life" (2001, xvii). It was our modern world, infatuated with technology and science, that eventually elevated *logos* and rationalism over *mythos*—to its own detriment.

When we eliminate the negative connotations of the term "myth," it becomes clear why phenomenologists of religion pay similar attention to various tribal legends and Christian Scriptures (without diminishing the veracity of the latter) and why scholars of biblical studies are able to reconcile myth with Christianity. For instance, in *Slaying the Dragon: Mythmaking in the Biblical Tradition* (1992), Bernard F. Batto, who analyzes the origins and transformations of biblical texts, argues that "myth is one of the chief mediums by which biblical writers did their theologizing" (1). Scholars who advocate in favor of the historical literalism of the Bible would certainly not agree with Batto's perception of the Scriptures as myth. Yet Batto, like many other critics, is convinced that historical literalism was never of real concern for the authors/editors of the Bible—hence, for instance, the two creation stories present in Genesis: one describes God's work in the Garden of Eden, while the other focuses on the seven days of divine creation. As Batto points out, "The notion that something is true only if it is historically accurate is a prejudice we moderns inherited from our Enlightenment mentors. For P [the Priestly Writer] these primeval stories were vehicles that enabled one better to approach the *mysterium tremendum* of the divine" (99).

Likewise, scholars and writers of fantasy fiction have similarly reconciled the category of myth with Christianity, and related both to fantasy literature. Dickerson and O'Hara argue, for instance, that since Greek *muthologeuo* ("to mythologize") originally meant "to relate word-for-word" (32) and *phantasia* stood for "representation,"[8] both terms denote "*accurate representations or accounts of real things*" (50–51; italics in the original). It was the digitalized modern world that eventually turned the categories of myth and fantasy into amusing, but otherwise trivial concepts, which should not be applied to "serious" biblical studies. Dickerson and O'Hara mediate between these two notions—mythological and biblical—by describing three ways in which myth is present in the Bible (67–74). First, some biblical tales, such as the accounts of creation in Genesis or the conversations between God and Satan in the Book of Job, are purely mythic, because embedding them in a historical context is neither possible nor necessary. Second, the Bible contains historical tales, e.g., about Jesus' youth in the Gospel of Luke, in which verifiable context is significant—yet the stories are not completely devoid of mythos. Third, Dickerson and O'Hara introduce the concept of the "Grand Myth" and argue that "the whole Bible should be taken into account as speaking mythically, but not all parts of it in the same way" (70–71). This third category is the most potent one, because it accepts the different voices of biblical tales and unites them into a coherent yet complex whole whose main goal is to present religious truths and beliefs on several planes of understanding.

J.R.R. Tolkien likewise perceived myth as a category of Christianity, and argued then that fantasy can be a means to spiritual enlightenment. Tolkien expressed his ideas very clearly in a conversation with fellow writer C.S. Lewis, initially an agnostic fascinated with mythology, who cogitated whether the Christian God was the answer to his spiritual searching. In a moment of *status quo*, when Lewis struggled with the belief in Christ's death and resurrection, Tolkien, a devout Catholic, elaborated on the nature of myths and stories, and argued that by creating stories, i.e., by assuming the position of a creator in the process of sub-creation, a person can grasp some truth about the world, which has its source in God, because God is both the source of all Truth and the ultimate Truth. When Lewis accepted the idea that Christ's death and resurrection are part of a "true myth," i.e., a sacred story which really happened in the distant past, he was able to fully embrace Christianity and the worship of Jesus Christ (Carpenter 1995, 150–152). In an interview with Bill Moyers, Joseph Campbell voices a similar idea when he argues that myth is not as a lie, but "penultimate truth—penultimate because the ultimate cannot be put into words" (1991, 206). In fact, Tolkien and Campbell seem to be of one mind as far as Christianity and myth are concerned. Campbell so reminisces on his childhood: "I was brought up as a Roman Catholic. Now, one of the great advantages of being brought up a Roman Catholic is that you're taught to take myth seriously and to let it operate on your life and to live in terms of these mythic motifs" (1991, 12). Thus, it is clear that Campbell did not regard myth as something contradictory with Christianity.

Finally, one more compelling explanation of the prominence of myth within the Bible appears in Carlos Ruiz Zafón's[9] novel *The Angel's Game* (2008). Andreas Corelli commissions David Martín, the protagonist, to write a book that will allow him to create a new religion. Though Martín agrees to complete this task, he eventually realizes that he has no idea how to proceed with it. Because the variety of available religious theories and doctrines only confuses the writer, Corelli instructs him that religious texts are:

> all tales about characters who must confront life and overcome obstacles, figures setting off on a journey of spiritual enrichment through exploits and revelations. All holy books are, above all, great stories whose plots deal with the basic aspects of human nature, setting them within a particular moral context and a particular framework of supernatural dogmas. [...] From now on I'll ask you to start reading the stories of the Brothers Grimm, the tragedies of Aeschylus, the Ramayana or the Celtic legends [124].

But first of all, Corelli tells Martín that he should read the Bible, because it is "one of the greatest stories ever told" (123).

Every religion, Christianity including, operates through a sacred story—a myth—which unites believers separated by time and space. These myths can be transmitted into new media where they might become, as Trocha and Attebery claim, distorted and exploited by writers, yet they might as well reconnect readers with the sacred, re-mythologize the modern world and, as Oziewicz suggests, form a new mythology for the unified humanity. The analysis of the chosen fantasy series demonstrates whether their incorporation of biblical themes and motifs corresponds to any of the above claims, i.e., whether the chosen narratives distort and exploit the Christian tradition or whether they become a new medium for conveying Christian truths—a medium which can perhaps partially satiate the nostalgic longing diagnosed by Svetlana Boym in *The Future of Nostalgia* (2001):

> [m]odern nostalgia is a mourning for the impossibility of mythical return, for the loss of an enchanted world with clear borders and values; it could be a secular expression of a spiritual longing, a nostalgia for an absolute, a home that is both physical and spiritual, the edenic unity of time and space before entry into history [8].

Phenomenology of Religion and the Study of Fantasy Literature

Inarguably, the complex relationship between the fantasy genre and myths has significantly affected the shape of secondary religions which appear in contemporary fantasy fiction. Consequently, in order to study a given fantastic religion thoroughly, it becomes necessary to divide it into separate elements which should be analyzed in terms of their origin, content, and purpose. Only such analysis will determine to what extent a particular fantastic religion has been informed by the Christian tradition. For that reason, the methods used by the phenomenology of religion for analyzing the manifestations of the sacred in the real world (which henceforth is called "primary" in contrast to the secondary manifestations present in fantasy fiction) seem to be suitable for this study.

James L. Cox argues that the phenomenology of religion[10] has dominated religious studies for several decades and is still its prominent component (ix). Because Rudolf Otto and Gerardus van der Leeuw are two scholars whose works have made a lasting impression on the concepts and methods applied by phenomenologists, their works are used as the main point of reference. Though Otto's and van der Leeuw's studies are devoted to manifestations of the primary sacred and human experiences of it, their terminology can be successfully transmitted to the study of the secondary sacred manifested in fantasy literature. This has already been partially demonstrated by the works of Bogdan Trocha and another Polish scholar, Jolanta Łaba, as well as by Chris Brawley, whose research is discussed further in this chapter. The study of fantasy literature through the prism of Otto's and van der Leeuw's phenomenology is a fairly recent approach to the genre, hence it offers thought-provoking and inspiring readings of well-known texts.

In *The Idea of the Holy* (1917),[11] Rudolf Otto focuses primarily on analyzing people's experiences of the sacred (divinity), and their emotional responses to such experiences. Otto claims that rationality, logical thinking, and knowledge about the historical development of religions do not play a vital role in experiencing the sacred, because divinity is in itself an irrational entity. Otto does not negate the presence of rational elements inside religious systems, because, after all, every religion is a structure consisting of aims, values, principles, goals, and other constituents. Still, he cautions his readers: "it is salutary that we should be incited to notice that Religion is not exclusively contained and exhaustively comprised in any series of rational assertions" (4). The adjective "irrational" implies that religious experiences cannot be explained with logic or defined with generally understandable terms (hence they cannot be fully represented by any system). While logical thinking can help in contextualizing religion in the course of history, intuition and emotions are the channels through which people might experience that which is not directly available to their physical senses—the divine.

Observing that the words "holy" and "sacred" have become associated with absolute goodness (5–7), Otto invents the concept of "the numinous" (derived from Latin *numen* which means "a deity") which allows him to approach divinity in a different way. Otto understands the numinous (divinity) to be an inexplicable and unattainable entity which frightens people and fascinates them at the same time. The numinous cannot be defined as being either good or bad, because it may order people to perform both acceptable and unacceptable deeds: some of the examples provided by Otto are the Old Testament episodes in which God tests his chosen people (e.g., Abraham and Job), and the events of Jesus' suffering and subsequent rising from the dead in the New Testament (Otto 108–129). Otto argues that people can experience the numinous through their intuition and emotions, but cannot determine its nature through the logic of the mind (4–9). He insists, in fact, that rational attributes related to God are so far "from exhausting the idea of deity, that they in fact imply a non-rational or supra-rational Subject of which they are predicates" (2). Also, the numinous is constructed as a concept *a priori*, independent of history, culture, or institutionalized religion (Otto 116–120, 179–182). Since it might appear in every religion or be experienced by any individual, a hierarchy of religions is neither something possible nor desirable.

Having argued that the numinous can be experienced through emotions rather than the mind, Otto then extensively analyzes people's emotional reactions in response to the numinous. While initially he calls a person's reaction and attitude to divinity a "creature-consciousness or creaturefeeling"—"the emotion of a creature, abased and overwhelmed by its own nothingness in contrast to that which is supreme above all creatures" (10)—he then delves deeper into human psychology and proposes more specific categories associated with religious experience: *mysterium tremendum*, *majestas*, *fascinas*, and *augustum*. Otto argues that "the nature of the numinous can only be suggested by means of the special way in which it is reflected in the mind in terms of feeling" (12). In other words, human reaction to the numinous speaks not only about the emotional state of the individual in question, but simultaneously reveals something about the nature of the numinous.

The category of *mysterium tremendum* indicates that the numinous is a mysterious and frightening divine force, "the 'wholly other' [...] which is quite beyond the sphere of the usual, the intelligible, and the familiar" (Otto 26). Apart from wonder and astonishment, the presence of the numinous evokes limitless awe that verges on dread which is different from natural fear (Otto 12–13). Otto also insists that the encounter with that divine "Mystery" can be so overwhelming that "the soul, held speechless, trembles inwardly to the furthest fibre of its being" (17). *Majestas* refers to the staggering magnitude of the numinous, which evokes in those who witness the manifestation of the divine a sense of "absolute overpoweringness" and the "feeling of one's own abasement, of being but 'dust and ashes' and nothingness" (Otto 20). *Fascinas* indicates that in spite of their dread and feelings of abasement, people can be utterly enraptured by the numinous and drawn to its presence (Otto 31). The attribute *augustum* signifies a person's reverential submission to the tremendous subject of the numinous, through which the person acknowledges, with fearful awe, the supremacy and might of the divine (Otto 54). It is clear that the attributes designated by Otto are not clear-cut categories, but interrelated notions which describe different aspects of the same entity and experience. Otto explains that the numinous—this incomprehensible entity that eludes human reason and morality—can be directly experienced through prayers and holy scriptures, and more indirectly expressed through sacred images and miracles, which evoke numinous feelings (62–68).

Gerardus van der Leeuw's phenomenological research on the variety of human religious experiences is presented in a vast work entitled *Religion in Essence and Manifestation: A Study in Phenomenology* (1933).[12] Van der Leeuw defines a phenomenon as "an object related to a subject, and a subject related to an object; although this does not imply that the subject deals with or modifies the object in any way whatever, nor (conversely) that the object is somehow or other affected by the subject" (671). The scholar explains that a phenomenon's "entire essence is given in its 'appearance,' and its appearance to 'someone.' If (finally) this 'someone' begins to discuss what 'appears,' then phenomenology arises" (671). The goal of phenomenology of religion is to identify, name (e.g., a prayer, a savior, a myth), and describe various religious phenomena present in human life, which are manifestations of the human experience of the divine (van der Leeuw uses the term *homo religious* to describe people who cherish religious experiences and who wish for their lives to possess a religious depth). Successful identification, naming, and description of individual phenomena allows the researcher to grasp their objective meaning and, therefore, understand not only them, but the entire religion in question. Van der Leeuw points out that in order to attain full comprehension of the studied phenomena, the researcher "must withdraw to one side, and endeavour to observe what appears while adopting the attitude of intellectual suspense" (688). By "intellectual suspense" van der Leeuw understands the application of phenomenological epoché, i.e., aiming for comprehension not based on prior judgment or evaluation, but on the collected data. As in philosophical phenomenology, in the phenomenology of religion epoché allows the researcher to take his knowledge, presuppositions, and prejudices into "brackets" in order to minimize their influence on the object of the study.

While analyzing various manifestations of divinity, van der Leeuw introduces the categories of will, form, and name, which define a divine figure that possesses a will, a form, and a specific name. At the same time, van der Leeuw firmly states that God cannot be treated as the object of phenomenological analysis, because God is not a phenomenon and does not manifest in any way that would allow phenomenologists to analyze His nature or understand Him. The scholar contends that God is visible only through Revelation which he perceives as the domain of theology, not phenomenology. Theology and phenomenology are therefore two distinct disciplines (671–689).[13]

In his study of religious phenomena, van der Leeuw establishes diverse categories which constitute man's complex experience and perception of the sacred. First of all, divine powers and religious ideology can be related to elements of the natural world (e.g., stones, metals, mountains, trees, water, fire, sky, light, animals). Second, divine powers can be channeled through intermediary figures (e.g., kings, priests, prophets), embodied by the figure of a savior, and represented by otherworldly beings (e.g., demons, angels). People's attitudes toward the divine are conveyed through speech (words of devotion, prayers, promises, magical formulas, blessings, and curses), ceremonies, rites of passage, taboos, sacred scriptures and objects (tools, amulets, totems), as well as through the entire life of a family, society, and nation, which might adopt various attitudes to the divine—such as avoidance, servitude, covenant, and adoration (23–590).

Van der Leeuw's study of religious phenomena was further developed by Mircea Eliade whose analysis of diverse hierophanies, i.e., manifestations of the sacred, is complemented by his remarks on the position of the sacred in the modern world. In *Patterns in Comparative Religion* (1949),[14] Eliade investigates the spheres of the sacred and profane—two modes of human existence—respectively filled with or devoid of religious manifestations and experiences. Eliade perceives the sacred as a fluid sphere which is comprised of several elements, since divinity might be expressed through numerous symbols, myths, and ceremonies related to the sky, the sun, the moon, water, earth, stones, plants, trees, agriculture, hunting, sacred places, and sacred times (1996, 38–409). These representations vary across cultures, and Christianity is only one of the several forms of religious experience available. However, in contrast to other forms, Christianity has become universal, instead of remaining the property of a particular society or nation (1959, 136–137; 1971, 7–30).

In *The Sacred and the Profane: The Nature of Religion* (1957),[15] Eliade claims that modern society is unable to understand past concepts of the sacred. In fact, modern society might be living in a de-sacralized world altogether, because its perception of religion has been altered too greatly—and what was once part of the sacred has now become profane (1959, 12–13). Eliade is convinced that such a shift is detrimental for people, because a religious person, whose existence is submersed in the sacred, can shape his life according to the models provided by religious and mythic patterns. A non-religious person is devoid of such guidance. As a result, his/her actions are limited to the profane dimension of life and stripped of transcendent value. On the one hand, such people will not be able to enrich their spiritual life; they will only satisfy their everyday needs, which will eventually block them from fully realizing their potential. On the other hand, they are still the descendants of the people who were once immersed in the sacred, so even if they change their world into a de-sacralized one, they cannot completely eradicate the sacred from their life, but only strip it of meaning, secularize it, and forget about it. This conclusion leaves some hope for modern secular people, because the religious depth of life might still be retrieved. What is more, even an irreligious person might retain elements of the sacred in his/her life, though s/he might not be aware of their nature and presence, e.g., in the celebrations of marriage and birth (1959, 105, 202–205). In *Images and Symbols* (1952),[16] Eliade writes: "The progressive de-sacralisation of modern man has altered the content of his spiritual life without breaking the matrices of his imagination: a quantity of mythological litter still lingers in the ill-controlled zones of the mind" (1961, 18). These words are more than a suggestion that the mythological heritage lingering in the human mind can reappear in various forms of art and literature—including contemporary fantasy fiction.

Though the application of the phenomenology of religion to the study of fantasy literature is a fairly recent approach, the works of Otto, van der Leeuw, and Eliade contain statements which suggest that the scholars were aware of a connection between their concepts and the literary representations of the sacred. Otto, for instance, claims that the experience of the numinous is not entirely restricted to rituals and holy places, and that through the notion of the sublime, the numinous is present in such forms of art as architecture, music, and painting. In the case of literature, the mystery and allure of the numinous "became an untiring impulse, prompting to inexhaustible invention in folk-tale and myth, saga and legend [...] and remaining till to-day [...], whether in the form of narrative or sacrament, the most powerful factor that keeps the religious consciousness alive" (Otto 66). When commenting on the position of fairy stories, Otto concludes that "the fairy-story proper only comes into being with the element of the 'wonderful,' with miracle and miraculous events and consequences, i.e., by means of an infusion of the *numinous*. And the same holds good in an increased degree of *myth*" (126). For the purpose of my work these claims are particularly significant, because they presuppose that modern fantasy—as the descendant of myths and fairy tales—can also offer its readers an experience of the numinous through its encounters with fantastic gods and secondary religions.

Similarly to Otto, van der Leeuw accounts for the role of myths in the preservation of religious experience when he writes: "myth not only evokes or recalls some powerful [religious] event, but it also endows this with form" (414). Van der Leeuw also emphasizes the link between myths and fairy tales, and states that fairy tales "have deep significance not merely for the history of religion, since they contain much ancient religious material, but for religion itself also. Telling fairy tales is therefore no affair of pure delight in fabulous narration, but has a magical effect" (416). Thus, van der Leeuw's words indirectly confirm the claim that modern fantasy becomes infused with religious themes thanks to the manifestations of the sacred preserved in myths and fairy stories, whose structures the genre reworks.

A similar idea is expressed by Eliade who claims that "[a] whole volume could well be written on the myths of modern man, on the mythologies camouflaged in the plays that he enjoys, in the books that he reads" (1959, 205). Eliade argues that the sacred may appear in uncountable variants and forms, and he does not perceive any variant to be less important than the other. Instead, he prefers to regard the multitude of existing forms as complementary and providing equally significant insights (1971, 29–30). In view of this claim, fantasy literature can be recognized as yet another means for preserving the sacred expressed by myths, including Christian myths. Eliade declares that even if a myth's form changes, even if it acquires a new setting and other decorative elements characteristic for a new artistic form, the meaning and the value of the original patterns and archetypes are still preserved: "A myth may degenerate into an epic legend, a ballad or a romance [...] for all this, it loses neither its essence nor its significance" (1971, 431). What is more, Eliade argues that mythological symbols "never disappear from the *reality* of the psyche. The aspect of them may change, but their function remains the same; one has only to look behind their later masks" (1961, 16). These claims again indicate that fantasy fiction, which reconstructs mythological symbols and patterns, can be regarded as one of these "later masks" and as a repository of mythological and religious structures in the modern de-sacralized world.[17]

Phenomenology of religion has been applied to the study of fantasy fiction by two Polish scholars: Bogdan Trocha and Jolanta Łaba, and more recently by Chris Brawley in his *Nature and the Numinous in Mythopoeic Fantasy Literature* (2014). As the title suggests, Brawley focuses mainly on Otto's concept of the numinous, which he links with mythopoeic fantasy. Analyzing the works of, among others, Tolkien, Lewis, and Le Guin, Brawley claims that mythopoeic fantasy (with its reverence for the natural world) presents nature as a source of the numinous, i.e., as a space filled with otherworldly entities and as the subject of the characters' religious-like awe, fascination, and fear, which readers also get to experience indirectly through the act of reading. Such depictions of the natural world allow readers of mythopoeic fantasy to regain awareness of their surroundings, which will perhaps persuade them to curb the dominant anthropocentric perspective on the world. By analyzing selected fantasy narratives, Brawley illustrates the complexity of the relationship between their heroes, their imaginary lands, and their non-human inhabitants.

On the other hand, in *Idee religijne w literaturze fantasy* [*Religious Ideas in Fantasy Literature*], Łaba investigates selected novels for their secondary religions and the characters' responses to religion. By applying the concepts of phenomenology, she is able to identify the boundaries of the secondary sacred and provide examples of the heroes' religious experiences, which she then analyzes in order to comprehend the religious massage of a given narrative. Łaba's analysis is not concerned with judging the theological correctness of the identified images or with juxtaposing them against a particular denomination. Instead, she refers to Eliade's remarks on the life of *homo religiosus* and the degradation of the sacred in the modern world in order to indicate that the religious phenomena present in fantasy literature denote a constant human need for the divine, which the genre might—at least partially—satiate (13–21). Łaba limits her study to American and British narratives belonging to the categories of heroic/sword and sorcery fantasy written between the years 1930 and 1975, which she perceives, arguably, as the period of the genre's greatest development. Her selection encompasses the works of Robert E. Howard, Ursula K. Le Guin, Andre Norton, Roger Zelazny, Peter S. Beagle, J.R.R. Tolkien, and C.S. Lewis.

The first level of the secondary sacred identified by Łaba is related to power and magic, which presuppose the existence of a spiritual sphere that affects the heroes' moral choices and requires them to follow a particular code of behavior. In the worlds of fantasy, magical forces are often described by secondary myths, which provide additional explanation about the cosmology, theology, and philosophy of the imaginary universe. The act of acquiring power is often paired with the characters' spiritual growth and a transition from a profane life to a life engulfed by the sacred. The search for and later the possession of power frequently involve actions and behaviors of a religious nature: undergoing the rites of passage, participating in sacred rituals and ceremonies, encountering gods and supernatural creatures, gathering secret knowledge, entering sacred places, and following a set of coded rules. All these elements contribute to the experience of the divine (Otto's numinous). The heroes granted access to power are then elevated to a special status of wizards, mages, shamans, or priests. However, there is always the risk of corruption: the craving for power can become a character's obsession, and the acquired power is used egoistically. In the context of Christianity, the issue of magic and power might pose a problem, because magical powers are often inborn or obtained from the external world (e.g., through laborious studies), yet rarely do they have their source in God (41–78).

Another level of the sacred, according to Łaba, is evoked by the presence of mythological patterns—themes, symbols, archetypes—borrowed from various myths. One of the major mythological patterns ubiquitously present in fantasy fiction is the cosmic struggle between good and evil (paired with the quest motif), which usually entails difficult moral choices and personal sacrifices, but in return offers redemption and ascension to a higher status. Rites of passage also play a significant role, because they allow fantastic heroes to mature, acquire power, and become full members of their society. Łaba is convinced that the ubiquity of these and other mythological and religious patterns in fantasy fiction is indicatory of their strong presence in the minds of contemporary fantasists. Consequently, the act of reading fantasy novels can reinforce these patterns in the minds of readers (79–116).

Finally, Łaba argues that the fictional sacred is related to the literary heroes who are modeled on mythological figures of warriors, kings, and mages, and set on their quests by myths or prophecies. These heroes frequently operate within a frame of messianic ideology: they are the predestined saviors of a fantasy land, who will sacrifice their safety and life to overcome evil forces. The non-human heroes (giants, mermaids, dragons, etc.) are important as well, because they have their origins in various mythologies, introduce a dimension of otherworldliness, and point to an ancient past when humanity did not even exist in the secondary reality (Łaba 117–154). Timothy K. Beal contends that the appearance of a monster is frequently "a revelation of the holy," because the monster is "an envoy of the divine or the sacred as radically other than 'our' established order of things" (6). Deriving the word "monster" from Latin *monstrare* ("show" or "reveal") and *monere* ("warn" or "portend"), Beal argues that "a *monstrum* is a message that breaks into this world from the realm of the divine" (7). In fantasy fiction, monsters may also function as representatives or embodiments of the sacred, and any encounter with them becomes an encounter with the divine.

Taking everything into consideration, Łaba manages to successfully identify manifestations of the secondary sacred within the chosen fantastic worlds, which allows her to argue that fantasy literature has the potential of providing modern people with stories that they desire and need—i.e., stories in which good is confronted with evil, and characters deal with the mysteries of life and death. What is more, by providing a literary experience of the sacred, these stories, Łaba suggests, are able to restore people's connection with religion and make them aware of the sacred present, though perhaps neglected and marginalized, in the primary world (155–161).

One area of Łaba's research which would perhaps merit from a more detailed examination is her approach to phenomenological methodology, since her work seems to lack precise description of how the methods of phenomenological analysis can be applied to the study of the imaginary worlds of fantasy. To avoid similar imprecision in this book, it is necessary to recapitulate the main steps of the phenomenological method and to adapt them to the study of secondary religions. James L. Cox (48–72) outlines the principal stages of phenomenological research. First, Cox emphasizes the importance of epoché, both at the onset of the study and throughout it, because epoché limits the influences of the researcher's knowledge and emotions on the observed phenomena, and allows him to adopt a neutral approach to the object of his study (and avoid conversion to the religion he is analyzing). Emphatic attitude and the technique of interpolation enable the researcher to examine the elements of alien religious traditions and to translate them into (or, at least, relate them to) his own culture and cognition. A proper phenomenological analysis includes the stages of naming (classifying) individual phenomena (the act of naming does not evaluate, e.g., whether a prayer can really get a deity to respond, it only assigns names which distinguish one phenomenon from another), describing their properties and categories, and accounting for their mutual relations. It should also incorporate the stage of "making 'informed comparisons'" (Cox 62), i.e., the research conducted should juxtapose the studied phenomena and similar phenomena from other traditions, because "comparing the phenomena as they are understood and practised within different traditions enables the scholar to develop a statement of meaning regarding the core concern or overriding principle characteristic of any specific religious tradition" (Cox 62). In the end, once the researcher is able to comprehend the complexity of individual phenomena of a given religious tradition, he might then be able to grasp the nature of the entire tradition in question.

The phenomenological approach to the primary sacred can be easily adapted to the study of the secondary religions and manifestations of the divine appearing in fantasy literature.[18] Epoché, emphatic attitude, and interpolation allow a researcher to address the images of alien gods and concepts of fictional religions without bias or prejudice, and to provide their accurate and thorough descriptions. These descriptions should account for the names, properties, and inter-relations of particular religious phenomena, as well as for their position within the imaginary world conceived by the author, so that it will subsequently be possible to determine the nature of the fantastic religion in question. The stage of "making informed comparisons" is, in fact, the main goal of this book, because the identified secondary religions and manifestations of the divine are juxtaposed against the biblical tradition and Christianity theology. Such juxtaposition becomes the basis for determining the extent to which a particular series is inspired by the biblical tradition and Christian morality, and evaluating the degree to which the borrowed elements retain their original Christian connotations.

Arguably, applying the phenomenological method to literary studies can pose certain problems. First of all, phenomenologists conduct their work by interacting with a community whose religion is the object of their study; they observe the people's actions and evaluate the influence of religious beliefs over their behavior. In the case of literary studies, the acts of reading and exploring an imaginary world have to become an equivalent to the interaction with a chosen community. Assuming the role of a phenomenologist, a literary critic needs to be also an impartial observer of an alien (fantastic) community, whose task it is to extract and categorize fragmentary information pertaining to fantastic religions and their gods. While the phenomenologist might always ask members of the community for clarification, the literary critic has to rely solely on his own observations. Second, the concept of phenomenological epoché, be it in philosophy or religious studies, is frequently discarded on the grounds that a researcher can never completely separate himself from his preconceptions and previous experiences, which will inadvertently, but inevitably, influence the result of his research. Though a dose of skepticism toward the possibility of attaining full epoché is justifiable, it is pointless to argue that researchers can in no way temporarily withhold from previous assumptions and prejudice to produce unbiased verdicts, lest we should question the point of conducting any research altogether. Third, the phenomenological method emphasizes the necessity of thorough descriptions, which in literary studies can be regarded as attempts at summarizing the plot rather than at providing valuable criticism. Yet without the background of solid description behind every identified phenomena, the phenomenological analysis is not complete. Finally, phenomenology, whether as a study of religion or as philosophy associated with Edmund Husserl or Roman Ingarden, does not judge the object of the study for its merits or flaws. Instead, it focuses on analyzing the essence and nature of the manifestation. Some critics might argue that the novels chosen for analysis in this book are not of the highest literary quality or the best representatives of the fantasy genre. Nonetheless, these novels contain valuable material in terms of religious and cultural studies.

Christianity in Fantasy Literature—Recent Studies

This chapter has so far contrasted the notion of the fantasy genre with related terms, discussed the development of American and Canadian fantasy literature, investigated the relationship between fantasy and myth, analyzed the concepts of the phenomenology of religion, and presented them as applicable to the study of fantasy fiction. In order to complete the theoretical background for the analysis of the selected novels, it is vital to investigate the relationship between the fantastic, fantasy literature, and Christianity, and to summarize some recent studies which have examined this relationship. The majority of these studies are focused on the works of British writers (J.R.R. Tolkien, C.S. Lewis, Philip Pullman, J.K. Rowling), whose popularity—particularly in the case of Tolkien and Rowling—has soared due to the success of movies based on their books, and generated debates on the moral and religious dimensions of fantasy fiction. Though these debates concentrate on British works, their remarks pertain to the relationship between fantasy and Christianity in general. Thus, it is worth recalling some of their key arguments, particularly since there are significantly fewer critical works devoted to the secondary religions of American and Canadian fantasy.

"Literature and religion lie at the very roots of culture" (xi)—write Robert Detweiler and David Jasper to underline the extent to which religious ideologies and experiences have conditioned the creation of oral and written narratives. The Bible in particular has long been recognized as a major influence on the body of Western literature. Following William Blake's words that the Bible is the Great Code of Art, Northrop Frye argues that "elements of the Bible had set up an imaginative framework—a mythological universe [...]— within which Western literature had operated down to the eighteenth century and is to a large extent still operating" (1982, xi). It is impossible to assume that modern fantasy could have escaped the influence of the Bible. The Bible can be, therefore, perceived as an influence on the fantasy genre on the grounds that it has affected the development of Western literature in general. Yet this relationship can be further analyzed in the context of two related claims: first, that there are fantastic elements within biblical narratives and, second, that other texts (not included in the fantasy genre proper) have employed fantastic elements in order to deliver or emphasize a Christian message.

The first issue is addressed by Colin Manlove in *Christian Fantasy: From 1200 to the Present* (1992). Manlove narrows the gap between fantasy and biblical tales by pointing out that the Bible employs several fantastic motifs, such as "mythic paradise, talking beasts, gods, dragons, angels, visions, many miracles, accounts of other worlds" (1992, 2). The presence of these elements should not be surprising, Manlove claims, since "God's imagery is often wholly different from ours, or may be quite other from our capacity to represent it except through fantastical imagery: therefore, if He speaks to men, they can only represent His truth through images that will look strange to us" (1992, 3). Since the world of the Bible is one that borders the otherworldly and the divine, it should not be limited by the dictates of reason, because only a fantastic discourse allows man to grasp the infinite and inexplicable. In this context, there is no disagreement or contradiction between fantasy and Christianity.

Several scholarly works have explored the fantastic dimensions of certain biblical episodes. For instance, in *The Phantom Messiah* (2006), George Aichele argues that the Gospel of Mark can be read as fantasy using Tzvetan Todorov's notions of the "uncanny" and the "marvelous." In his structural approach to fantasy, Todorov claims that the fantastic is the moment of uncertainty and hesitation experienced when a person faces an occurrence transgressing the laws of nature (25). The uncertainty—and the fantastic—lasts as long as the person is unable to decide whether the odd, anomalous element should be treated as something non-existent and metaphorical or as something real, but previously unknown. Choosing one of the interpretations results in leaving the sphere of the fantastic and opting for either the marvelous or the uncanny. Using Todorov's notion of fantasy, Aichele studies Jesus' parables (e.g., about the seed), miracles (e.g., exorcism and raising from the dead), and identity (e.g., as the Son of God and Messiah), and argues that because they are described as remaining on the borderline between reality and metaphor, they are, in a sense, fantastic.

Aichele has also edited three works with Tina Pippin—*Semeia 60: Fantasy and the Bible* (1992), *The Monstrous and the Unspeakable: The Bible as Fantastic Literature* (1997), and *Violence, Utopia, and the Kingdom of God: Fantasy and Ideology in the Bible* (1998)—which, on the one hand, study fantastic elements within the Bible by using theories previously applied to research on the fantasy genre, and on the other, search for biblical motifs within fantasy fiction. Like Manlove, Aichele and Pippin argue that the Bible contains numerous examples of magic and the supernatural (1997, 11). The essays in their collections explore several such examples and juxtapose biblical themes with their counterparts in fantasy literature. Some of the topics discussed are the motif of the forbidden fruit, which has been successfully reconstructed in the fairy tale "Rapunzel," and Nathaniel Hawthorne's short story "Rappaccini's Daughter," the presence of the Nephilim and other semi-divine angelic beings in modern fantasy, and the theme of the Apocalypse which is often creatively reconstructed within fantasy. Jack Zipes goes as far as to claim that:

> The Bible is the seminal work of all fantasy literature. While seemingly providing a world order through the narrative about the origins of the universe and the events that lead, in the Old and New Testament, to the foundation of a Judeo-Christian morality, it subverts this order with promises of other worlds/ other spaces. The Bible transports us back in time to a legendary past to encourage us to look forward [...] to another and better world. The Bible undermines reality and will not let us rest content with conditions as they are [in Aichele and Pippin 1992, 7].

Inarguably, fantasy fiction also undermines reality as we know it. By the means of their fantastic realms, writers address social, psychological, and religious problems pertaining to the real world, and then encourage readers to solve these problems so that, like the fantastic heroes, they too can look forward to a "better" world. All things considered, the volumes edited by Aichele and Pippin support the claims that biblical themes and motifs continue to exist within the structures of modern fantasy, and that the fantastic—defined as a literary mode which can introduce supernatural elements into any narrative—can be identified in the contents of biblical narratives.

Laura Feldt has a similar objective in her study on *The Fantastic in Religious*

Narrative from Exodus to Elisha (2012). Feldt argues that since the fantastic continuously reappears in the biblical narratives she chose for analysis (e.g., in the hyperbole of the Israelites' fertility, in Moses's mystical encounter with the burning bush, in the horror of the plagues, and in the miraculous parting of the sea), studying the fantastic dimensions of these episodes can enhance our understanding of the Hebrew Bible. According to Feldt, the fantastic elements—phantasms in the forms of metamorphoses, hyperboles, paradoxes, and violations of natural categories—appear in biblical narratives to evoke not only respect toward divinity, but also fear, doubt, and uncertainty, which might stimulate further reflection on the nature of the divine (78). What is more, they make readers aware of the transformative period in Israel's history (the ethnogenesis), and stimulate reflection about God's identity and about human interaction with and experience of the divine.

The research conducted by Manlove, Aichele and Pippin, Feldt and others support the first claim that the fantastic is a significant part of biblical narratives. The second claim—that certain texts, which are not part of the fantasy genre, have employed fantastic elements in order to deliver a Christian message—is supported by a range of works dating back as far as the Middle Ages. Dickerson and O'Hara point out that the Old English epic poem *Beowulf* is a blend of Germanic heroism and Christian morality (121), and that Snorri Sturluson's *Prose Edda* connects Norse myths with the Gospel (118). Manlove argues that during the first millennium the supernatural was accepted in Christian writing only in the form of *miraculosus*, i.e., deriving from God. The supernatural as *mirabilis*, i.e., the marvelous, combined with Christian morality, began to appear more often in the 12th century, e.g., in the tales about Tristan and Isolde, and in the Arthurian romances (1992, 12–13). In *The Encyclopedia of Fantasy* the category of "Christian fantasy" is exemplified by Dante's *Divine Comedy*, John Milton's *Paradise Lost*, and John Bunyan's *The Pilgrim's Progress*, which combine fantastic imagery with a Christian message (191). This list may be complemented by several other works, e.g., the poem *Pearl* with its allegorical vision of heaven, Edmund Spenser's magic-filled *The Faerie Queene* with its representations of Christian morality and grace, Christopher Marlowe's *Doctor Faustus* with the themes of divine damnation and salvation, and William Blake's poetry which, as Manlove aptly summarizes, "helped to let God out of the Bible and the Church" (1992, 155). These and other works combine their narratives with elements of the fantastic in order to investigate the religious, and often distinctly Christian, dimension of human existence.

The connection between fantasy and Christianity was further strengthened in the 19th century, because works which shaped the developing fantasy genre operated with fantastic imagery and Christian undertones. Though frequently they contained no explicit references to the Bible or Christian theology,

Christian themes were disguised as a pervading sense of divine presence, the hero's acute spiritual yearning, or providence that miraculously delivered the hero from harm. Such motifs appeared in the works of George MacDonald (*At the Back of the North Wind*, *The Princess and the Goblin*, and *The Princess and Curdie*), Charles Kingsley (*The Water-Babies*), and Charles Williams (*Descent into Hell* and *All Hallows' Eve*). In *Christian Mythmakers* (2002), Roland Hein rightly argues that these writers "see the Bible as the repository of ultimate Truth and salute its authority in all matters of faith and doctrine. Their literary myths are replete with its imagery and precepts" (11). It is vital to remember that these works shaped modern fantasy and inspired the next generation of writers, including Tolkien and Lewis, whose novels are imbued with Christian morality and symbolism. In fact, in recognition of the Christian nature of the works of MacDonald, Williams, Tolkien, and Lewis, Elise Brooke calls them "theological fantasy" (7), because they speak "of God and of our right attitude towards Him and therefore also of our living with and for other men" (9).

The works of Tolkien and Lewis, as well as those of Philip Pullman and J.K. Rowling, have been at the center of the debate on whether or not modern fantasy literature can be reconciled with the Christian faith. A brief summary of the main arguments introduced both in favor and against such reconciliation, as well as a concise analysis of the religious contents of the works of the abovementioned British writers, will shed more light on the complex relationship between Christianity and the fantasy genre.

As Tolkien was a devout Catholic throughout his entire life, it is not surprising that his religious convictions were reflected in his literary work. Tolkien's theoretical approach to writing fantasy literature, as well as his thoughts about fantasy being a mirror of Christianity, are best expressed in his three shorter works: the essay "On Fairy-Stories," the short story "Leaf by Niggle," and the poem "Mythopoeia."[19] In the beginning of "On Fairy-Stories" (1947), Tolkien first explores the connection between fantasy, myth, and religion by using the metaphor of the Cauldron of Story (in *Tree and Leaf* 29-31). Any story invented by an author or delivered by a teller, Tolkien argues, comes from the Cauldron, which is full of "bits"—old and powerful motifs and themes taken from myths, fairy tales, and even history—which are boiled together until some of them are ladled out by a Cook (a writer or storyteller) and turned into a tale. Thus, all the particles present in the Cauldron constantly interact with each other, undergo changes, and reappear in new forms. Tolkien's idea of the Cauldron of Story is a clever, even if a bit exaggerated, explanation for the ubiquity of certain literary motifs and for the presence of biblical themes within fantasy fiction, since this type of fiction is also produced from the rich material blended in the Cauldron.

The concept which is by far more influential than "the Cauldron of

Story" theory is the notion of sub-creation, investigated by Tolkien during his analysis of the four qualities of fairy stories: Fantasy, Recovery, Escape, and Consolation. Tolkien defines sub-creation as the act of creating a believable secondary world which is governed by a set of laws and which convinces the reader to temporarily suspend his disbelief. Tolkien bestows the act of sub-creation with religious prominence and argues that a writer's powers of sub-creation as well as his secondary world are a fragmentary reflection of God's divine powers and an echo of His grand creation *ex nihilo* (in *Tree and Leaf* 52).

The qualities of Recovery and Escape pertain to the reader's reception of fantasy. Recovery means that fairy stories present familiar things from a new perspective, which allows readers to gain a fresh awareness of what they have already taken for granted. The Escape offered by fantasy is an escape from the injustice and ugliness of everyday life, from the boundaries of impossibility, or even an escape from Death (in *Tree and Leaf* 59–61). When discussing the same attribute of fantasy, Rabkin is even more explicit about the genre's escapist qualities: "The real world is a messy place where dust accumulates and people die for no good reason and crime often pays and true love doesn't conquer much. In one sense all art is fantastic simply because it offers us worlds in which some order, whatever that may be, prevails" (1979, 3). Thus, for Rabkin it is perfectly reasonable that readers should seek liberation from the confusion and oppression present in the world around them (1979, 23).

Tolkien combines the last quality—Consolation—with the concepts of a Eucatastrophe, i.e., the good catastrophe which unexpectedly offers comfort and joy despite the previous sadness and tragedy (a similar quality has been identified by Campbell in reference to myths: "at the bottom of the abyss comes the voice of salvation. [...] At the darkest moment comes the light" [1991, 44]). Tolkien argues that Eucatastrophe is inseparable from the Christian Gospel and that it appears most prominently in Christ's birth and resurrection (65). If all of these claims are taken into consideration, it becomes clear that Tolkien perceives the categories of fantasy and Christianity not only as reconcilable, but also interrelated: the act of literary sub-creation mirrors the act of divine Creation, and similar qualities are present both in fairy stories and the Gospel. Tolkien, therefore, concludes that God reigns over everyone (angels, men, and elves), and that fantasy should not be rejected by Christians, but embraced for its potential (in *Tree and Leaf* 66).

Though all of these theoretical claims are successively realized in Tolkien's works set in the imaginary Middle-earth, the short story "Leaf by Niggle"—rightly called by Margaret Summitt "a Catholic allegory" (182)—is a particularly explicit example of Tolkien's convictions. The eponymous Niggle is an artist who is passionately devoted to completing one particular painting of a tree and its leaves. Niggle is meticulously working on every detail, so that even simple leaves become unique and beautiful. He is so immersed in the task that he abandons his other artistic projects or incorporates them into the painting of the tree, which grows vast in size and becomes an enormous landscape. However, Niggle cannot devote to it as much time as he would like to, because there are other duties he must tend to and an unspecified journey he must get ready for. The journey, however, revels the truth about the nature of his artistic creation.

The story of Niggle's painting is, first of all, a dramatic account of an artist's struggle to complete his work within his lifetime, while his attention is diverted by several duties. Such an interpretation reflects Tolkien's private life: as meticulous and devoted to detail a writer as Tolkien was, he frequently had to postpone his artistic projects in favor of academic and family obligations. Second, "Leaf by Niggle" can be read on a religious plane. The artist, forced by Death to abandon his work, is first sent to purgatory, where he works in order to repent for his sins, but may be offered "Gentle Treatment" for his good deeds, and eventually go to heaven led by the shepherd. Heaven is only hinted at by the metaphor of the Mountains—a distant land which even the narrator cannot describe. Though "Leaf by Niggle," like Tolkien's other works, never explicitly mentions religion, Christian overtones reverberate throughout the story: Niggle's earthly life is measured according to Christian standards of morality before he is finally deemed worthy of salvation, and the shepherd leading him into the mountains symbolizes Jesus Christ.

What is more, "Leaf by Niggle" implies that Art is the medium through which the artist and his audience might catch a glimpse of the ultimate Truth which underlies all creation. A similar idea is expressed by Tolkien's poem "Mythopoeia" (in *Tree and Leaf* 97–101) which presents Philomythus's address to Misomythus. Philomythus insists that not only logic and science, but also imagination is necessary for comprehending the world (98)—an idea which corresponds to Otto's claims that man can experience the divine only through emotions and intuition. Tolkien's poem also praises the "legend-makers," because they are able to preserve the ultimate Truth in the face of the modern industrialized world (99).

Tolkien's dedication to Christianity is visible also throughout his creation of Middle-earth which, though it never mentions Christianity directly, is steeped in Christian symbolism. In *The Silmarillion* (1977), Tolkien unfolds the divine creation of Middle-earth's world, Arda, performed by Eru Ilúvatar, an omnipotent figure resembling the Christian God. Eru creates the Ainur who function in the roles of angels and assist him in the further creation of the world and its inhabitants. Peace lasts until one of the Ainur, Melkor, rebels—in a Luciferian manner—against the Creator, because of his own selfish desire to take control over the god's creation. Melkor's rebellion is the beginning of corruption and fall, which ruins the god's perfect work. *The Silmarillion* presents an intricate cosmogony of a secondary realm, which is clearly indebted to Christian tradition.

In contrast to the poignant *Silmarillion*, *The Hobbit* (1937) is a light and humorous tale about Bilbo Baggins's adventures with a groups of dwarves who try to retrieve their treasure from the dragon Smaug. Though the book displays hardly any religious references, it can be, nonetheless, read on a Christian level. In *Walking with Bilbo* (2005), Sarah Arthur[20] relates every major stage of Bilbo's adventure to a corresponding passage from the Bible. By juxtaposing the hobbit's behavior and choices with the experiences of Jesus' first disciples and their spiritual development, Arthur argues that the images created by Tolkien remain in agreement with the biblical ones, and may, therefore, serve as lessons in godly Christian life. Arthur argues, for instance, that Bilbo is similar to many biblical figures (e.g., Moses, Paul) in that he begins his adventure as an ordinary person who is called to perform a great task and succeeds in spite of his initial insignificance. She concludes that the story about Bilbo, like the stories about biblical prophets, contains an uplifting message for ordinary people who struggle with daily challenges (12–16). In addition, Arthur focuses on the values conveyed by Tolkien's fiction, which—she argues—remain in accordance with Christian morality: Tolkien presents mercifulness as a desirable feature of character, which guarantees the final victory over evil (67–73), and condemns greed which leads a person to their downfall (161–169). Every chapter of Arthur's work is followed by a list of questions for self-reflection and recommended passages from the Bible. Though Arthur's devotional reading of *The Hobbit* can undoubtedly be inspiring and prompt some reflection on the nature of one's religious commitment, there is but one problem: it contains little in terms of literary criticism. Arthur does not provide an in-depth analysis of the religious dimensions of Tolkien's Middle-earth (or Lewis's Narnia in her other publication). Instead, she selects certain elements of the plot and uses them as a springboard for discussing various aspects of Christian ethics. Her analysis is strongly affected by her personal religious beliefs, and a devotional reading of the selected novels appears to be a more significant goal than objective literary criticism.

Tolkien's *The Lord of the Rings* also renders itself to devotional reading, as has been manifested by Kurt Bruner and Jim Ware's *Finding God in The Lord of the Rings* (2001). Yet numerous other publications contain more objective critical studies of the trilogy, which demonstrate that Christian themes appear on various levels of the narrative, though, paradoxically, God or faith of any kind are never directly mentioned. This, however, remains in line with Tolkien's approach to writing fantasy, since he was against treating his works as allegories of the Bible. Instead of writing conspicuous allegories, which might weaken readers' immersion in the secondary world, Tolkien preferred to reconstruct and embed the essence of biblical truths in a fantastic context.

On the most general level, *The Lord of the Rings* trilogy is Christian because it presents a cosmic struggle between good and evil, in which evil, embodied by Sauron, has to be conquered. Conquered not by powerful wizards or outstanding warriors, but by the joint efforts of all good people whose actions are measured against the Christian standards of selfless love and sacrifice. Frodo represents the common person who is motivated in his fight against evil not by heroism or a desire for recognition, but by the feeling of responsibility: for the Ring, for his community, and for his world. The hobbit uses his free will to volunteer as the Ring-bearer, carries the accursed item—the symbol of temptation, corruption, and sin—for hundreds of miles, and fights against its influence over his mind and soul. He is what Russell Dalton calls "a Christ figure," i.e., a hero who displays some characteristics of Jesus. Dalton explains that "Christ-imagery can be most thought provoking when some aspects of the character are quite different from Jesus Christ. This technique—known as defamiliarization—can help us reflect on aspects of the Christ story in new ways" (138–139).[21] In the context of Christ imagery, Frodo bearing the Ring resembles Christ bearing the Cross, and both the Ring and the Cross stand for death, human corruption, and sin. But Frodo is not the only Christ figure in the trilogy. His loyal companion, Sam, who never wavers in his support and love, represents the humble side of Jesus who provided His disciples with lessons in servant leadership. Gandalf the Grey is another representation of Christ: he sacrifices himself to protect the fellowship and is then restored to life as Gandalf the White, so that he may aid the heroes in their struggle against evil. Aragorn functions in the messianic context of Christ's Second Coming: he is the long-awaited, benevolent, and wise king who begins his reign over humankind after the Ring is destroyed (and marries Arwen, his bride from the angel-like elves). Though God is never directly mentioned in the trilogy, His presence is known through the miraculous grace bestowed upon the heroes, e.g., the Ring is destroyed only because Frodo had previously shown mercy to Gollum, who becomes the final agent of the Ring's destruction. The analyses conducted by Arthur, Bruner and Ware, and other scholars almost unanimously agree that the world of Middle-earth is permeated with Christian symbols and morality.

A similar conclusion has been reached about Lewis's *The Chronicles of Narnia* (1950–1954) in which the Pevensie children learn about the goals of human existence, the nature of one's relationship with God, and the significance of faith against all odds. The seven volumes of *The Chronicles* draw upon various biblical themes unified by the figure of Aslan, the lion who—

according to Lewis's idea that an alternative world should have an alternative version of incarnation—is the Narnian embodiment of Jesus Christ. Among the series' most prominent Christian images there are Aslan's *ex nihilo* creation of Narnia and its inhabitants, the temptation posed by a forbidden fruit found in a garden, Aslan's sacrifice for the sins of others and his subsequent resurrection, the appearance of a fake Aslan (the anti–Christ), and the battle for Narnia, which is followed by the vision of Aslan's Country—a heavenly place available to those who believed in him and acted according to his laws. The series promotes such virtues of character as perseverance, loyalty, and obedience; it also teaches readers that God loves his children, that they may rely on Him when they are in need of help, and that good always prevails over evil. Like Tolkien's Middle-earth, Lewis's Narnia is a land immersed in Christian spirituality. However, Andrzej Wicher points out that Tolkien's and Lewis's works approach Christianity in distinctly different ways. First, there are certain differences between Lewis's and Tolkien's representations of the sacred, which derive from the different source materials used by both authors, e.g., the figure of Gandalf is a mixture of Christian and mythological references (Christ vs. Odin), while Lewis's Aslan is "a venture to visualize and represent a pure, unadulterated experience of the sacred" (Wicher 27). Second, Lewis's and Tolkien's works differ in terms of their heroes' attitude to religion:

> Generally speaking, in Lewis's represented world the characters have usually a religious mindset, and religion is a problem for them, while in Tolkien's world they are too hard-pressed to take sides in the struggle of good and evil to have time to think about religion. In other words, the logic of Lewis's fantastic stories is that of a philosophical or religious parable, while the logic of Tolkien's creations is that of the tale of magic, or the fairy tale, and consequently they are highly autonomous and do not lend themselves so easily to an ideological, or theological, exegesis [Wicher 307].

The novels chosen for analysis in this book could be similarly divided into those in which the heroes are challenged to (re)define their religiosity and those in which religion and religious motifs are a significant component of the secondary world, but the heroes are not forced to resolve personal problems of religious nature. This issue is taken into consideration in the following chapters.

In contrast to Tolkien and Lewis, Philip Pullman uses the fantastic world of *His Dark Materials* trilogy (1995–2000) to severely criticize Christianity and institutional religion. The trilogy follows the adventures of two children, Lyra and Will, who have to participate in a conflict between the malevolent Authority (God) worshipped by the Magisterium (a fictional Church) and the Republic that intends to destroy them. Among the trilogy's numerous references to Christianity there is Lyra's position as the New Eve, the story's focus on human sin, and the motif of the angels' rebellion against their God. Apart from reworking these biblical concepts, Pullman introduces two original elements: Dust which is a mystical energy permeating the universe and connected with all living creatures, and daemons—manifestations of a person's inner-self in animal form.

Pullman's fictional Church and god are a literary prop that allows him to criticize institutional religion and the Christian God. The Magisterium is a tyrannical organization and the Authority is a usurper who appropriated divine status; both are presented as a constraint on human freedom. The promised heavenly afterlife turns out to be a hoax: afterlife is a dreadful underworld in which the souls of the dead are tormented for all eternity. In Pullman's universe, religion is just a façade of lies. For these reasons, Dickerson and O'Hara state that the entire trilogy presents the writer's "unrelenting animosity toward God, church, religion in general, and especially Christianity. […] Everything that has ever gone wrong in any of the universes, it seems, is the fault of the Church or of those who believe in God" (199–200). Nevertheless, in *Shedding Light on His Dark Materials* (2007) Bruner and Ware attempt to present some arguments in defense of the trilogy. For instance, they suggest that the tyrannous deity should be perceived not as the Christian God, but as the disobedient Lucifer who wanted to claim the Creator's powers and who was actually able to do so in Pullman's universe (2007, 78–80). Thus, to rebel against such an entity is a natural thing to do for the protagonists. What is more, the trilogy never attacks Jesus Christ, and Christ does not appear even once in the narrative.[22] Finally, as the scholars argue, the trilogy ends with the triumph of good over evil, and morality over egoism (2007, 155). Taking everything into consideration, Bruner and Ware go as far as to suggest that the trilogy's disturbing portrayal of a religion and world from which the benevolent God is absent is the result of Pullman's private struggle to comprehend God and the Church (2007, 153-164). However, confronted with numerous interviews in which Pullman explains that *His Dark Materials* is what he intended for the trilogy to be—a critique of Christianity under the guise of fantasy fiction—Bruner and Ware's claims might seem to be a forced apologia. Inarguably, though fantasy fiction can be a medium for conveying religious values, its subversive alternative worlds can also be an effective vehicle for religious criticism.

Like Pullman's *His Dark Materials*, J.K. Rowling's *Harry Potter* series (1997–2007) has received mixed criticism for its treatment of morality and spirituality. Part of the negative commentary focuses on the heroes' questionable moral conduct. While the series extols such virtues as friendship, loyalty, and sacrifice, the young protagonists frequently break the rules and generally misbehave in order to obtain their goal. Though that goal is to protect the world from the evil Voldemort, the rule-breaking heroes might not be the best role models for young readers. The other argument against the series, which raises concern among Christian readers and is repeated in reference to many fantasy books, is the inappropriate portrayal of magic, witches, and wizards, which might boost readers' interest in real-world magic, i.e., occult practices (Abanes 132–140, 150–164). Though magic powers and items are standard elements of fairy stories and fantasy narratives, in the *Harry Potter* series they are presented as parts of a marvelous world hidden from ordinary (British) citizens. What is more, in contrast to the worlds of Tolkien and Lewis, in which the use of magical powers is very restricted and the final victory is achieved only because of divine grace, in Rowling's creation readers learn about a system of spells and potions, which can be freely used by positive and negative characters. Though it is doubtful whether the *Harry Potter* novels can be treated as a manual instructing in occultism, religious-conscious readers might be rightfully concerned about its depiction of magic. While the sole appearance of magic in fantasy fiction is not something requiring instant condemnation, its inappropriate portrayals, i.e., when the boundaries between good and evil are blurred, and magic is presented as a solution to everything, can be questioned—that is why Dickerson and O'Hara suggest that the fairy tale about Aladdin is much more controversial than *Harry Potter*, since the hero enslaves a genie and uses his powers for his own benefit (238).

Nevertheless, in *Fantasy and Your Family: Exploring The Lord of the Rings, Harry Potter and Modern Magick* (2002), Richard Abanes rightfully points to a certain group of urban fantasy novels whose representations of magic and attitude to the occult might raise serious concern. Abanes argues that in recent years the quality of fantasy fiction has markedly decreased, because it fell prey to commercialization which has produced hundreds of books thriving on a few sellable patterns, meant to provide simple and accessible (and addicting) entertainment for pre-teen and teen readers (38). These patterns include the ubiquitous presence of the supernatural which manifests itself in the ordinary world and which is saturated with occult, neopagan, or Wiccan symbolism. Another characteristic element is a predictable protagonist: a young witch or wizard who discovers his/her magical powers and studies witchcraft. Abanes argues that books based on such patterns "reinforce the idea that magick and occultism are harmless forms of entertainment unworthy of serious moral objections" (129)—spelled with "k," the word magick refers to practices connected with the occult. Thus, the scholar is very critical of writers such as Cate Tiernan (the *Sweep* series), Isobel Bird (the *Circle of Three* series), and Lynne Ewing (the *Daughters of the Moon* series), whose works repeat such patterns.

Taking everything into consideration, the works of Tolkien, Lewis, Pullman, and Rowling exemplify different approaches to the Christian tradition. Tolkien's and Lewis's novels, though they never directly mention Christianity, contain numerous parallels to biblical tradition and are structured upon Christian morality, for which they have frequently been praised. Pullman is, or at least attempts to be, explicitly anti–Catholic and uses his novels as a medium for delivering religious criticism. Rowling, whose portrayal of morality and magic has been both defended and criticized, does not seem particularly interested in addressing religious issues or in intentionally inserting them into her narrative—it is her readers that measure her imaginary reality against Christian standards. It is clear from these examples that fantasy literature can address religion in several ways and for several reasons.[23] First of all, fantasists develop fictional religions, often inspired by real traditions, to complement the process of literary worldbuilding, and to create a moral and spiritual background for their characters' actions. Second, in some cases fictional religions become the core of the entire narrative and the protagonists' ability to (re)define their religiosity is a prerequisite for the successful completion of the quest. Thirdly, fictional religions can serve as the means through which the author promotes or criticizes a particular religion of our world. The first type can be exemplified by George R.R. Martin's *The Song of Ice and Fire* cycle, while the second by Celia S. Friedman's *The Coldfire Trilogy*. These two categories might, of course, overlap since they differ in terms of the degree to which a given writer develops his fictional religions—a factor which might change within a single lengthy cycle. Writers such as Tolkien, Lewis, and Pullman exemplify the last category, as they are either implicitly or explicitly supporting and criticizing Christianity. What is more, there are several works which introduce Christianity as an antagonistic element (e.g., Poul Anderson's *The Broken Sword*, 1954; Jack Vance's *Lyoness* trilogy, 1983–1989; Clive Barker's *Weaveworld*, 1987) or which support those characters who favor humankind's mythic past with its pagan traditions whenever a clash between Christianity and the old traditions ensues (e.g., Robert Holdstock's "Thorn," 1986; Charles de Lint's *Greenmantle*, 1988).[24]

In terms of the aforesaid categories, the works analyzed in the following chapters—Stephen R. Donaldson's *Chronicles of Thomas Covenant*, Guy Gavriel Kay's *Fionavar Tapestry*, Celia S. Friedman's *Coldfire Trilogy*, and Brandon Sanderson's *Mistborn* series—represent mostly the second category, because their fantastic religions are a prominent component of their imaginary realms and the motif of the heroes' (re)discovery of faith significantly affects the plot of each work. Nonetheless, certain parts of the chosen cycles do participate in the discourse defined in the third category—implicit/explicit promotion or criticism of a particular religion—which are also acknowledged during the analysis.

The proposed analysis is intended to become a new thread in the discourse established by the works of Manlove, Aichele and Pippin, Feldt, Bruner and Ware, and other scholars who have examined the complex relationship between the fantastic and the Bible, and between Christianity and the fantasy genre. Before we end this theoretical introduction and proceed with the main task, we should reiterate the stages of the phenomenological method according to which the selected American and Canadian novels are investigated. Every chapter, first of all, gathers information (often scattered throughout the series) on the secondary religions and religious institutions present in a given work. The information is divided into related phenomenological categories, e.g., religious figures, sacred rituals, holy scriptures, etc., and thoroughly investigated both in terms of their own properties and their interrelations. These categories are further complemented by description of a given series' pantheon of deities, concepts of cosmology, manifestations of the divine, and the heroes' experiences of and attitudes toward divinity. Only when all of these elements are taken into consideration are we able to determine the structure of the fictional religions, discuss the nature of the fictional numinous, and acknowledge the impact of religion on the development of the plot and the characters. Epoché (withholding from prior judgment) and emphatic attitude toward the object of the study, which characterize phenomenological research, are indispensable, because they allow us to address the alien concepts of secondary gods and religions without prejudice.

Once the phenomena which constitute every fantastic religion are thoroughly established, they are contrasted with Christianity so that we can determine to what extent they are inspired by and reconstruct the biblical tradition (though parallels to other religious and mythological traditions are acknowledged, they are not studied in detail). The areas analyzed in terms of their relatedness to Christianity include: presence/absence of a divine Creator and his attributes; presence/absence of a divine antagonist; the nature of other deities and minor divine beings; the source and nature of magic and supernatural powers; motifs of creation, temptation, sin, fall, destruction, sacrifice, redemption, and salvation; secondary mythologies and prophecies; structures of religious institutions, including their internal hierarchy, sacred scriptures, holy rituals, prayers, etc. In addition, Christian interpretation is applied to some of the major symbols appearing in the chosen narratives to reveal their Christian connotations. To complement the examination of each series, the characters' behavior is contrasted with Christian morality in order to assess whether the values upheld by a given novel correspond to Christian ethics. The level of the characters' religious awareness is also investigated in order to determine if their spiritual development is a significant part of the plot. At the end, every chapter indicates whether the chosen series reflects its author's private religious beliefs and whether it contains the author's personal remarks about Christianity. To avoid any preconceptions about the results of my analysis and to work in agreement with phenomenological epoché, I searched for information about a given author's denomination and religious beliefs only at the end of my research on a particular series. That way, my analysis was not pre-determined: without knowing about the author's beliefs, I was not deliberately searching for their reflection in the text. Only after my analysis was complete did I compare its results with background information on the author's religious affiliation (if any such information was available).

2

The Christian Foundation of Stephen R. Donaldson's *The Chronicles of Thomas Covenant*

Introduction to The Chronicles

Stephen Reeder Donaldson (b. 1947), an American writer of fantasy and science fiction, began his literary career with the publication of *Lord Foul's Bane* (1977)—the first installment in a multivolume series featuring Thomas Covenant's adventures in a secondary reality modestly called "the Land." Over the years, Donaldson expanded the single book into a vast and complex cycle:

> *The Chronicles of Thomas Covenant, the Unbeliever* (also called *The First Chronicles*): *Lord Foul's Bane* (1977), *The Illearth War* (1978; followed by an independent novella, *Gilden-Fire*, from 1981), *The Power That Preserves* (1979);
>
> *The Second Chronicles of Thomas Covenant: The Wounded Land* (1980), *The One Tree* (1982), *White Gold Wielder* (1983);
>
> *The Last Chronicles of Thomas Covenant: The Runes of the Earth* (2004), *Fatal Revenant* (2007), *Against All Things Ending* (2010), *The Last Dark* (2013).

While Donaldson was not working on the adventures of Thomas Covenant (the *Second* and the *Last Chronicles* are separated by more than twenty years), he published his other acclaimed series, a science fiction epic called *The Gap Cycle* (1991–1996).

Because of the vastness of *The Chronicles*, the analysis of the series' imaginary religions and their Christian references should be preceded by a brief introduction of its protagonists and a short delineation of its plot. *The First*

Chronicles follow Thomas Covenant's three visits to the Land, a beautiful fantastic world that is under the onslaught of Lord Foul the Despiser, who intends to destroy the realm because it is his eternal prison. Covenant is chosen to aid the Land's protectors with a rare power—white gold magic—lying dormant in his wedding ring. Yet Covenant, a man ruined by leprosy, is not a typical or predictable fantasy hero who immediately rushes to graciously save the world. Before the onset of his illness, Covenant was the embodiment of the American Dream: he was a writer from a Midwestern American town who became a bestselling author, earned a fortune, and lived happily with his wife and infant son (Senior in James and Mendlesohn 191). After the diagnosis, Covenant's American Dream collapses. Left by his family and shunned by the society, the protagonist is reduced to "a mechanical derelict" (*The Chronicles...* 15) who lives in the ruins of his former prosperity. Covenant's only remaining purpose in life is to survive and fend off the threat of becoming another maimed victim of leprosy. Unending VSE—Visual Surveillance of Extremities, i.e., the act of scrutinizing his body in search of injuries that might be affected by the illness—is his only means to achieving the goal.[1]

After being transported to the Land, Covenant manages to survive his first encounter with Lord Foul, who gives him a prophecy of destruction which the leper delivers to the Council of Lords in Revelstone. To postpone the prophecy's fulfillment, Covenant journeys with the Lords to retrieve an instrument of power—the Staff of Law. Though the adventures are fraught with physical dangers, the Land's influence over the protagonist as well as the people's expectations toward him are even more dangerous, because they constantly threaten his integrity and sanity. For Covenant, the numbness and impotency of leprosy have become the prism through which he experiences the world around himself, and the measure which he uses to judge his surroundings. Not surprisingly then, he is deeply disturbed by the Land's vibrant potency and his own miraculous healing. The sudden restoration to health results in Covenant's mindless rape of a young girl, Lena. This crime, in turn, further exacerbates his psychological torment. Covenant constantly struggles with his status as the Land's mythical savior and his general inability to believe in the realm's very existence. Having eventually rationalized the existence of the Land as a figment of his restless mind, the leper reluctantly allows himself to be involved in the realm's affairs, believing that the fulfillment of the assigned quest will return him to sanity. When the Staff of Law is finally retrieved, Covenant regains consciousness in his own world.

W.A. Senior recognizes the protagonist's behavior as typically American. On the one hand, Covenant refuses to give credence to occurrences not grounded in logic and material reality as he knows it, and dismisses the fantastic fancies of the Land—or at least tries to convince himself that he has dismissed them. On the other, he behaves as a stereotypical arrogant and demanding American abroad, who focuses on his own feelings and comforts so strongly that he disregards the people around him. On top of that, like many Americans affected by the Vietnam War, the protagonist strongly distrusts all instances of power, even if the power in question can save the world from ultimate destruction (Senior 1995, 29–31).

In the second volume, the leper is again summoned to the Land to aid the Lords against the evil Lord Foul and to accompany the High Lord Elena—his daughter begotten in rape—in her quest to find ancient knowledge and power. Unfortunately, Elena's misuse of power results in her downfall. Though Foul's armies are temporarily defeated, Covenant returns to his world deeply embittered both by his daughter's doom and his own failure to understand the wild power of his white gold ring.

As a result, the third volume begins with Covenant's acute psychological suffering, which is further exacerbated by his knowledge of the havoc wrought by Lord Foul in the Land. Covenant resolves to destroy the oppressor, but the journey to Foul's dwelling becomes a harsh trial which forces the man to reexamine his earlier failures and to acknowledge various sacrifices made for his sake. Even during the final fight, Covenant is able to defeat the evil deity only thanks to the help of others. Paradoxically, such a victory enables him to accept his own inadequacies, and the man returns to the "real" world with a better understanding of his illness and his identity.

The Second Chronicles begin ten years after the original trilogy and introduce the cycle's second protagonist, Linden Avery. While at the beginning, Linden, a physician, might seem a natural antithesis to Covenant—a man ruled by his illness—the narrative eventually reveals the similarity of their experience. Covenant became a social outcast because of leprosy, whereas Linden emotionally isolated herself from others because of a traumatic childhood. Linden is a woman deeply wounded by her parents: her father forced her to helplessly observe his suicide and then her hospitalized mother harassed Linden until the tormented girl killed her. Marred by her past, Linden cannot escape the belief that she is evil, and mistrusts herself on various occasions.

Linden and Covenant are lured to the Land by Lord Foul who has again risen to power (4,000 years after his last defeat—the Land has a different flow of time than the primary world). The fantastic realm is horribly corrupted by a distortion in the cycles of nature (the Sunbane), and by Foul's servants (the Clave). Covenant, who struggles against uncontrollable bursts of his wild magic, eventually discovers that the Land may be restored only if a new Staff of Law is created from the wood of the One Tree. The first volume ends when he and Linden depart on a sea journey to find the mythic Tree.

The journey of the second volume takes the heroes to new places within the secondary world and introduces new characters. The powerful *Elohim* not only reveal the location of the One Tree, but also force Covenant into a state of mental dissociation. The heroes are then confronted by Kasreyn of the Gyre, a malevolent wizard craving the white gold ring. Compelled by events, Linden "possesses" Covenant's mind in order to free him from his dissociation, and the heroes flee. They eventually arrive at the Isle of the One Tree, but the leper is unable to obtain the holy wood, because the Tree is protected by an apocalyptic beast—the Worm of the World's End. Only Linden's intervention prevents the man from rousing the Worm and initiating the world's destruction.

The third part follows the heroes' desperate return to the Land, whose corruption has been exacerbated by the blood-thirsty Clave. To stop further atrocities, Covenant conquers the Clave's fortress, destroys the leaders, and even manages to curb his violent power. However, his new perception of power and obligations inspires him to submit his ring to Foul. Though the leper is killed, his spirit unites with and then protects a divine construct, the Arch of Time, until Foul drains all of his powers in an attempt to shatter it. Using the white gold ring, Linden creates a new Staff of Law and heals the Land. She then returns to the primary world with the memory of Covenant's love.

The Last Chronicles begin by showing Linden's bitter-sweet life with her adopted mentally ill son, Jeremiah. The boy is suddenly kidnapped by Roger, Covenant's now adult son, and all three are transported to the Land, which is again assaulted by Foul. Though Linden gathers a group of companions and retrieves the Staff of Law, the realm is inevitably falling into chaos. The woman is then approached by false Jeremiah and Covenant, whom she accompanies into the Land's past, where they are supposed to find a remedy to the realm's disintegration. Linden eventually discovers her companions' true identities, and the cruel masquerade leaves her deeply hurt. Consequently, she obtains another instrument of power to realize her greatest desire: she resurrects Covenant, hoping that he will help her retrieve her son and defeat Foul. Her abuse of power first awakens the apocalyptic Worm, which accelerates the Land's destruction, and then another monstrous being, She Who Must Not Be Named. Aggravated by her failures, Linden decides to concentrate her efforts on restoring her son's mind, while Covenant departs to deal with his mad ex-wife, Joan, who threatens the integrity of the divine Arch of Time. Despite several obstacles, Jeremiah finally returns to his senses, whereas Covenant puts an end to Joan's madness. Though the Worm continues its progress, the heroes decide to forsake any attempts at stopping it, and instead concentrate on defeating Lord Foul, so that he will not be able to corrupt the entire universe. Thanks to the combined efforts of their friends, Covenant, Linden, and Jeremiah manage to overcome their fears, trap Foul, and re-create the Arch destroyed by the Worm. Afterward, the Land and the heroes are restored to greatness and happiness.

2. Christian Foundation of *The Chronicles of Thomas Covenant*

Following the types of religious phenomena established by van der Leeuw and Eliade, the analysis of the secondary sacred constructed by Donaldson in *The Chronicles* is divided into the following categories: deities and divine powers, including their attributes, manifestations, and the religious institutions which address them; religious institutions, including their perception of divinity, internal structure, principles, practices, holy places, and symbols; lesser divine beings and people with access to power; secondary mythology, instruments of power, sacred places, and sacred events. The analysis of the nature of these individual phenomena becomes the basis for investigating the Christian elements used by Donaldson in the construction of his imaginary world and its fictional religion(s).

Images of the Numinous

As far as Donaldson's fictional numinous is concerned, even a brief summary of *The Chronicles*' plot reveals that its universe is grounded in monotheism and determined by a contest between two antagonistic forces—the Creator and Lord Foul the Despiser—that can be described in terms of Otto's definition of the numinous as *mysterium tremendum et fascinas*. In Donaldson's realm, the nature of divinity remains a mystery (*mysterium*) beyond human reason, understanding, and grasp (at least until Covenant temporarily achieves a state similar to godhood). Whenever the characters face the Creator, Lord Foul, or any of the lesser divine entities—and thus become exposed to the overpowering divine majesty and potency (*majestas*)—they are repeatedly humbled by the experience of their own mortality, insignificance, and weakness. Encounters with the malevolent Lord Foul are particularly unsettling, because he evokes nothing but terror associated with the terrifying aspect of the numinous. Foul is the epitome of Otto's *tremendum*, and every confrontation with him is an experience of "grisly horror and shuddering" (Otto 13). As the heroes strive to protect the Creator's Land from destruction planned by the Despiser, both deities and the lesser divine beings become the objects of their prevailing fascination and unending attention (*fascinas*). Yet even though the protagonists' attitude toward the awful majesty of the numinous frequently resembles the state of reverential submission or even self-abasement which Otto defines as *augustum*, the knowledge of their own morality and vulnerability never incapacitates the heroes nor does it deter them from fighting for what they hold dear.

Fragments scattered throughout *The Chronicles* allow a careful reader to learn more about the series' fictional gods and the characters' approach to them. Donaldson's Creator is a benevolent but distanced deity responsible for the making of the Land and its inhabitants. Several of the characters occasionally refer to the realm's creation myths, and it is worth examining, because these myths reveal valuable knowledge about Donaldson's imaginary cosmology and the beliefs upheld by the Land's denizens. Covenant, who at some point gains very intimate knowledge of the Land and its existence, describes the fictional Creator as a supreme figure residing in an otherworldly sphere, surrounded by his children and other immortal beings, and passionately devoted to his creation (*The Wounded...* 125). According to other genesis myths, the Creator first formed the Arch of Time and then used the power known as wild magic as the Arch's keystone, so that Time would resist chaos (*The Chronicles...* 212, 238). Inside the Arch, he created the Earth and the Land, and remodeled them—with "the greatness of his love and vision as tool" (*The Wounded...* 125)—until he achieved perfection. Finally, he gave life to the world's inhabitants, who were also meant to reach for perfection with their abilities to create and love (*The Wounded...* 125). Thus, the Land's inhabitants believe that divine creation was an act guided by love and benevolence, and that they—bestowed with gifts which liken them to the Creator—are intended to achieve their own level of greatness. Unfortunately, the newly formed Earth was at some point stealthily corrupted by the evil Despiser (Lord Foul), whom the Creator then fought and cast out the infinity—an event which is also recounted by secondary myths (*The Chronicles...* 239). Covenant later says that the Despiser is the son or brother of the Creator's heart (*The Wounded...* 125). Neither he nor Lord Tamarantha is able to precisely define the relationship between the two deities, which contributes the inexplicability of the fictional numinous. Using concepts understandable to human logic (in this case, family and kinship), both heroes can only suggest that there exists a kind of bond (if not a union) between the gods. This idea is later supported by a statement that even the Law, which defines and regulates the structures of divine creation, is not the opposite of Despite (*The Chronicles...* 786)—Despite being the deivine force associated with Lord Foul (the Despiser). Regardless of their bond, the Creator proved to be the mightier of the two deities and punished the Despiser by imprisoning him within the Arch, i.e., within time and space. Yet as a result, the Creator cannot stop his antagonist's subsequent corruption of the Land, because the Laws which govern creation (the Law of Time, Life, and Death) prohibit any form of external divine intervention. A breach of the Law may shatter Time and release Despite into infinity, hence the Creator's withdrawal.

Another of *The Chronicles*' secondary myths similarly highlights the Creator's impotency to aid his children. According to this myth, the Creator once lived in joy and peace in the company of his children (*The Chronicles...* 156). Because he wanted to delight his children, the Creator "descended to the great forges and cauldrons of his power, and brewed and hammered and cast rare theurgies" (*The Chronicles...* 156), and thus formed a beautiful rainbow, which joined his abode with the heavens of the Earth. The god then discovered that the rainbow was tainted by the Enemy (*The Chronicles...* 156). While the Creator was seeking a way to mend his newest creation, his children crossed the rainbow bridge and lit the earthly sky. Unaware of that, the god removed his imperfect work and trapped the children in exile; they cannot return until the Enemy (Lord Foul) is defeated.

Both the genesis myths and the myth about the rainbow reaffirm the Creator's might and benevolence, the existence of his beloved children, and his striving for perfection which is countered by the Despiser's corruption. They also suggest that he is neither an omnipotent nor omniscient deity, but a fallible god who cannot foresee the actions of his adversary and who, blinded by wrath, unconsciously traps his children in exile—qualities which seem to contest Otto's notion of the overwhelming might of the numinous. Yet since Donaldson rarely engages into an in-depth discussion of the nature of godhood (perhaps recognizing, like Otto, the futility of any attempts at defining godhood through human logic and language) and the relationship between the Creator and the Despiser is never explained, it is not clear whether the Creator's fallibility is a feature ascribed to him by secondary myths in an attempt at translating the god's transcendental nature into terms understandable for the recipients of these myths or whether Donaldson deliberately portrays an imperfect god.

As if to further emphasize the mystery (*mysterium*) and inexplicability of divinity, Donaldson hardly ever allows the Creator to make a direct appearance. Though the deity may don a physical body, he never materializes in the Land due to the constraints imposed by the Laws of creation. Thus, readers encounter him only twice, when he challenges Covenant and Linden in their primary world, disguised as an old beggar in an ochre robe (the Creator's ability to enter Covenant's world but not the Land raises questions about the deity's relationship with and status in the primary world—an issue never explored by the series). In *Lord Foul's Bane*, the Creator appears to test Covenant and, once he has acknowledged the leper's humility, to reassure the man of his worth. Like in the creation myths, the beggar–Creator is kind and benevolent, yet his eyes and stature reveal divine majesty which Covenant cannot oppose and which have little to do with actual physical appearance. Linden, when it is her turn to be tested, is also affected by the beggar–Creator's otherworldly aura. Though both protagonists are specifically chosen by the god to save the Land—he calls the man his son (*The Chronicles...* 1146) and the woman his daughter (*The Wounded...* 28)—the deity respects human autonomy and does not control their actions, because the necessity of human freedom is also one of the Laws of creation. Thus, for most of the time, the Creator is the *Deus Absconditus*, the hidden god, that seldom reveals himself to humankind.

It was probably because of his withdrawal that the Creator has never become the object of any institutional worship in the Land. While many inhabitants of the secondary realm praise the Land's beauty and the Creator's generosity, there are no temples, rites, or scriptures which would regulate the worship of the Creator in any form. In fact, when High Lord Prothall, the leader of the Council of Lords, is asked about worship, he replies that the word is obscure to him (*The Chronicles*... 278), and instead talks about serving the Land and respecting its Law. The Land's inhabitants preserve their scant knowledge about the Creator in the form of myths, but they do not combine it with religious rituals. Thus, the secondary numinous in the figure of the Creator is not only a force that escapes human rationalization and cognition (including moral categories: though the Creator is presented as a benevolent entity, the heroes are continuously exposed to suffering because of their status as the deity's chosen ones), but also one completely independent of institutionalized religion and formal worship, which corresponds to Otto's perception of the numinous as an *a priori* concept.

Similar claims can be made in the case of Lord Foul, though it must be repeated that Foul, more than the Creator, embodies the terribleness of the numinous and elicits the feelings of abasement and dread. The origins of Lord Foul the Despiser (also known as a-Jeroth of the Seven Hells), the Creator's malevolent antagonist, are never explored beyond the assumptions that he might be some part of the Creator, which adds to the mystery of the numinous. For the sin of corrupting Earth, he was punished with expulsion from infinity and imprisoned within the Arch of Time; to shatter the Arch with white gold and gain freedom is thus Foul's chief desire. Feared and abhorred by the Land's inhabitants, he has been given names such as Satansheart, Soulcrusher, Fangthane, Corruption, and the Gray Slayer (*The Chronicles*... 41). Though Foul, like the Creator, is an incorporeal being existing on a different plane than the material world, he may manifest his presence in various ways (also in Covenant's "real" world): as a malicious and contemptuous voice deriding the heroes, as a pair of fang-like wicked eyes, or as a shadowy figure encompassed by power and the smell of attar. At rare moments, when he is forced to adopt a physical body, he appears not as some abhorrent monster, but a patriarchal figure of great power and dignity (*The Chronicles*... 1139); even his dwelling, Ridjeck Thome, is not a filthy lair, but an example of unnaturally perfect stonework that mirrors the nature of its master (*The Chronicles*... 1124). Also Foul's conversation with Covenant reveals that he is not a mad deity obsessed with destruction, but rather an embittered and cynical god disgusted with puny, shallow humankind and their hopeless world (*The Chronicles*... 1139). Foul clearly loathes people, so he strives to corrupt them by offering them immortality or by distorting their relationship with the Land and the Creator. Thus, though his armies often wreak havoc among the realm's inhabitants, he does not depend on the brute force of destruction to achieve his goals, but prefers to shame people with his divine majesty, and lure them into despair with his many intrigues. Donaldson's depiction of the numinous in the form of Lord Foul underlines the negative and dreadful aspects of the numinous experience, which reverberate in Otto's definition of the creaturefeeling as "the emotion of a creature, abased and overwhelmed by its own nothingness in contrast to that which is supreme above all creatures" (10). In the presence of the malevolent Lord Foul, the characters are challenged by the knowledge that in his eyes they are but lowly beings whose only value lies in their usefulness to the deity.

While the Creator and the Despiser are the two divine entities which dominate in the universe of *The Chronicles*, the numinous imagined by Donaldson is represented also by three impersonal powers linked to the gods and the material world: Earthpower, Despite, and white gold magic. All three share the attributes previously ascribed to the deities: they are great and terrible forces whose potency is the cause of fascination and temptation, and which remain beyond complete human comprehension, control, and moral judgment. Even Earthpower and wild gold magic, which can be used by the heroes for growth and protection, will wreak havoc when abused or misused, and therefore become as dangerous as Despite. Interestingly, the inhabitants of the Land seem to have developed a more complex relationship with these powers rather than with their deities. Thus, while it is still significant that we analyze Earthpower, Despite, and wild gold magic as other instances of the numinous in Donaldson's world, it is equally important to discuss their relationship with institutionalized religion.

The Numinous and Institutionalized Religion

Earthpower is presented as the natural essence of creation and a force which permeates the entire Land (*The Chronicles*... 278). Though it is neither an omniscient nor omnipotent divine entity, it attracts more religious-like attention of the Land's inhabitants than the Creator, and by the end of the series it becomes, together with wild gold magic, the core of Donaldson's secondary sacred. In the background of the series' main plot, attentive readers can find plenty of information about the inhabitants' perception of and attitude to Earthpower, and discover the fate of three subsequent religious institutions—the Lords, the Clave, and the Masters—which wish to regulate the inhabitants' relationship with Earthpower, but do so for different purposes and in very different ways.

In *The First Chronicles*, the denizens of the Land possess exceptionally strong senses which allow them to fully comprehend the beauty and health of their realm. This knowledge strengthens not only their love for the Land, but also their devotional respect for Earthpower—the divine essence permeating the material world and responsible for its well-being. The life of the Land's inhabitants is one of constant spiritual awareness and engulfed in the sacred. The harmony between the realm and its inhabitants consequently gives some of the people mystical knowledge about nature. The lore of the stone, *rhadhamaerl*, allows Stonedown craftsmen to work with "living" stone,[2] while the wood-lore, *lillianrill*, gives the Woodhelvennin similar skill to work with wood. These lore-wise people may also use Earthpower hidden in the instruments of power—*orcrest* (pieces of the One Rock, i.e., the heart of the Earth) and *lomillialor* (white-wood rods from the One Tree)—to aid their communities. These practices, together with the people's love of the natural world and their loving respect for Earthpower, become manifestations of their religious piety. Christine Barkley is right to note that while the Land's people have no institutionalized religion to worship the Creator, they engage in a form of deism: though they seldom refer to the Creator and possess neither temples nor scriptural knowledge of their god, they acknowledge him and ascertain his divinity through their devotion to his creation (94).

The Council of Lords from Revelstone is the first of three religious institutions which appear to formally regulate the spiritual life of the realm's inhabitants. The Council is a group of men and women led by a High Lord, who willingly devote their lives to the study of Earthpower in order to "consecrate themselves to Earthfriendship" (*The Chronicles...* 94). They are able to invoke Earthpower with knowledge and songs, and then channel it through their staffs to heal the Land or destroy its enemies. The strongest invocation is the Seven Words, which are considered to be a part of the language of creation (*Fatal...* 257). Within the circle of Lords, the Unfettered Ones are people who underwent the Rites of Unfettering in order to free themselves from earthly bonds and pursue lore according to their private visions.

One of the few presented religious doctrines pertaining to Earthpower is the Oath of Peace. The Oath is an affirmation of life and beauty established after one of the ancient Lords, Kevin Landwaster, unleashed Earthpower to commit a Desecration (destruction) of the Land (in that way revealing its terrifying and destructive potency). Kevin's descendants swore to be masters of their emotions, so that anger, despair, and desire for power would not fool them to repeat his mistake. Thus, the Oath promotes self-discipline and moderation, and condemns any acts of violence. One of the denizens, Lena, explains that abiding by the Oath is a conscious choice made by the Land's people at the age of fifteen. The extent of the Oath's influence is particularly visible in two cases: Atiaran, Lena's mother, never punishes Covenant for raping her daughter, and the Lords refrain from killing and are deeply grieved when they have no other choice but to kill even in defense of the Land. However, this ideology of pacifism is eventually overruled by High Lord Mhoram who realizes that to successfully protect the Land, its people need to revise their spiritual commitment and establish a new path of service. This shift in perception is only one of the several changes in the people's understanding of and attitude toward the numinous.

In Donaldson's world, the sacred is a dynamic sphere and even the embodiments of the numinous are susceptible to change. Earthpower, for instance, is gradually diminished by the consecutive breaking of the Laws of creation. The violation of the Law of Death (when ghosts appear in the material world) and the destruction of the Staff of Law (an attribute of the High Lord) allow Foul to steadily corrupt Earthpower and produce the Sunbane, an emanation which distorts the energy of the sun and the cycles of nature. The four random stages of the Sunbane—the desert sun, the fertile sun, the sun of rain, and the sun of pestilence—change nature into humankind's worst enemy. The Council of Lords is, by then, substituted by the Clave, the second religious organization, secretly controlled by Foul's allies. The Clave is a hierarchical congregation comprised of the leader (called na-Mhoram), his helpers (na-Mhoram-in and na-Mhoram-wist), and novices (na-Mhoram-cro). Following the Rede, a distorted version of the Lords' knowledge, the Clave performs bloody sacrifices to appease the Sunbane. The triangle and the number three are its main symbols. Every member of the Clave bears a *rukh*—a rod with a triangle which allows them to draw power from the Sunbane. The number three appears also in the Clave's holy creed together with "The Three Corners of Truth" (*The Wounded...* 307). The "Three Corners of Truth" is the doctrine defining the Clave's service: firstly, no power compares to the force of the Sunbane; secondly, the Sunbane is the Land's doom; thirdly, the Clave sheds blood in order to gain control over the Sunbane and use its power against it (*The Wounded...* 308). However, since the Clave is secretly led by Foul's ally, its actions only aggravate the Land and further sever people's link with true Earthpower. As a result, the realm's inhabitants no longer perceive the numinous as a benevolent force, but as a threat and monstrosity. Those who still retain any mystical power need to sacrifice their own or their people's blood—and thus pervert their knowledge—to help their communities: the Gravellers use blood, *orecrest* stones, and invocations to grow food in an unnatural way, whereas the ehBrands use blood and *lianar* wands to foretell the next stage of the Sunbane.

Though the Clave and the Sunbane are eventually destroyed, the people's intimate relationship with Earthpower visible in *The First Chronicles* is not restored. On the contrary, it is altogether put into obscurity by the third religious organization—the Masters of the Land. The title is adopted by the *Haruchai*, an ancient race of people who measure their worth through combat, have a strong sense of communal identity, and communicate mind to mind (this ability allows them to preserve memories for thousands of years). In the distant past, the *Haruchai* were once defeated and sorely humiliated, so their only purpose in life is to reaffirm their worth. Yet their inability to accept the slightest failure undermines all of their efforts. The *Haruchai* first serve the Lords as the Bloodguard and their Vow is consecrated by Earthpower, so that the men live for hundreds of years without love (in fact, *Haruchai* women never make an appearance and the men seem to live in constant celibacy), sleep, or death. But after three of them are corrupted by the power of evil, the entire Bloodguard feels unworthy of further service and withdraws altogether. Secondly, when two of the *Haruchai* fall into the temptation of some female monsters, the decide they are no longer fit to serve Covenant and abandon him. Finally, they become the Masters of the Land[3] and deprive the inhabitants of their spiritual heritage, because they are convinced that since people are weak and prone to temptation, and since even Earthpower itself may be corrupted, it is altogether better to withhold any knowledge of it from the Land's denizens. Thus, they execute stringent control over the communities. The leader of the Masters is called the Voice, but the most revered ones are the Humbled: the three strongest *Haruchai* who earn the privilege to be maimed in commemoration of the mythical Berek Halfhand and Covenant (both men are missing two of their fingers). The *Haruchai* also revere a legendary figure called ak-Haru Kenaustin Ardenol who is the protector of the sacred Isle of the One Tree.

Covenant and Linden desperately challenge the Masters' ideology and religious tyranny in order to reestablish the people's awareness of Earthpower and reintroduce the numinous into their lives. Covenant passionately declares that the Masters can never achieve perfection, because they are mortal. So instead, they should accept their human fallibility and put more trust in humankind's inborn goodness (*Against...* 631). What is more, Covenant's words not only highlight the two aspects of the numinous—its capacity for wonder and terribleness (and its amoral nature)—but also point to a serious violation on the part of the Masters: they thwart the freedom given to people by the Creator (*Against...* 631). The *Haruchai* eventually recognize their mistake and denounce control. When the Land is reborn after the apocalypse, its inhabitants can reestablish their bond with Earthpower and perhaps they will form a new religious institution that will be able to properly address both their spiritual needs and the numinous permeating the secondary world.

It is clear that the shape of Donaldson's imaginary numinous is largely determined by the existence of opposing forces and entities, which struggle for supremacy: the Creator is contested by Foul, whereas the benevolent and life-sustaining Earthpower is countered by Despite—the essence of Foul's malevolence and his ancient contempt toward all creation (and, in that way, an extension of the numinous). Nonetheless, Despite cannot be defined as the absolute antithesis of Earthpower. Rather than being, like Earthpower, a supernatural force which can be obtained or manipulated, Despite appears in the series as a moral category whose closest synonym is evil. Mental weakness, susceptibility to violence, sin, and despair may ultimately turn a person into a victim of Despite and Foul's (un)willing servant. Consequently, only by resisting temptation, consciously refusing the allure of violence, and willingly surrendering their egoism (rather than by simply using their "magical powers") do Donaldson's characters triumph over Despite and prove their valor.

The ambiguous contradiction between Earthpower and Despite is balanced by a third impersonal force: white gold magic. While Earthpower embodies primarily the benevolence of divinity and Despite—its malevolence, white gold magic is neutral. It is the power of chaos, capable of both creation and destruction: it can be used to shatter the world (because the Creator used it to seal the Arch of Time) or to defeat Foul. Thus, its wielder is able to overrule both Earthpower and Despite. Yet at the same time, white gold magic is severely constrained: it is bound to a metal that does not even exist in the Land, and cannot be used unless the white gold ring is willingly submitted by its rightful wielder. The latter suggests that Donaldson conceived the power as related to the divine gift of human freedom, which in turn implies that white gold magic's role as the keystone of the Arch of Time (the construct which was the culmination of creation) was also to guarantee the freedom of will to the Land's inhabitants. This claim is supported by Donaldson's remarks that both human will and white gold magic must be intentionally renounced for Foul to triumph, that they are characterized by imperfection, and that both may wreak havoc. People may use their freedom to serve either the Creator or the Despiser, whereas white gold's "imperfection is the very paradox of which the Earth is made, and with it a master may form perfect works and fear nothing" (*The One...* 264). As a result, both white gold magic and human freedom are powers of paramount importance in Donaldson's vision of the fantastic universe. It is not surprising then that in the Land white gold has become the object of prophecies which emphasize both its redemptive and destructive nature (the so-called paradox of the white gold).

Other Faces of the Numinous

The contest between the Creator and Despiser, as well as the clashes between Earthpower, Despite, and white gold magic, demarcate the boundaries of Donaldson's imaginary numinous, which becomes a complex and dynamic sphere that fascinates and frightens humankind with its majesty and potency. The heroes' experience of the divine is further diversified by their encounters with lesser divine beings and creatures possessing power. In *The Last Chronicles*, Donaldson introduces a feminine element into his vision of the numinous—She Who Must Not Be Named. Originally, this female entity was known as Diassomer Mininderain and was the divine embodiment of Love and desire (*Against*... 296). The Land's mythology describes her as a divine consort who was seduced by a-Jeroth (Foul), betrayed by him, and then trapped on Earth (*The Wounded*... 158–159). The betrayal transformed the female entity into a mad being consumed by hatred, who devoured the souls of other betrayed women. When the heroes encounter She Who Must Not Be Named, she is a wrathful monster whose force obstructs even Earthpower (*Against*... 260). Blinded by her rage, She Who Must Not Be Named is the Despiser's tool, and is not freed until Linden is able to restore the creature's forgotten identity ("I am myself!" announces Diassomer). Afterward, the female reclaims her former place somewhere outside the material world. Diassomer does not play a significant role as an individual character—Donaldson invents her simply to test Linden's spiritual strength. Yet her appearance shifts the Land's balance of divine powers: like white gold magic, female love and hatred (which Diassomer apparently represents) are an unpredictable force that can override both Earthpower and Despite. And like Lord Foul and white gold magic, She Who Must Not Be Named brings into focus the dangerous and threatening aspects of the numinous.

The balance is further tipped by the appearance of an apocalyptic beast called the Worm of the World's End. Though the Worm's role is to consume the world, the protagonists cannot destroy it, because the existence of the fantastic world depends on the existence of the beast (*Against*... 50). Thus, the very presence of the Worm suggests that everything in Donaldson's universe must one day come to an end, even the Creator's beloved world. In fact, one of the secondary genesis myths attributes the creation of Earth to the Worm, rather than to the god. In the distant past, after the beast fed on stars, it desired a rest, during which its body transformed into the surface of the world, which was then filled with people and animals (*The One*... 52–53). If the beast is ever roused, and not "opposed by the forgotten truths of stone and wood, *orcrest* and refusal," it will destroy the Earth (*Against*... 159). Which is exactly what happens in *The Last Chronicles*, but even then readers are offered only glimpses of the Worm's body and its staggering power: "a shape within the hermetic mass of the storms, a dark form limned by the heavy rise and fall of the lightning" (*The Last*... 169). The Worm clearly embodies the unfathomable destruction and amorality inherent to the numinous. It also corresponds to certain sacred imagery which Mircea Eliade identified in several mythological traditions. According to Eliade, dragons "are the emblems of water; hidden in the depths of the ocean, they are infused with the sacred power of the abyss [...]. Dragons dwell in the clouds and in lakes; they have charge of thunderbolts [...]" (1996, 207).

The protagonists are similarly confronted with the mystery, grandeur, and monstrosity of the numinous whenever they encounter creatures that are embodiments of Earthpower and Despite. The former is represented by the *Elohim*, Forestals, Ranyhyn, and Fire-Lions, while the latter by the Ravers. The *Elohim* were originally the Creator's bright children living in heaven (*The One...* 52), who were accidentally trapped on Earth where they became shadows of their former selves. Still, they possess powers that transgress mortality and the physical world, so they distance themselves from humanity, assume a sovereign position, and serve the Land according to their own merciless visions. They inhabit *Elemesnedene*, an enchanting land inaccessible to mortals, described as the center of everything (*The One...* 117). The vain *Elohim* similarly deem themselves the core of creation, not subjected to any external force or judgment (*The One...* 119). They name themselves the Würd (Wyrd or Word) of the Earth, and even substitute "Worm" with Würd when they talk about the beast's presence, thus implying the existence of an inherent connection between them, the Worm, and the act of creation (*The One...* 120). Despite their claims to power and knowledge, the *Elohim* are neither omnipotent nor omniscient: they cannot act outside the stricture of the Law, they never directly combat the Despiser, and they are more than once proven wrong in their judgments. Their main contribution to the fate of the world is the selection of "the Appointed"—an *Elohim* chosen to risk his/her existence against some threat posed to the Earth.

The leader of the *Elohim* is Infelice who adopts the form of a gorgeous female and believes herself to be "the crown of Creation" (*The Last...* 289). Infelice acts on behalf of her race and conducts the *Elohimfest*, a ceremony which takes place on the eftmound—a low hill surrounded by a ring of dead elms and illuminated by a spectral light. For mortals, participation in the *Elohimfest* (another direct contact with the numinous) is a highly unsettling and belittling experience: the protagonists are awed with the *Elohim*'s majesty and might, and grieved by their own insignificance and frailty—a response which perfectly fits into Otto's definition of *augustum*. However, it is eventually the divine *Elohim* that must acknowledge their own belittlement: they are saved from ultimate destruction only thanks to the protagonists' endurance and selflessness.

While the *Elohim*'s service is based on self-centeredness, the Forestals, called "guardians in the Creator's stead" (*Fatal...* 385), serve by humbly tending to the forests, which are a central part of divine creation. They were created by the sentient One Forest (the primeval woodland) from the Earthpower of an *Elohim*. Through signing and otherworldly music—"an arboreal melody more numinous than speech" (*The Last...* 329)—they protect the woods from evil and from the humankind whose actions have destroyed the One Forest. Like the *Elohim*, the arboreal guardians appear in human form, e.g., Caerroil Wildwood of the Garroting Deep is presented as a patriarchal figure clad in a robe and carrying a staff made from a branch, and two subsequent Forestals are created from human men (Hile Troy becomes Caer-Caveral of Andelain, and Mahrtiir—who renounces his humanity for the sake of the world—becomes Caerwood ur-Mahrtiir). Their transformation is an act of transubstantiation in which both men are elevated from the constraints of their mortality into another, divine-like state of existence.

The forests and the Forestals are repeatedly presented as a central point of divine creation: the proatgonists are instructed that it is impossible to preserve the Land unless its forests are also preserved, and that only the Forestals' power (the Forbidding) may stop the apocalyptic Worm. Thus, in Donaldson's vision, the health of the natural world is presented as a pre-requisite for the preservation of the realm. It is not surprising then that both Covenant and Linden are "anointed" by nature: the moss stains on Covenant's clothing are a message interpreted as the forest's act of redemption (*Fatal...* 609), whereas the grass stains on Linden's jeans are an encoded map which allows the woman to realize that the realm is doomed without its arboreal guardians (the grass stains mysteriously disappear after ur-Mahrtiir is created). The protagonists' experiences prove that in Donaldson's universe nature is a sentient entity filled with or reflecting the majesty and might of the numinous.

The same idea prevails in Donaldson's depiction of the Ranyhyn (the Great Horses of Ra) described as "majestic and ineffable, as vital as the Land's pulse of Earthpower, and as numinous as the Hills of Andelain" (*Against...* 531). Because of their beauty and might (their connection to Earthpower allows them to transgress time), the horses are treated with almost devotional respect, particularly by the Ramen—the people of the plains who willingly take care of the beasts. In the Ramen culture, any crime against the Ranyhyn is severely punished, and the act of riding a Ranyhyn is an unbreakable taboo (which eventually has to be broken, since in Donaldson's world the people's relationship with the sacred is in constant change). Even the Ramen's vision of paradise accounts for their devotion, since its central idea is the peaceful coexistence of people and the Ranyhyn (*The Chronicles...* 312). In exchange for their service, the Ramen develop a mental understanding of the horses' identities and intentions. In contrast to the vain *Elohim*, the Ranyhyn are humble creatures who willingly serve as mounts. They represent the gentleness of Earthpower, whereas the Fire-Lions are the quintessence of its ferocity. The Lions are fiery creatures made of Earthpower, lying dormant on Mount Thunder. They figure prominently in the Land's secondary mythology, but seldom make a direct appearance, because they can be called only by a figure of power, who is in dire need of divine intervention.

In contrast to the array of beings united with Earthpower, Despite is embodied only by three malicious creatures called the Ravers. Though the Ravers bear individual names—*turiya* Herem, *samadhi* Sheol, and *moksha* Jehannum (or Fleshharrower, Satansfist, and Kinslaughterer)—hardly anything else distinguishes them as individuals. Originally, they were three brothers created out of human malevolence, who came into Lord Foul's service because of their loathing for life. *Turiya* Herem proudly claims that hatred is what makes Foul and them immortal, because true hatred/Despite evades death (*The Chronicles...* 1020). To bring about the world's end, they tempt people into Foul's service or possess their bodies like parasites. However, possession eventually becomes their own downfall: though the Ravers seem immortal, the power of a self-sacrifice—when a host willingly accepts a Raver and his own death—proves capable of rending their spirits, so ultimately all three are obliterated. Apart from the Ravers, Donaldson invents other evil creatures, e.g., the serpentine *skurj*, the succubus-like *croyel*, ice beasts called *arghuleh*, and Horrim Carabal—an enormous tentacled monster worshiped by acid wraiths, the *skest*. Yet though these creatures also evoke terror and despair in the heroes, only the Ravers represent Foul's transcendental Despite.

Though at this point not all of the categories of religious phenomena have yet been discussed, it is clear that Donaldson's *Chronicles* present an imaginary world permeated by the numinous. Even if the dominant deities seldom manifest their presence in the material world, the protagonists constantly encounter lesser divine beings and confront divine powers circulating in the realm. The numinous of the Land evokes in the protagonists an entire palette of emotions signaled by Otto in his characterization of humanity's experience of the sacred: awe and gratitude, fear and despair, abjection and insignificance. On the one hand, the protagonists can use Earthpower and white gold magic to protect the fantastic realm, which they treat with utmost devotional respect. On the other, the true nature of those powers is beyond their comprehension, they are constantly cowed by the magnitude of these powers, and diminished by divine indifference and malevolence. Though none of the deities or minor beings is worshipped by a gathering of the Land's inhabitants, there do exist "para-religious" institutions which professionally address these divine powers and regulate the spiritual life of the Land's denizens. Both the numinous and the religious institutions are dynamic entities prone to transformation: the former due to the contest between the gods, which affects the balance of divine powers, and the latter due to the changes in the inhabitants' perception of the nature of the numinous, which affects their relationship with it.

Secondary Mythology, Instruments of Power, Sacred Places and Events

The phenomenological analysis of how the numinous manifests itself in the realm of *The Chronicles* and how its people conceptualize the sacred needs to be further complemented by the categories of secondary mythology, instruments of power, sacred places, and sacred events, which define and regulate people's relationship with the Holy. As far as secondary mythology is concerned, apart from the myths of creation and destruction the Land's mythological tradition recounts the deeds of ancient heroes whose fate offers both consolation and admonition. Berek Halfhand (known as Earthfriend, Hartthew, and Lord Fatherer) is remembered as a great champion, protector of the Land, and progenitor of the first Lords. He is the central figure of the Land's quasi-soteriological doctrine as people believe that he will return when the Land is again in need of a savior—and since Covenant's hand is maimed like Berek's, the inhabitants believe that he is their hero reborn. Among Berek's descendants, the High Lords Damelon Giantfriend and Loric Vilesilencer are commemorated for their great knowledge and service to the realm. In contrast, High Lord Kevin, called Landwaster, is remembered for his failure. Believing that good ends justify bad means, Kevin wielded power in an act called the Ritual of Desecration to destroy Foul. While Foul survived, the Land became a desolation, and Kevin's mistake—a warning for others (nonetheless, the New Lords still rely on Kevin's lore hidden in the Seven Wards). Finally, Thomas Covenant also joins the Land's pantheon of mythic heroes. A cult is formed after Covenant's first victory over evil, which reveres the leper as the Land's savior and prophesizes his future return, thus establishing another soteriological doctrine. Though the cult eventually declines, Covenant becomes a permanent element of the Land's mythology. What is more, after his second victory over evil, the man actually undergoes deification and becomes a part of the fictional numinous (a process that fantasy fiction, in contrast to phenomenology of religion, can acknowledge and describe). After the protagonist's death, his spirit is united with the Arch of Time and Covenant is transformed into a divine-like being: omniscient and omnipresent, though not omnipotent. When Linden forcefully resurrects Covenant, she immediately becomes aware of the alteration within his nature: "He had spent uncounted millennia among the essential strictures of creation, participating in every manifestation of the Arch: he had been as inhuman as the stars, and as alone" (*Against...* 21). The act of resurrection restores Covenant's mortality and deprives him of his divine knowledge and status. Covenant's elevation to the state of godhood is an exception which emphasizes the leper's position within the secondary mythology and his very intimate connection with the Land. Because he eventually manages to protect the Land, he confirms his status as the prophesied savior. All in all, though the secondary myths provided by Donaldson are not extensive, they outline the genesis of the imaginary realm and highlight the people's reverence for their ancestral leaders and their attachment to tradition.

Among the instruments of power, Covenant's white gold ring is by far the most significant object, because it channels the redemptive/destructive white gold magic. However, the ring is not a practical magical item that can be used whenever the bearer wants or needs to use it. White gold magic is the power of chaos and freedom, and bearers of white gold rings (Covenant, Linden, Joan) constantly struggle with their inability to fully control or understand the force. The main instruments of Earthpower and Despite are respectively the Staff of Law and the Illearth Stone. Wielded by a High Lord, the Staff (made from the wood of the One Tree, which highlights the connection between the divine force and the natural world) is the ultimate defense against evil. The original Staff is destroyed by Covenant, which significantly weakens Earthpower, and a new one is fashioned by Linden (from fragments of the old Staff, sacred wood, and a Forestal's signs of theurgy). The new item reflects the emotional states of its wielder: it becomes black when Linden is tormented by grief, and retrieves purity only after it is claimed by Linden's son, Jeremiah. The Illearth Stone is the antithesis of the Staff; it is the only instrument serving Despite, because Despite is, in general, the flaw in human nature and as such can be invoked by human despair and failure, rather than by magical tools. The emerald-green Stone grants its user immense power, but also corrupts, so that s/he becomes a servant of evil. Interestingly, while white gold rings and the Staff of Law can do both good and evil (according to the user's intentions), the evil Stone can never be used to serve good purposes, as if to emphasize the author's message that bad means never serve good ends. The last item of power is Loric's *krill*—a dagger incrusted with a transparent gem which reacts to Covenant's white gold magic. Though the *krill* possesses its own formidable power, its main ability is to reconcile contradictory forces: by using the *krill* Linden can simultaneously wield white gold magic and the Staff of Earthpower. This grants her almost divine omnipotence (which she abuses to resurrect Covenant): "She could have raised or leveled mountains, divided oceans, carved glaciers. She had become greater than her most flagrant expectations: as efficacious as a god, and as complete" (*Fatal...* 760). All of the instruments of power are extensions of the numinous and, like the subjects of the numinous, they evoke awe, fascination, and terror in their users.

As far as sacred places are concerned, earth and water are two elements particularly strongly imbued with the essence of Earthpower, so the most prominent sacred places are all natural locations (which, as Eliade's research proves, is a common element of different mythological traditions). The entire Land—with its vitality, beauty, healing hurtloam, and nourishing fruit of *aliantha*—is treated with respect and religious-like piety. Yet some locations are particularly potent, e.g., Lake Glimmermere which reflects its surroundings, but not people, as if their mortal lives were too fleeting to create a reflection (the only exception is Covenant after his purification in fire). People who swim in the lake's numbingly cold waters usually experience a spiritual revival. A similarly significant location are the Hills of Andelain, which lie almost in the Land's center and are called "the quintessence of Law" (*The Wounded...* 343). The holiness of Andelain is highlighted by Covenant's need to symbolically cleanse himself by wading the river barefoot before he enters the sacred region (*The Chronicles...* 129). Andelain's status as the center of creation is further confirmed when the Law of Death is broken and ghosts can enter the material world through Andelain.

Yet for all of Andelain's transcendental beauty, the greatest reservoir of undiluted Earthpower is the Earthroot hidden under a mountain named *Melekurion* Skyweir—a place where mortals become acutely aware of divine majesty and their own flawed nature (*The Chronicles...* 748). In Earthroot, Covenant and his daughter, Elena, discover a red stream whose source is a bleeding rock. The red liquid, the EarthBlood, is the very essence of Earthpower. The imagery of blood suggests that the entire Land is a living being sustained by Earthpower coming from a hidden heart. Anyone who drinks the red liquid gains the Power of Command to alter anything within the Arch of Time. Linden's partaking of the EarthBlood is vividly described as a clash between mortality and divinity (*Fatal...* 349). By partaking of the EarthBlood, the heroes experience a fleeting moment of divine omnipotence and supremacy, which threatens their mortal existence. The dual nature of this experience parallels the duality of the numinous whose majesty and might are both irresistibly alluring and utterly frightening to the mortal witness of a divine manifestation.

The other sacred bastion of Earthpower is the Isle of the One Tree, the resting place of the apocalyptic Worm of the World's End. The One Tree is presented as enormous, leafless, and somehow connected to the Worm (*Against...* 52). In fact, the Tree begins to decline when the Worm awakens and ventures to partake of the EarthBlood hidden under *Melekurion* Skyweir. Thus, both the Tree and the mountain are sacred locations related to a divine entity and to the cosmic plan of creation and destruction. Their prominence corresponds to the divine quality which Donaldson bestowed on the Land's entire natural environment. Their depiction might have been inspired by several religious traditions in which, as Elidae explains, cosmic trees and mountains function as the "Axis Mundi"—the axis of the world (1996, 99, 111), which links the sphere of the divine with the material world.

As for sacred events, *The Chronicles* recount several ceremonies performed both by the Land's human and non-human inhabitants. While in Revelstone, Covenant witnesses the Vespers, a ceremony consecrated to the service of the Land. The Vespers are performed in the Close, which is a sanctuary illuminated by only two flames. The High Lord, accompanied by other Lords, commences the ceremony by blessing the gathered people. Afterward, he intones a hymn which recalls the Lords' past and present commitment to preserve the Land, and which reminds everyone of "Seven hells for failed faith" (*The Chronicles...* 192). The gathered people reply by avowing not to perform another Desecration and to keep their Oath of Peace; they also sing and repeat hymns intoned by the Lords. The traditional formulas are followed by the High Lord's direct address to the congregation, in which he expresses his fears about the future. The listeners are apparently not barred from responding, since the High Lord receives a reassuring reply from one of the participants. It is clear that the purpose of the Vespers is to offer consolation, commemorate the people's heritage, and bond the participants as members of one community. In contrast, the two other religious institutions that eventually replace the Council of Lords—the Clave and the Masters of the Land—are less concerned with communal bonding and more with exercising control. They never enact the ceremony of the Vespers or any other that would offer people consolation and spiritual guidance, which is an apt summary of the differences between these three institutions.

While the Vespers provide communal bonding, the Giants' ritual of *caamora* focuses on physical and spiritual purification. The Giants are a people known for their love of stonework, sailing, and storytelling; though they are not the Land's indigenous race, they acknowledge the divinity hidden in material creation and nature (*The Wounded...* 446). Thanks to the properties of their flesh, the Giants are not hurt by fire, though they experience the pain of being burnt. Thus, in the act of *caamora* a Giant willingly subjects himself to flames, so that pain may cleanse him of grief and guilt. *The Chronicles* offer some powerful descriptions of such cleansing. For instance, Foamfollower is so anguished by the slaughter of his race that he immolates himself by crossing a lake of burning lava (Hotash Slay), described as "the open throat of hell" (*The Chronicles...* 1109). He returns from it transmogrified: cleansed physically and spiritually, yet at the same time marked by "a transcending pain" (*The Chronicles...* 1117–1118). In *The Second Chronicles*, Covenant performs the *caamora* to cleanse the spirits of the murdered Giants and send them to the afterlife (while ghosts do appear in the series, Donaldson hardly ever comments on the nature of the afterlife, so it remains an inexplicable state beyond human comprehension). When the protagonist himself is in need of bodily and spiritual restoration, he enters the horrible Banefire and emerges visibly changed (*White...* 290). Covenant's self-immolation is not only a physical and mental restoration, but also a step to his deification (the chapter is revealingly entitled "Apotheosis"): like his white gold ring which is an alloy of metals, the man becomes an alloy of mortality, white gold magic, and evil venom coursing in his veins.

The non-human inhabitants of Donaldson's realm possess their own rituals. The Wraiths of Andelain, tiny flame spirits, participate in *Banas*

Nimoram—the Celebration of Spring—during which they perform an elaborate Dance. The words which Covenant uses to describe the event emphasize its sacred nature: "conclave," "apotheosis," and then "sacrilege" when the Dance is interrupted by enemies (*The Chronicles*... 136–138). The Ranyhyn's horserite, *Kelenbhrabanal*, is their way to commemorate the sacrifice of the Father of Horses (Stallion of the First Herd) who exchanged his life for Fangthane's (Foul's) promise to spare the Herd. Though the Stallion was slain, Foul did not respect the promise, and the Ranyhyn would not have survived if it had not been for the service of the people. Once in every generation, the sentient horses commemorate the sacrifice, also to remind themselves that actions motivated by despair (even noble ones) are more prone to failure than steadfast service. During *Kelenbhrabanal* the horses drink from a tarn whose potent water unites their minds, and they run in frenzy until they drain their sorrow. On rare occasions, people are allowed to participate in the rite to share the Ranyhyn's knowledge. Elena, Covenant's daughter, described the ceremony as a restorative communion (*The Chronicles*... 753). These rituals prove that Donaldson perceives the natural environment as permeated by divinity, and that the Land's non-human inhabitants are sentient beings with their own intimate and personal relationship with the numinous.

Taking all of the elements into consideration, the phenomenological analysis of *The Chronicles* reveals the complexity of Donaldson's vision that consists of layers of representations of the secondary numinous and religious practices, which actively shape the narrative and the fantastic world. After all, the protagonists are transported to the imaginary realm because they are yet another piece in the millennia-old conflict between two antagonistic deities. Covenant's and Linden's quests are then motivated by their (un)willing participation in the divine battle, and their responses to spiritual and religious dilemmas determine their progress. Donaldson does not reject the traditional hallmarks of fantasy writing such as spectacular battles and bizarre creatures. Yet instead of relying on them to push his narrative forward, he concentrates on his protagonists' psychological and spiritual transformations after they are exposed to the Land's overwhelming numinous.

Fluidity and continuity are two features which define the nature of the fictional numinous and religions crafted by Donaldson. Fluidity denotes the constant changes which the subjects of the numinous undergo in the course of the series, and which then affect both the inhabitants' perception of the divine and the state of their religious institutions. Between *The First* and *The Last Chronicles* divine powers rise and fall, while people protect, lose, and rediscover their spiritual heritage. Such alterations give plausibility to Donaldson's imaginary world, because it changes and develops instead of remaining a static background serving the requirements of the plot. Also, because of these alterations the heroes' personal struggle to understand and fulfill their spiritual needs becomes more meaningful and dramatic.

In spite of the changes, there is a strong sense of continuity and unity in the inhabitants' past and present relation to the numinous. Covenant, Linden, and the readers quickly learn that the Land's past is not really in the past; it is being constantly reenacted by new generations. Though the storylines of the three *Chronicles* are separated by thousands of years, the Land's existence depends on the same millennia-old divine conflict, and the characters' actions are invariably conditioned by memories of what their ancestors did centuries ago. As a result, generations of people are united by a living heritage and a shared objective—to protect the Land from a malevolent deity. This unity encompasses not only the human inhabitants of the Land, but all sentient creatures affected by Earthpower and Despite. Both groups are subject to the Laws of creation, serve the Land according to their own ideals, and eventually share the same fate: preservation or destruction by the apocalyptic Worm. Donaldson more than once highlights the connection between humanity and nature, humans and non-humans: they all live in a world which belongs to one and the same Creator.

Biblical References in the Figure of Thomas Covenant, the Unbeliever

References to Christianity present in *The Chronicles* are so numerous and ubiquitous that they condition the shape of the imaginary world and regulate the protagonists' behavior. However, the portrayal of Christianity as an institutional religion is rather ambiguous. On the one hand, the narrative borrows numerous motifs from biblical tradition and creatively incorporates them into the structures of its imaginary numinous and sacred. References and allusions to the Bible can be identified in the name and portrayal of the main hero, in the structure of the Land's cosmology, and in the motifs, symbols, and language used by the author. In addition, the protagonists' moral development is strongly embedded in Christian ethics. On the other hand, the series enters into a dialogue with Christian theology, often using the decisions and actions of the protagonists to challenge or reject Christian dogmas. Yet most importantly, Donaldson advocates salvation through works rather than divine grace, and paints an unfavorable picture of institutional religion, which is illustrated by his protagonists' failed relationship with the Church. The latter seems to be grounded in the author's private experiences with the Church, which is discussed at the end of this chapter.

The figure of the main protagonist combines several elements from the Old and New Testament. Thomas Covenant, called the Unbeliever, is described as a lean, gaunt, bearded man whose face reflects moral anguish. More than once Donaldson compares him to a tormented prophet, which emphasizes the spiritual nature of the protagonist's quests. Covenant is an also amalgam of two biblical figures—Job and Doubting Thomas. The Old Testament Job is a devout man who is suddenly deprived of his family, friends, and fortune, and stricken with an incurable skin disease in a test of faith administered by God. Yet because Job does not succumb to despair, he proves worthy of God's love; in recognition of the man's fidelity, Yahweh restores him to health and fortune. Covenant's fate resembles the biblical episode in that his life is also devastated by an unexpected illness, leprosy, which leaves him bereft of happiness: his embittered wife deserts him and takes their infant son, while his frightened fellow citizens would rather see him dead than among them. But even though Covenant makes mistakes, like Job he does not yield to evil. By surpassing his shortcomings and egoism, the leper manages to save not only his own soul, but the entire imaginary world, in which he achieves a new divine state of existence in the company of his beloveds.

The Chronicles frequently describe leprosy in biblical terms, which strengthens Covenant's likeness to a biblical figure. In the Bible, incurable skin disease was seen as God's punishment for one's sins and as a stigma of guilt and disgrace, so a leper was shunned by the society and banished from the community (Ryken et al. 507). In the modern-day world of *The Chronicles*, Covenant's wife, Joan, still treats leprosy not as an illness, but a spiritual stigma and proof of divine judgment (*Against...* 691). Covenant is also mercilessly excluded from his society, and seldom does anyone sympathize with him. One of the few exceptions is a doctor who describes leprosy in reference to medieval representations of Christ's Crucifixion (*The Chronicles...* 377). A comparison to the unending horrid pain of Crucifixion not only elevates leprosy to a divine experience, but also establishes Covenant-the-leper as a figure similar to Christ-the-savior, which is a premonition of the protagonist's soteriological role in the Land.

While Covenant's physical state points to his affinity to Job, his mentality likens him to Doubting Thomas. Originally called Thomas the Apostle, the man became known as "Doubting Thomas" after he received the news of Christ's resurrection with skepticism and disbelief. Only after Thomas was approached by the resurrected Christ and could put his fingers into his wound did he believe in the resurrection. Which, however, did not stop him from doubting the Assumption of the Virgin Mary, until she lowered her belt from heaven as proof. Despite his initial disbelief, Thomas became one of the missionaries who spread the revelation of Christ's resurrection throughout the ancient world (Sill 15). It is interesting to note that Thomas the Apostle became a prominent figure in the Indian branch of Christianity known today as Saint Thomas Christians—a community from the region of Kerala. Given that during his stay in India Donaldson attended the Kodaikanal International School which is located in a neighboring state to Kerala, perhaps the protagonist's name and character were inspired by Donaldson's knowledge of this particular Christian faction. Thomas Covenant's behavior is strikingly similar to that of his biblical namesake. He repeatedly refuses to believe in the Land's existence, and treats his experience as a figment of a restless mind. To express his inability and unwillingness to believe in the Land, he names himself "the Unbeliever," which vividly corresponds to the Apostle's title of "Doubting Thomas." Thereafter, *The Chronicles* often refer to Covenant's "Unbelief" which serves as his psychological mechanism for self-defense: if the Land does not exist, the man cannot be held accountable for his failures to save it.

Nonetheless, Covenant eventually acknowledges the ineffectuality of his attitude and decides that whether the Land exists or not is not really the point; what matters is that he cannot remain passive in the face of destruction. By placing himself in "the eye of the paradox" (*The Chronicles*... 1132), i.e., by accepting his desire to protect the Land regardless of its material existence, he can preserve both the realm and his own mental integrity. In fact, the Unbelief is what allows Covenant to persevere, because he does not believe in the inevitability of Lord Foul's victory (*The Chronicles*... 1137). And even after his victory, the protagonist is still the Unbeliever who, like Doubting Thomas, does not refrain from questioning what he cannot see: when the Creator offers the leper a reward for his deeds, the man responds with "'I'll believe it when I see it'" (*The Chronicles*... 1147). Nonetheless, having once reconciled his dilemma, Covenant is less troubled by the question of the Land's actual existence in the following volumes.

Another element linking the protagonist to biblical tradition is his surname. The concept of a "covenant" (agreement) figures prominently in the Christian scriptures, because it defines the relationship between God and His chosen people (Ryken et al. 176–178). The Old Testament abounds with accounts of divine covenants. In Genesis, God promises Noah that the world will never again be flooded; He also promises Abraham that if the man follows Divine command, he will receive Canaan and protection. In Exodus, the divine covenant pertains to an entire nation—God establishes a covenant with the Israelites and frees them from Egypt. When they swear their obedience, they receive the Ten Commandments, which they place in the Ark of the Covenant. These covenants are not earned, but granted out of divine mercy, because biblical covenant is "an agreement between unequals. God is the sovereign being who initiates the covenant, who announces its conditions to people and who rewards the human recipients of the covenant with promise and blessing" (Ryken et al. 177). In the New Testament, Old Testament covenants are renewed through the Last Supper and, subsequently, by the Eucharist which reenacts the Last Supper: by sharing Christ's flesh and blood, people pledge themselves to God and are rewarded with the promise of salvation, sealed by Christ's death on the cross (Ward et al. 47, 254). This New Covenant is superior to others, because it is the final one and delivered through Christ himself (Ryken et al. 178).

W.A. Senior argues that "Donaldson's naming methodology produces a metaphoric, connotative lexicon for understanding the quintessence and role of the individual or things" (1990, 260). The protagonist's surname is not an exception. The man is hardly ever called by his first name, and even his beloved Linden realizes that she always uses only the man's surname, because his identity and actions are defined by his commitments (*Against...* 447). What Linden means is that the leper frequently tries to cope with problems by offering pacts and promises (his own covenants), for instance, that he will never mount one of the sentient horses, that he will protect his companions from harm, or that he will refrain from using power (yet bound by human fallibility, he manages to maintain intact only the first promise). Moreover, the concept of a "covenant" defines not only the protagonist's relations with others, but also his own existence. Donaldson, who was educated by Christian fundamentalists, consciously used the Old Testament idea of the "covenant of law" and the New Testament "covenant of grace" to delineate the development of his protagonist. According to Donaldson, the "old" Thomas Covenant is a man controlled by his illness, whereas the "new" Thomas Covenant, redeemed by his self-sacrifice and Linden's love, does not need these old laws ("Gradual Interview," May 27, 2004). Finally, Covenant can be also recognized as the embodiment of a covenant between the Land's inhabitants and their god, the Creator, who personally chose the man as the Land's savior. Thus, for the denizens of the Land Thomas Covenant is an incarnation of the "covenant of grace" with the Creator, a symbol of divine protection and care. If all of these biblical references pertaining to "Thomas Covenant, the Unbeliever" are taken into consideration, it is clear that the protagonist is a multifaceted figure—an innocent sufferer, a hardened skeptic, a chosen savior. The acknowledgment of these layers allows readers to deepen their understanding of the spiritual and religious dimensions of Covenant's struggle with his illness, his disbelief in the existence of the Land, and his divine appointment.

Christianity and Donaldson's Fictional Gods

Donaldson transports Covenant to a secondary world whose cosmology is embedded in the Christian perception of divinity and material creation. First of all, the imaginary realm is suspended in a dichotomy of good and evil represented by the two (at least partially) antagonistic and antithetical forces of the Creator and the Despiser. Aside from white gold magic, which in Donaldson's realm is synonymous with humankind's free will, there are no other supernatural powers or deities which could challenge the supremacy of the Creator or annihilate the Despiser (the appearance of the monstrous She Who Must Not Be Named is too brief and ambiguous to exert impact on the balance of powers). This imagery is compatible with the Christian perception of the universe as belonging to God, the Supreme Lord, who is opposed by Satan, whereas humanity's freedom allows it to choose either good or evil.

Secondly, the divine creation described in *The Chronicles* corresponds in many respects to the biblical imagery of genesis. Donaldson's supreme deity forms the Earth out of nothingness, in which act he is likened to a craftsman (*The Chronicles...* 238). Afterward, the fictional god creates people whom he destines for happiness and perfection, which they can pursue according to their free will. But the perfection of divine creation is corrupted by the Despiser, who is then cast out of infinity and imprisoned on Earth, where he tempts people to sin. All of these elements find their reflection in the biblical Book of Genesis. In Genesis, God creates the world out of a void and darkness, and once the world is ready, He fills it with life. Donaldson's imagery of a craftsman corresponds to the imagery used in Genesis 2 where God "works with his hand, taking pride in his creations. Like a potter, he shapes man from dust. Like a gardener, he plants trees. With a surgeon's skill, he removes a rib from the sleeping man" (Ward et al. 17). The first people, Adam and Eve, are said to be made in the Lord's likeness, which scholars interpret either as a physical resemblance or a spiritual one, because people possess soul, intelligence, and conscience. Their blissful existence in Eden is then shattered by the serpent's temptation, which results in expulsion. The motif of the original sin is a point of divergence between *The Chronicles* and Genesis, because though in both narratives humankind is modeled on God's perfection and destined for prosperity, *The Chronicles* never mention the first sin and the Fall. Perhaps the imaginary Land should be perceived as the pre–Fall equivalent of the biblical Eden, so then by analogy, the Despiser functions as the biblical serpent that is still trying to shatter the realm's heavenly bliss.

Thirdly, the attributes of Donaldson's Creator and Despiser suggest that they might have been modeled on the Christian God and Satan/Lucifer respectively. Like the biblical Yahweh, Donaldson's Creator is presented as a Heavenly Father dwelling in an immaterial dimension surrounded by his angel-like bright children. Though he is a generous and benevolent deity, he does not yield from testing the virtue of his chosen people (Covenant and Linden). In this respect, his actions mirror those of Yahweh who repeatedly tests his appointed prophets (e.g., Abraham is ordered to sacrifice his son Isaac). What is more, Donaldson's Creator is represented by a symbol that frequently appears in reference to the Christian God—the rainbow. In the biblical tradition, the rainbow is a sign of God's forgiveness for humankind's disobedience and of His covenant with Noah (it appears in the sky after the great deluge); it is also one of the symbols of the new covenant between Christ and humankind (Steffler 118). In Christian art, the rainbow may serve as a throne to Christ or God (Sill 4, 41). In Donaldson's realm, the rainbow functions in a similar context. It is first mentioned as one of the Creator's masterpieces (a symbol of his divine power), which linked the heavenly sphere and Earth. It does not appear for the second time until the Land is restored from apocalyptic destruction. This second rainbow is a substitution for the Creator's bodily manifestation in the material world and, like the rainbow of Christian tradition, it serves as an announcement of the reestablished connection between Heaven and Earth. Nonetheless, for all the parallels between Donaldson's Creator and the Christian God, some descriptions of the fantastic deity do not correspond to the imagery of the Scriptures and Christian theology. One of the secondary myths, for instance, explains that the Creator used forges, a cauldron, and theurgies in his divine work, which resembles some magical practices rather than the divine creation *ex nihilo* advocated by Christianity. Another secondary myth describes the deity's anger and thoughtlessness, which cloud his perception and judgment. In contrast, Christianity assumes that God is an indubitably omnipotent and omniscient entity who does not err. Thus, some of the attributes ascribed by Donaldson to his supreme deity would be considered inappropriate and unacceptable in reference to the Christian God.

The figure of Lord Foul the Despiser is less ambiguous as it is strongly embedded in the image of Satan/Lucifer. Foul's affinity with the former is grounded in his names and actions, whereas that with the latter in his origins and punishment. Though "the Despiser" is the deity's main title, he is also known as Corruption, Fangthane, Gray Slayer, Soulcrusher, and Satansheart— the last name could not have been a more obvious reference. The multitude of Foul's titles is also a reference to Satan, because the biblical antagonist is similarly known under many names, e.g., Adversary, Devil, Great Dragon, Prince of Demons (Ward et al. 223). Also, like Satan who is the "Liar and the father of lies" (Ward et al. 223), Foul deceives people to lure them into his service, to corrupt them, and eventually to thwart divine creation.

Foul's likeness to Lucifer, the rebellious fallen angel, is visible in his ambiguous origins and fate. *The Chronicles* cryptically describe Foul as the son or brother of the Creator's heart. While the idea of brotherhood is obscure and never explored in the series, the father-son relationship finds support in Christian imagery and is thus a more plausible explanation. If Foul is the Creator's son, i.e., one of his creations, then it is clear that he occupies an inferior position. Thus, after his "rebellion"—an attempt at corrupting the divine creation—he is cast out from infinity and imprisoned on Earth; though he may still try to oppose his maker, he cannot regain freedom. Foul's fate is an obvious paraphrase of Lucifer's. Being the first among the angels created by God, Lucifer rebelled against his Maker because he did not intend to accept Adam's exaltation. Consequently, he was banished from heaven together with his supporters. Donaldson's portrayal of Foul might have also been inspired by the image of the proud Lucifer from Milton's *Paradise Lost*, since Lord Foul the Despiser—the Lucifer of Donaldson's universe—is similarly depicted not as an abhorrent monster, but a majestic figure full of pride, dignity, and contempt for humankind.

The lesser divine beings that Donaldson incorporates into his imaginary numinous—the *Elohim* and Diassomer Mininderain—could have also been partially inspired by Christianity. The *Elohim*, described as the Creator's children, are beings of spiritual substance who do not change, die, or procreate (*Against...* 51); they were accidentally trapped on Earth,[4] on which they have remained ever since, striving to preserve it from corruption and destruction. They call themselves "the Creator's surrogates" (*Against...* 51), believe in their own superiority, and attempt to control the protagonists' actions. The multiple parallels between the *Elohim* and Christian angels are easily discernable. First, it is the nature of the *Elohim* that renders them similar to angels, since the latter are also described as non-physical beings who may assume corporeal appearance to serve as God's messengers, provide guidance, and deliver divine judgment (Ryken et al. 23–24). Second, there is the case of their name. Angelic names typically end in "-el," because in Hebrew *El* stands for "God," so the names emphasize the angels' bond with their Maker. However, the Hebrew plural *Elohim* stands also for "God," and this form implies that "God in his majesty represents all aspects of divinity" (Ward et al. 39). Interestingly, in a psychoanalytical study of *The Chronicles*, Kate Simons compares the *Elohim*'s leader, Infelice, to the Christian God on the basis that Infelice demands humility and abasement, and is not concerned with lesser beings (183). Yet Simons obviously neglects other aspects of the Christian God such as mercy and benevolence. Donaldson has confirmed that he was aware of the word's meaning when he chose it as the name for his imaginary race: the name was meant as an irony, since the *Elohim* are such vain and self-centered beings ("Gradual Interview," July 27, 2005). Yet even their self-centeredness can be related to biblical tradition. The proud *Elohim*, who are trapped on Earth and want to control the untrustworthy people, resemble the rebellious angels who supported Lucifer and thus suffered banishment from Heaven. What is more, *The Chronicles* reveal that one of the *Elohim* (Kastenessen) once took a mortal lover. This story is reminiscent of the biblical tale of "the sons of God"—angels or other heavenly beings—who married "the daughters of men" (Ward et al. 26–27). Both in Christianity and in Donaldson's realm, unions which blur the boundaries between mortality and divinity are treated as a sin and transgression.[5]

As for the pitiful Diassomer Mininderain, it is possible to see her as a combination of imagery pertaining to the Virgin Mary and Eve. On the one hand, Donaldson describes Mininderain as a divine consort and "stars' and heaven's chatelaine" (*The Wounded...* 158–159), which is reminiscent of how Mary is elevated as the Queen of Heaven by the Christian Church (Ryken et al. 690), though she is never presented as God's spouse. On the other hand, Diassomer functions as the embodiment of a fallen female. Like Eve, tempted by the serpent and then driven out of Eden, Diassomer responds to Foul's coaxing which deprives her of her heavenly position and results in her imprisonment on Earth. Her subsequent transformation into the monstrous She Who Must Not Be Named accentuates the depth of her earthly torment. Yet since Donaldson never clarifies what happens to Diassomer after she is liberated from her agony, it is impossible to determine her exact position within the imaginary numinous.

Christian Undertones in the Selected Themes of The Chronicles

In addition to biblical references present in the portrayal of the protagonist, dominant deities, and other divine beings, the influence of Christian Scriptures is noticeable in the series' treatment of such themes as the divine creation of life, humankind's free will, significance of self-sacrifice, and destruction of the world. As far as the theme of creation is concerned, the analogies between the Donaldsonian and Christian perception of genesis have already been analyzed. Yet this analysis should be further complemented by two episodes pertaining to Donaldson's imaginary races—the *jheherrin* and the Viles. By contrasting the acts of divine and artificial creation of sentient life, Donaldson indirectly comments on the nature of good and evil.

According to *The Chronicles*' myths, the supreme deity formed the Land as a place of beauty, and allowed its inhabitants to pursue love and fulfillment. His divine work is then contrasted with Lord Foul's actions, which are presented as corruption and a miserable parody of the Creator's perfection. Foul is the Maker of the *jheherrin*, a race of sentient mud "people" who are a byproduct of his gruesome experiments. The vulnerable and pitiful *jheherrin* find consolation in a compelling soteriological myth which accounts for their origins, their corruption from the hands of the Maker (Lord Foul), and their subsequent torment; the myth also contains a promise that a savior will eventually deliver the *jheherrin* from enslavement if they are found worthy (*The Chronicles...* 1101–1102). Thus, though they are weak, the *jheherrin* strive to oppose their Maker in order to prove worthy of salvation. In the context of the balance between the powers of good and evil, their case suggests that even though evil may corrupt originally perfect divine creation (the *jheherrin* call Foul "seedless" which means he cannot procreate or create life *ex nihilo*), good can prevail and seek restoration. This is a very Christian outlook, since Christianity affirms that everything created by God is inherently good, and evil appears when the good creation becomes corrupted (Jonas 248). Lord Foul's downfall in the first trilogy liberates the *jheherrin* and restores their ability to reproduce. Covenant later meets their descendants: the *sur-jheherrin*, the *skest*, and the Feroce, who are still seeking spiritual guidance, but misplace their faith and choose a monstrous beast as their High God. As pathetic and pitiful as these creatures might be, their yearning for a spiritual depth of existence is dramatic and poignant, and adds another layer to the series' already complex religious dimension.

The *jheherrin*'s story implies that something which had originally been a part of divine creation may be redeemed and restored to goodness even if it was at some point corrupted by evil. The case of the Viles and their descendants reveals that also artificially created life strives to become part of the divine whole. The Viles were creatures of miasma who cherished beauty and therefore loathed their own forms. To perfect their race, they used secret lore and produced the semi-corporeal Demondim. Unfortunately, the Demondim shared the fate of their makers: they succumbed to self-loathing, destroyed the Viles, and then produced creatures consisting of both flesh and lore—the ur-viles and the Waynhim. Both groups are deeply disturbed by their artificial origins and ensuing exclusion from the natural Law (*The Wounded...* 290–291). Inspired by self-loathing, the ur-viles serve evil, whereas the Waynhim seek to justify their existence through humble service; both races believe that they must adhere to their Weird (fate). In Donaldson's universe, the word "Weird" is often substituted with Würd, Worm, and Wyrd. Donaldson has admitted that he deliberately used these words interchangeably, because all of them sound like "Word," which is reminiscent of divine creation described in Genesis 1. This similarity allowed him to create a more intricate concept which might imply that everything—be it in the real or imaginary world— is united by its participation in divine creation and by its relation to One God ("Gradual Interview," January 22, 2006). As for the ur-viles and Waynhim, they eventually experience an apotheosis which liberates them from the constraints of their artificial origin, and both races are finally accepted within the structures of divine creation (they become the new Forestals). Their struggle to justify their existence and to become a part of the divine whole might illustrate the Christian belief that every living being should strive to reach God.

In Donaldson's world, the relationship between people and their god is complicated by their inability to understand the nature of divinity and their gift of free will. The series' treatment of both issues finds support in Christian thought. In the face of evil, Donaldsonian heroes—like numerous Christians appalled by the unfairness and cruelty of their world—wonder whether their god has abandoned them or whether he ever existed at all (*Against...* 75). Only a few of them suggest that the human mind cannot pierce a god's intents (the *mysterium* of the numinous) and that perhaps the Creator's "abandonment benefits his creation" (*Against...* 76), i.e., it is a necessary part of the divine plan. These boundaries of perception are well summarized by the Theomach:

> neither I nor anyone may grasp the mind of this world's Creator. The needs and desires of that which is eternal surpass finite comprehension. Yet I deem that the Earth, and within it the Land, were formed as a habitation where living beings may gaze upon wonderment and terror, and seek to emulate or refuse them [*Fatal...* 258].

Also Covenant, after his own experience of godhood, makes an insightful comment on divine nature and its limitations:

> No wonder only people like Roger and creatures like the *croyel* wanted to be gods. The sheer impotence of that state would appall a chunk of basalt [...]. Absolute power was as bad as powerlessness for anybody who valued someone else's peace or happiness or even survival. The Creator could only make or destroy worlds: he could not rule them, nurture them, assist them. He was simply too strong to express himself within the constraints of Time [*Against...* 325].

While Covenant's words aim to logically explain the deity's absence from the material world,[6] the Theomach's remark about the inexplicability of divinity and humanity's duty repeats the Christian belief that though people cannot meet God on request or comprehend His nature because God is the Ultimate Mystery, they nonetheless need to preserve their faith and submit themselves to His worship (Jonas 244).

Seldom do Donaldson's heroes realize that the Creator's withdrawal is dictated by the gift of freedom granted to his children. In fact, "the necessity of freedom" is the condition of the world's existence (only the protagonists' willing submission to evil may destroy the world) and a right that no living being should be deprived of, not even by gods: "That's the paradox of the Arch of Time [...]. If Foul just conquers us, if we're under his control, the ring won't give him the power to break out. But if the Creator tries to control us through the Arch, he'll break it" (*The One...* 87). Donaldson continuously tells his readers that everyone is entitled to their own choices, even if these choices are not the best ones, because the freedom to choose between good and evil is a divine gift. Thus, even if the heroes err and fail to make the correct decision, they are not doomed by their failure, and may still gain salvation through repentance—that is why Covenant is able to save the Land even though he is not a paragon of morality and virtue. This imagery of sin and repentance corresponds to Christian teachings. In Christianity, humankind can also exercise the power of free will to follow or reject God (Ryken et al. 788). The greatest denial of the relationship with God was performed by Adam and Eve when they ate the forbidden fruit. That did not, however, stop Yahweh from renewing covenants with His chosen people in the course of the entire Old Testament and offering them His forgiveness and mercy. Similarly, the New Testament teaches that even if people oppose God and commit sins, repentance and divine mercy will allow for spiritual renewal, since mercy is one of God's chief attributes (Ryken et al. 548).

The most highly valued form of repentance in *The Chronicles*, as well as the act invoking the greatest power, is the self-sacrifice. The three victories over Lord Foul are achieved not by the raw force of massive armies or the heroes' insurmountable magical skills, but by their ability to renounce themselves for the preservation of the Land. In *The First Chronicles*, Covenant defeats Foul only because the malevolent deity is already diminished by the pure joy of life reverberating in the laughter of Foamfollower who is willing to forfeit his life in exchange for the realm's safety.[7] When Covenant later confronts Foul in *The Second Chronicles*, he has no intention of fighting with the god to prove which one of them is mightier. Instead, Covenant tells the Despiser: "'We aren't enemies. That's just another lie. Maybe you believe it—but it's still a lie. You should see yourself. You're even starting to look like me. [...] You're just another part of me. Just one side of what it means to be human. The side that hates lepers. The poisonous side. [...] We are one.'" (*White...* 463). With these words Covenant not only acknowledges the human capacity for despair and evil, but also delivers a prophecy which will be fulfilled in *The Last Chronicles*. Afterward, the leper willingly surrenders his ring and his life to Foul. Though the protagonist dies, his soul is united with the divine Arch of Time, which he protects from Foul's onslaught. By passively accepting the attacks, the man forces the Despiser to overspend his power and disappear. Meanwhile, Linden performs her own sacrifice. The woman willingly exposes herself to evil in order to cleanse the Land from the corruption produced by the Sunbane. Her consciousness merges with the malevolent force so that she may purify it and restore to the Land as Earthpower (*White...* 487). Without Linden's willingness to subject herself to suffering, the restoration of the Land would not have been possible.

In *The Last Chronicles*, both Covenant and Linden have to renounce themselves for the final time. Linden challenges her greatest fears, while Covenant faces Foul and proclaims that neither of them will survive without the other. Because Covenant has finally understood the meaning behind the deity's existence, he decides to accept the Despiser into himself: "'All that malice and contempt is just love and hope and eagerness gone rancid. He's the Creator's curdled shadow. [...] He gives us the chance to do better. [...] taking a stand against him is what makes us who we are'" (*The Last...* 700).

For this reason, the Despiser could never have been defeated in a mere contest of powers. Only repentance and self-sacrifice could provide the protagonists with enough strength to conquer evil.

Such a perception of the restorative and redemptive power of self-sacrifice corresponds to the Christian tradition in which the act is epitomized by Jesus' crucifixion. Christ's death on the cross and subsequent resurrection are not only the climax of the biblical story of salvation, but also the ultimate victory over Death and Satan (Ryken et al. 442). Through Jesus' sacrifice, humanity is delivered from eternal death and offered the promise of salvation as a grace from their merciful God. Donaldson's descriptions of the protagonists' sacrifices contain hardly any references that would point to the biblical imagery surrounding Christ's ordeal on the cross. It is the author's elevation of the act of a self-sacrifice that brings to mind the Christian tradition: performed as a willing renunciation of oneself, the self-sacrifices of Donaldsonian protagonists have the ultimate power to vanquish evil and to deliver the people of the Land from the threat of death and damnation.

Certain elements of the apocalyptic destruction envisioned by Donaldson also correspond to the biblical vision of the Judgment Day and the coming of the Kingdom of God. Firstly, both in the universe of the Bible and in the universe of *The Chronicles* the unraveling of material reality is part of the divine plan, which will commence the spiritual renewal of the world and its inhabitants. Secondly, in *The Chronicles* the Apocalypse is embodied by the Worm of the World's End which consumes and destroys everything on its way. Since "worm" is an archaic name for "dragon," Donaldson's beast can be interpreted as the great dragon of the Book of Revelation, which represents the devil (Ryken et al. 565). Thirdly, after the Worm fulfills its purpose, the protagonists combine their talents to reconstruct a Despiser-free world. The description of the restored Land bears notions of religious exaltation and divine glory: "Intimations of morning lifted birds into the air. Chirps and twitters began like introits, the preliminaries of worship. Every in-drawn breath was a sacrament" (*The Last...* 700). The protagonists' efforts are crowned by the appearance of a rainbow—the symbol of the supreme Creator. This vision corresponds to the biblical prophecies that after the Judgment, the world and humanity will be restored in the glory of God (Ward et al. 232).

Nonetheless, there are certain differences between the biblical vision and Donaldson's version of the Apocalypse. Firstly, in Christianity no one except God knows the hour of the final judgment (Ward et al. 232). Yet in *The Chronicles* the end is bound to come once the apocalyptic Worm is awakened by a great power, which can be wielded by reckless people or those tempted by the Despiser. Thus, in Donaldson's universe humanity is the agent that may, at any time, bring forth the prophesied destruction. Secondly, along with the analogies between the Worm of the World's End and the biblical

Dragon, Donaldson's beast can also be identified with Jormungand, the Serpent of Norse mythology, which lies at the bottom of the sea, encompasses the entire Earth, and is supposed to appear during Ragnarök (Cotterell 202). The Worm resting under the One Tree resembles also Nidhogg, the dragon of Norse mythology, which gnaws at the roots of Yggdrasil, causing its downfall (Eason 47–48). Given other allusions to Norse myths appearing in *The Chronicles*, the affinity between Donaldson's Worm and Norse beasts cannot be ignored. Thirdly, in Donaldson's version of events the world is recreated after the apocalypse by three mortals bearing divine powers, who are aided by the angelic *Elohim* (that remake Donaldson's *Axis Mundi*—the sacred One Tree—and put the Worm back to its sleep). Thus, the notion of agency is again removed from the supreme god and transferred onto people. Covenant, Linden, and Jeremiah reconstruct the world and then appear in it in the manner of prophets or patriarchs: barefoot, dressed in robes, and engulfed by power. Their number can be analogous to the three persons of the Holy Trinity: Father, Son, and the Holy Spirit, or to the three members of the Holy Family: Joseph, Mary, and Jesus. Soon after they manifest their presence, the protagonists disappear—they fade together with the rainbow, the symbol of the Creator—which suggests that they might have been given access to a higher state of being, perhaps in the Creator's presence, or even a state of godhood in their own right.

Christian Symbols and Language in The Chronicles

In addition to the themes and motifs discussed so far, two other areas in which *The Chronicles* extensively borrow from the Bible are the symbols and the language. The symbols which most strongly evoke biblical tradition are water, fire, and the plagues. In the Bible, both water and fire are the catalysts of spiritual renewal and symbols of God's presence. The Old Testament accounts, for instance, for the act of ritual washing which had to precede the Israelites' practices of worship. In the New Testament, Jesus' baptism in Jordan established that act as a way of bestowing forgiveness of sin and spiritual cleansing (Sill 42). The word "baptize" is derived from the Greek verb *baptizo* which means "to immerse" and "go under"; the first baptisms were performed by full immersion in running water, and the pouring of water over one's head is a later variation of the ritual (Ward et al. 117). Moreover, the New Testament describes the practice of washing another person's feet, which expresses one's humility—a sinful woman washed Jesus' feet with her tears and was forgiven for her sins, and Jesus himself washed the feet of his disciples in an act of selfless service. The act of washing one's hands signifies innocence, as Pilate washed his hands to emphasize that he is not guilty of sentencing Jesus to death (Sill 42). What is more, water is also the means through which divinity may manifest its presence and power in the material world (Ward et al. 213–215). In the Old Testament, God sent a deluge to punish humankind, chastised the Egyptians by turning water into blood, and then parted the Red Sea so that the Israelites could escape from Egypt. In the New Testament, Jesus' miracles also often involved water: he changed water into wine during a wedding and walked on the surface of a stormy lake.

Fire likewise represents the divine in the Christian tradition. In the Old Testament, God appeared to Moses in the form of a burning bush, a pillar of fire guided the Israelites during the Exodus, and Sodom and Gomorrah were destroyed by fire sent from heaven (Ward et al. 213). In the New Testament, tongues of fire appeared above the Apostles during Pentecost, which symbolized the presence of the Holy Spirit and spiritual renewal (Steffler 5, 41). In addition, fire was a significant part of the Israelites' religious practices as they prepared burnt offerings for Yahweh. This particular element can also be associated with the destruction of sin and purification (Ryken et al. 287).

Donaldson's usage of water and fire imagery has a lot in common with the biblical symbols. In the case of water, Donaldson frequently returns to the idea of baptism and spiritual cleansing. For example, when Covenant needs to cross a river to enter the sacred region of Andelain, he does so barefooted, because the river water "was as clean, clear and fresh as an offer of baptism. At the sight of it, Covenant felt a rushing desire to plunge in, as if the stream had the power to wash away his mortality" (*The Chronicles...* 146). This scene combines the images of baptism through immersion in running water, washing of one's feet as a sign of humility, and removing one's shoes when the person is standing on holy ground—like Moses when he was approaching the burning bush (Sill 134). Another reference to baptism appears when a parched Covenant finally finds water and experiences both physical and spiritual renewal (*Against...* 335). Moreover, a bath in Lake Glimmermere, whose waters are filled with divine Earthpower, is always presented as an moment of spiritual restoration similar to the act of baptism; e.g., after Linden bathes in the Lake, her companions notice a change in her demeanor and the woman wonders whether she "gleaned something sacramental from the lake" (*Fatal...* 67). Furthermore, Donaldson's use of water imagery establishes a parallel between his protagonists—the saviors of the Land—and the figure of Christ the Savior. When Covenant tries to retrieve a magic dagger hidden in Lake Glimmermere, he miraculously walks on water supported by his white gold magic and Earthpower. Linden also uses the element to perform her own "miracles": she brings a flood to save her companions and then uses water to help her son, Jeremiah. In addition, the woman is later restored from a coma only when Covenant holds her under river water in a scene vaguely reminiscent of Christ's immersion in Jordan.

In the case of fire, several images from *The Chronicles* emphasize the element's double nature and connection to the divine. First and foremost, the protagonists' white gold magic—the power that affects the entire material creation—is manifested in the form of an argent fire which can be used both for restoration and destruction. Another example is the Giants' ritual of self-immolation in fire, *caamora*, which illustrates the transfigurative and restorative nature of the element. The most striking performance of *caamora*—Foamfollower's descent into a lake of fire hidden under Lord Foul's dwelling—combines two biblical images: John the Baptist warns people of baptism in a river of fire that will be a part of the last judgment (Ryken et al. 288), and a lake of fire serves as the representation of hell (Steffler 5) and is a place into which Satan and the damned will be ultimately thrown by God (Ryken et al. 59). In Donaldson's reconstruction of biblical imagery, Foamfollower braves the liquid hell of the lake and, just as John the Baptist prophesizes, he emerges from it refined.

Apart from water and fire, Donaldson reworks also the motif of the plagues. The most famous are the Ten Plagues from the Old Testament, which God sent to punish the Pharaoh for his refusal to release the slaves. The plagues were respectively water turned into blood, frogs, gnats/fleas, flies, disease of livestock, boils, storms, locusts, darkness, and the death of first-borns. In *The Second Chronicles*, people of the Land are falsely instructed that the Sunbane (the distortion of nature) was sent by the Creator as punishment. Though the four forms of the Sunbane are not exactly the same as the biblical plagues, their effect is similar: the desert sun, fertile sun, sun of rain, and sun of pestilence ruin the environment and people's ability to sustain their existence. But while in the Bible the plagues are God's just punishment, in *The Chronicles* they are the works of the evil deity who wishes to torment the world and destroy people's inherent connection with the Land.

What distinguishes *The Chronicles* among many other fantasy series which reconstruct the biblical material is the language. The linguistic layer created by Donaldson abounds with metaphors, similes, and allusions which pertain either to religion in general or to Christianity directly by operating with various figures, events, and concepts from the Old and the New Testament. Thus, readers are more than once invited to consider the Christian dimensions of the described scenes and events. Below is a list of selected examples which demonstrate how religion and Christianity function on the linguistic level of Donaldson's narrative (thus reinforcing the series' religious themes):

> a forest's attack on Foul's army is described as an apotheosis [*The Chronicles...* 684],

when Covenant suffers during a winter journey, he is compared to a suffering penitent [*The Chronicles...* 921]; the cold and inanition are compared to the figures of priests [*The Chronicles...* 994],

the characters' manner of speaking, when they are revealing some crucial information, is described as a "profession of faith" [*The Runes...* 720],

events are often likened to "an act of grace" [*The Last...* 106].

Such connotative vocabulary, though it is not exclusively Christian, places many episodes within a spiritual context and hints at the spiritual dimension of the heroes' quest. These examples can be complemented by numerous expressions which point directly to Christianity:

Covenant's thoughts are described as litany [*The Chronicles...* 153],

there are references to baptism/christening: "the comfortable ease of the Mahdoubt's aura washed over her [Linden] like a baptism" [*Fatal...* 409]; "[t]heir High Lord they christened the na-Mhoram" [*The Wounded...* 341],

there are also references to Holy Communion and the Eucharist: the relationship between the Ramen and the sentient horses is described as "a form of communion" [*Fatal...* 585]; the non-verbal interaction between the *Haruchai* is called "mental communion" [*Against...* 88]; after eating the nourishing fruit of *aliantha*, Linden feels "as though she had partaken of a Eucharist" [*The Runes...* 366]; the scene when Linden receives a potent liquid, called *vitrim* [*Against...* 287], from a loremaster also resembles the Eucharist:

"an iron bowl as black as obsidian took form in its palms, apparently transubstantiated from within the creature's flesh. The bowl held a fluid that gave off the must aroma of *vitrim*. Because she was touched and did not know how else to express her gratitude, Linden sank to her knees in order to accept the bowl from the loremaster's hands." [*The Runes...* 540–541],

there are references to sacraments in general: one fragment describes "Earthroot's sacramental air" [*The Chronicles...* 749]; another states that the *Elohim* "sanctified the unnatural twilight as if their coming were a sacrament" [*The Last...* 295],

the ritual performed by the Lords—the Vespers—is a congregational meeting during which the participants sing hymns and repeat their promise of service to the Land. Various Christian churches also hold the Vespers—the evening prayer service (from Latin *vesper* which means "evening")—that consist of hymns, psalms and prayers,

the *krill* (a dagger) is likened to a cross [*The Chronicles...* 829], when Covenant reaches for the evil Illearth Stone, the Stone is compared to "the fruit of the tree of the knowledge of life and death" [*The Chronicles...* 1142],

the region of Andelain is described as "imitating paradise" [*The Wounded...* 218],

a hero's invocation is "like a liturgy of worship" [*The Wounded...* 377],

the Hall of Gifts in Revelstone, lofty and spacious, is likened to a cathedral [*Fatal...* 484]; similarly, Salva Gildenbourne is described as "a cathedral forest, solemn and sacral. With every step, the trees verged closer to transubstantiation" [*Fatal...* 705],

Mahrtiir's fate is likened to "that of a sacrificial lamb" [*Fatal...* 597],

the grass stains on Linden's jeans resemble "arcane stigmata" [*Against...* 97],

there are also references to hell and its inhabitants: monsters have "satanic faces" [*The Chronicles...* 661] or unfold "like crouching behemoths" [*The Last...* 660]; the Mithil river looks "black and viscid, like a Satanist's chrism" [*The Wounded...* 204]; when the heroes emerge from a distortion in Time (a *caesure*), it is as if they emerged "from the belly of Hell's own leviathan" [*The Runes...* 534]. Even the Land's inhabitants refer to hell: during the Vespers, the High Lord mentions "[s]even hells for failed faith" [*The Chronicles...* 192], and the evil a-Jeroth is said to have come from Seven Hells, which are "rain, desert, pestilence, fertility, war, savagery, and darkness" [*The Wounded...* 309].

Other references and metaphors center around the figure of Jesus Christ and are linked to:

crucifixion: a description of Covenant's appearance states that "his frown deepened until he wore the healing of his forehead like a crown of thorns" [*The Chronicles...* 442]; when Covenant saves a child, his suffering is described as "the nails of pain which crucified him" [*The Chronicles...* 835]; when he is snake-bitten and carried by his friends, he is portrayed as "crucified across the shoulders of his companions" [*The Wounded...* 160]; when he sacrifices himself for his ex-wife, he lays "crucified on the stone. But the wound was not in his hands or feet or side: it was in his chest" [*The One...* 460]; when Linden's hand is stabbed, the assault is similarly likened to crucifixion [*Fatal...* 356],

resurrection: Andelain's beauty reminds Linden of "loss and resurrection; of broken Law and death that enabled life and victory" [*Fatal...* 716]; the sunshine feels "like the light of resurrection" [*Against...* 360], salvation: when Linden fights to help those in need, she is described as "wreathed in a glory of fire and salvation" [*Fatal*... 575]; the stars on the Ranyhyn's heads are described as shining "instances of salvation" [*Against*... 706].

These metaphors and similes (and many other examples could still be provided) strengthen the religious dimension of the narrative, constantly remind readers of the spiritual connection between the characters, the Land, and the divine, and emphasize Covenant's and Linden's role as the realm's godsend saviors.[8] Covenant is most strongly related to Christ after his first victory over evil: revived by the Creator, the leper wakes up in his own world tied to the bed "as if he had been crucified" (*The Chronicles*... 1150). It is then revealed that he wakes up during Easter morning—the reference to the celebration of Christ's victory over death strengthens the impression that Covenant is a savior designated by the Creator, who has brought redemption to the Land through his own sacrifice. It is also worth pointing out that Covenant's venture into Foul's abode is a variant of the motif of katabasis, i.e., the hero's descent into the underworld. The motif appears in ancient narratives in the quests of Gilgamesh, Odysseus, Aeneas, Heracles and Orpheus, who all enter the underworld to obtain a certain object or to free a beloved person. Their ability to return from the land of the dead confirms their status of the hero. In biblical tradition, the motif of katabasis appears in the episode of the Harrowing of Hell, when Christ enters Hell after His crucifixion to conquer the devil, liberate people from eternal death, and then return triumphant (Resurrection). Covenant's katabasis is more akin to the Christian variant, rather than to the other ones, because the leper symbolically descends into the underworld not to retrieve an object or person, but to face evil, whose personification—Lord Foul—he manages to conquer for the sake of the Land's inhabitants. All in all, *The Chronicles*' multiple linguistic allusions to Christianity, together with the biblical references hidden at various levels of the text (protagonists, deities, motifs, symbols), strongly support the claim that Donaldson's imaginary world, as well as the entire story, are deeply embedded in the Christian tradition.

The Chronicles *and Christian Ethics*

What is more, the moral integrity of Donaldson's imaginary world is visibly rooted in Christian ethics whose fundamental tenets are religious piety and love. In Christianity, the faithful are instructed to praise the Lord and follow his commandments, as well as to express their religiosity by treating other people with kindness and respect. In the Sermon on the Mount,

Jesus explicitly urges his followers to discard hatred and "love their enemies," because only then will they be allowed to enter the Kingdom of God (Ryken et al. 668). The credo to love one's enemies advocates selfless service to others, self-giving love, and humility, which are epitomized by Christ's life and death. The Seven Virtues extolled by Christian teachings are Faith, Hope, Charity, Fortitude, Temperance, Prudence, and Justice (Sill 212). The Seven Vices, known as the Seven Deadly Sins, are Pride, Lust, Gluttony, Greed, Sloth, Wrath, and Envy. As for the conceptualization of sin, Christian doctrine teaches that Jesus' sacrifice has freed people from the bondage of sin (Ryken at al. 793), that Christians do not affirm sin itself, but the forgiveness of sin offered by the merciful God (Jonas 270), and that it is the sin that should be condemned, not the sinner who may always find redemption due to God's infinite mercy.

All of these elements constitute the moral premises of Donaldson's world and determine the protagonists' path to spiritual perfection. Humble service is a theme that recurs throughout the entire series. Humans and non-humans of great power devote themselves to others: the Lords dedicate themselves to the Land, common people abide by the Oath of Peace, generations of Ramen diligently protect the Ranyhyn, while the Ranyhyn—creatures of unrivaled beauty and dignity—serve as mounts to the Land's protectors. All of them feel elevated by the service they perform, because their efforts strengthen their union with their beloved world. This notion of a union is comparable to the Christian idea suggesting that since the name *Adam* is related to the Hebrew word *adamah* meaning "ground," there is "an intimate link between man and the earth from which he was created" (Ward et al. 18). Since God established man as the steward and protector of His creation (McGrath 73), it is therefore humankind's responsibility to dedicate itself to the preservation of their world. The inhabitants of Donaldson's imaginary world perceive that responsibility as their top priority.

Donaldson then demonstrates that service to others is meaningful only when it is defined by humility and knowledge of one's limits. When the characters feel unable to defeat evil, High Lord Mhoram comforts them by reminding them that every human service is unavoidably limited by the servant's mortality, so the only expectations toward people is that they should do their best: "Life or death, good or ill—victory or destruction—we are not required to solve these riddles. Let the Creator answer for the doom of his creation" (*The Chronicles*... 821). Donaldson then warns readers that service which is performed not with humility, but with arrogant pride, eventually becomes unworthy. Excessive pride is one of the sins repeatedly condemned by *The Chronicles*. The divine *Elohim*, for instance, strive to preserve the Land, but reject any judgment apart from their own. Eventually, they are humbled by the necessity to rely on fallible humans for protection. Similarly, the *Haruchai* are severely criticized for their desire of perfection and withdrawal of service whenever they are faced with mortal fallibility: "True service submits itself to the cause which it serves, deeming that cause holy [...]. True service does not judge the deeds which are asked of it. It does not consent to this and refuse that, according to the dictates of its own pride. It gives of itself because the cause which it serves is worthy" (*The Last...* 595). Because of their failure to acknowledge their own erroneous decision to become Masters of the Land, the *Haruchai* are accused by their mythic hero—ak-Haru—of simony (*The Last...* 84), which he defines as withholding knowledge and trust from others, and treating the Land as a thing that can be possessed. In the Christian tradition, simony is the sinful act of selling and buying consecrated objects and church offices. The name is derived from Simon Magus (Magician) who offered to buy from the Apostles the power of transmitting the Holy Spirit (*Britannica...* 1012–1013). Donaldson's usage of such a specific term not only strengthens the impression that the *Haruchai* are spiritual figures close to divine power, but also emphasizes the Christian dimension of their actions and failures.

Aside from pride and simony, other sins condemned by Donaldson are greed and wrath. The embodiment of greed are the Insequent—a group of people whose covetous desire for knowledge and power violated their mortality and turned them into capricious semi-immortal beings. They are known under pseudonyms, because their real names command them. The Vizard is obsessed with the destruction of the *Elohim*, the Mahdoubt collects tokens of gratitude for her help, the Harrow yearns for ultimate power, the Ardent seeks unique experiences, while the Theomach aims to be the greatest of them all. Though they do not have a sovereign ruler, all conform to the agreement that one Insequent should not go against another, lest s/he wants to become insane and disappear. Even though some of the Insequent help out the protagonists, they do so not because of their love for the Land, but because of their private (selfish) motivation. However, though they are fairly interesting characters, they seem a last-minute addition to even out the plot. In comparison to Donaldson's other characters who undergo complex psychological development (e.g., the *Haruchai*), the Insequent are not full-fledged characters, but a symbolic representation of greed. Like excessive pride, greed needs to be punished, or at least curbed. Thus, in one way or another, Donaldson diminishes or kills all of the Insequent, and at the dawn of the new world he introduces a single new one—the Acolyte. The pseudonym suggests that s/he will be a being intent on spiritual development rather than power or personal gain.

Wrath is ambiguous, as it can be both a virtue and a sin. The Christian tradition approves of just wrath: Yahweh of the Old Testament rages at his people's sins and metes out one punishment after another, the prophets become enraged on Yahweh's behalf (e.g., Moses is furious when the Israelites worship a golden calf), and even Jesus demonstrates his capacity for anger when he chases the money-changers out from God's temple. Otto speaks about Yahweh's (divine) wrath as an aspect of *tremendum*, i.e., a manifestation of divine majesty and might, which cannot be predicted or fully comprehended by mortal reason (18–19). Yet wrath can become a sin when people lose control over their emotions and behave unreasonably; such behavior is repeatedly condemned in the Bible, because it leads to evil (Ryken et al. 25–26). Both aspects of wrath are present in *The Chronicles*. At times, Covenant is like a wrathful prophet condemning evil and injustice. When Foul derides leprosy and shows the protagonist a vision in which all people are miserable lepers, the man's fury at such merciless mockery allows him to successfully oppose the evil god. Yet though wrath inspired by opposition to evil is empowering, it may be tainted by human capacity for hatred and desire for retribution, and thus become the source of evil. It is even directly stated in *The Chronicles* that Foul "may be freed only by one who is compelled by rage, and contemptuous of consequences" (*Against...* 41). When the protagonists' rage draws close to such a state, they are appalled by the massacres they are able to perform in the name of what they deem a higher cause. The experience of such wrath does not elevate the heroes, but diminishes them and instills a feeling of shame.

The question of what is allowed in the name of a higher cause, or more precisely whether bad means justify good ends, reappears throughout the series. *The First Chronicles* give a precise answer to this moral dilemma. Covenant is not condemned when he refuses to return and protect the Land because he needs to save a child in his own world. The man who summons Covenant affirms that even the life of a single child cannot be forfeit in exchange for the Land's protection. Thus, he acknowledges the sacredness of every life, which remains in accordance with Christian belief.

Linden's moral struggle is perhaps more acute than Covenant's, because while the man tries to renounce responsibility for his actions, Linden deems herself—with inadvertent arrogance—responsible for everything. While in the Land, the woman discovers that she possesses a health-sense, i.e., an ability to enter a person's consciousness and heal the injuries of the person's body. Since she is a compassionate doctor, Linden wonders whether she is entitled to make such intrusions into another person's psyche. Though by doing so she could save a person's life, such mental intrusion would be but a milder form of demonic possession—an act repeatedly condemned by *The Chronicles*. Linden's dilemma is one of the ways in which Donaldson reworks the motif of temptation.

The motif of temptation is a prominent one within the Bible since the biblical narrative revolves around people's choice between good and evil, which then reveals their true nature and identity (Ryken et al. 851–854). The same can be said about *The Chronicles*, because Donaldson constantly tests his heroes by demanding that they make difficult moral choices. For instance, Linden's obsessive desire to be reunited with her beloveds results in her abuse of power—she forcefully resurrects Covenant and thus awakens the apocalyptic Worm. Only the sheer terror of hurting her son stops her from possessing Jeremiah's mind in order to break his mental dissociation. The woman is appalled by her mistakes and begins to perceive her soul as carrion. Throughout *The Chronicles* temptation is also given other faces. As temptation for dominance, it revolves around the magical instruments whom many desire to possess. Donaldson's protagonists eventually learn to renounce power: Covenant willingly submits his white gold ring to Foul, and Linden twice gives up her Staff of Law. Such decisions become milestones in their spiritual growth. Another type of temptation is the one posed by evil. In exchange for worship, Lord Foul promises Covenant and others a share in ruling, restoration to health, or salvation from death. Such temptation corresponds to the Christian idea that Satan cannot gain mastery over a person's soul if s/he does not willingly accede to worship him. Both Covenant and Linden, regardless of their other mistakes, always refuse such direct temptation. Finally, the heroes have to deal with the temptation of believing in their own perfection and self-sufficiency. Perfection is a divine attribute precluded by mortal fallibility; aided by their companions and communities, people may only aim at fully realizing their human potential. Yet Linden, burdened with several tasks, assumes supreme responsibility and fails to acknowledge other peoples' right to bear responsibility for their own choices and errors. Thus, she is told: "you demean all who stand with you by believing that there can be no other fault than yours, and that no fault of yours can be condoned" (*Against...* 587). To make amends and become stronger, Linden must renounce her claim for perfection and her self-centered perception of the world.

Fortunately for the heroes, *The Chronicles* repeatedly ascertain that no mistake or sin is too great to be redeemed. Yet Donaldson creates a world in which salvation is achieved not by faith and divine grace, but by one's works, which is contrary to what has been accepted by the western Church (McGrath 153). Both the Old and the New Testament instruct the faithful to lead a moral life regulated by divine commandments and both, particularly the New Testament, extol God's love and mercy, which are given to people as a divine gift, regardless of personal merits (Wogaman 10). Following the Bible, Augustine of Hippo (354–430) argued that weak and sinful humanity can be redeemed only through divine grace (McGrath 150), though people are, of course, required to live in such a way as to become worthy of that gift. Augustine's view is still upheld by the Western Church:

> *All* persons have missed the mark of God's holiness; *all* persons fall short of God's glory. Once we have sinned and offended God, it is up to *God* to forgive *us*. It comes as a free

gift that has been offered to all through the death and resurrection of Christ. To say that we can save ourselves through our good deeds is to say that the death of Christ was not necessary [Fedler 197].

Augustine's teachings were challenged by Pelagius (390–418) who advocated salvation through works, i.e., achieved by good deeds. Pelagius emphasized the importance of human free will and believed that the notion of salvation through grace alone "encouraged moral laxity [...] and failed to emphasize the need for Christians to actively seek perfection" (McGrath 152). Pelagius argued that perfection, i.e., obedience to all of God's laws, was possible for humankind, and that humankind should not search for excuses in the idea of inborn sinfulness advocated by Augustine.

The fate of Donaldson's heroes clearly exemplifies the Pelagian worldview: the heroes do not gain their salvation by faith (they hardly have any religious faith at all), but by their conscious attempts at overcoming their weaknesses and repenting for their sins. They also hardly ever rely on divine grace to deliver them from harm; one of the few exceptions is when one of the heroes says: "*Attempts must be made, even when there can be no hope. The alternative is despair. And betimes some wonder is wrought to redeem us*" (*Against…* 76; italics in the original). Some wonder is indeed wrought: despite their mistakes, the protagonists are able to repent for their sins and, using their own divine-like powers, eventually restore the Land to its greatness. Yet that wonder is shown to stem more from the protagonists' dedication, hard work, and right decisions, rather than from divine grace and mercy.

Criticism of Institutional Religion

In addition to contesting the idea of salvation through grace, *The Chronicles* include an implicit criticism of institutionalized religion, hidden in the protagonists' personal experiences with Christianity (since the series shows modern-day people transported to a fantasy world, it can mention Christianity directly). Covenant and Linden can hardly be called religious people. Yet rather than describe them as declared atheists, it is more correct to say that they—like many modern people—have lost their connection with religion and the numinous (which they rediscover only in the Land). While both, consciously or not, yearn for a spiritual depth of life, the religious institutions of their world are shown as insufficient and ineffective in providing either spiritual meaning to their lives or even mere consolation in times of personal strife.

For instance, when Covenant is severely tormented by the death of his daughter and by his own failures, he happens upon a gathering devoted to spiritual healing and revival during the Easter season, organized by Dr. Johnson and Matthew Logan.[9] There, he hears a prayer as if designed to illustrate his emotional torment, since it highlights people's desperate need of Jesus' mercy and forgiveness (*The Chronicles...* 795). The pleading for divine intervention is then followed by passages from the Bible. The first reading is about the terrible punishment that will be meted out on people who do not follow God's commandments. For Covenant, that reading carries a very personal message: the pain and terror inflicted on him are divine judgment for his failures. The second reading is about the Apocalypse (*The Chronicles...* 797), and the passage's reference to "the unbelievers" becomes a direct warning for Covenant, the series' supreme Unbeliever (and Donaldson later reworks the image of fire and brimstone mentioned in the passage by having Covenant carried over a lake of lava and, in that way, delivered from the threat of death). Next, Dr. Johnson claims that sinfulness is expressed by one's bodily sickness, so he invites people to experience physical and spiritual healing. The preacher highlights human imperfection and then announces: "The Old Covenant says to you as plain as day, 'The leper who has the disease shall wear torn clothes and let the hair of his head hang loose, and he shall cover his upper lip and cry, "Unclean, unclean."'" (*The Chronicles...* 797). Again, these words strongly appeal to Covenant for whom the word "unclean" has become a personal mantra (his attitude can be also considered an extreme case of self-abasement in the face of the numinous—an emotional response to the magnitude of the divine that Otto discussed under the category of *augustum*). Thus, when Dr. Johnson promises that even lepers can be healed through Jesus, if they sincerely plead "I believe; help my unbelief" (*The Chronicles...* 799), Covenant yields to the promise of salvation. Unfortunately, Dr. Johnson is either a very poor preacher or a fraudster, because when Covenant reveals that he truly is a leper, the preacher has him removed from the congregation. Yet Covenant is also responsible for the treatment that he receives from the hands of the gathering. Though he wants help, he cannot make himself kneel and honestly ask for forgiveness. When pressed by Dr. Johnson, he reluctantly admits: "I do not believe" (*The Chronicles...* 800). This episode presents Covenant as a man unable to believe in divine providence and to establish a personal relationship with the numinous. Yet it also suggests that preachers and religious gatherings are not the best path to God: Dr. Johnson never sympathizes with Covenant, and the participants who pray for spiritual renewal never reflect on their treatment of the leper.

Linden's experiences with the church similarly suggest that spiritual development can be found in overcoming one's imperfections and serving those in need, rather than in a religious congregation. Traumatized by her father's suicide, Linden found support neither in her mother who yielded to self-pity and obsessive church-going nor in faith, because "[s]he spent too many hours as a child, wearing her one nice dress and fidgeting while a preacher levied strictures against her; a preacher who knew nothing about her pain—or her mother's" (*The Runes*... 270). Thus, as an adult woman, Linden proclaims that she does not need God (*The One*... 375), and she does not believe that any divine force will respond to her pleas for help (*Fatal*... 560). As a protagonist, Linden is never driven by faith in the divine, but by love: for Covenant, her friends, and the Land. It is only because of love and self-reproach that she is able to overcome her inadequacies and rise to the status of the Land's savior.

What is more, the case of Joan, Covenant's ex-wife, implies that misplaced faith can have detrimental, even fatal, results. After she flees from her husband's leprosy, Joan is tormented by anger and guilt. She cannot find consolation in mainstream religion, because it instructs her to acknowledge her own blame—something Joan is unwilling to do (*Against*... 693). Instead, she responded to Foul's teaching of despair and joined the Community of Retribution, which is a gathering of people who believe that others are to be blamed for all the sins and wickedness, and therefore they should be sacrificed to bring redemption for those truly faithful. The Community, together with the Clave operating in the Land, are images of corrupt congregations, which mockingly use Christian symbols: the triangle (which represents the Holy Trinity) and croziers (staffs carried by archbishops of the church, also associated with saints). Joan's misplaced faith eventually results in her madness and demonic possession. Though the woman can be chastised for the inability to acknowledge her own sins, her case is another example of the ineffectuality of religious institutions in dealing with traumatized individuals. As a result, despite their multiple and complex references to the biblical tradition, *The Chronicles* are strongly distrustful of institutional religion: the heroes have a very poor relationship with religious authorities and only *para*-religious institutions are present in the imaginary Land. Para-religious, because the Council of Lords simply supports people in their personal commitment to the Land without imposing any formalized practices of worship, whereas the Clave and the Masters function more in the context of tyrannical administrative bodies that intend to control all aspects of people's life and censor their knowledge, rather than encourage them to explore their relationship with the divine.

Stephen Donaldson and the Religious Dimensions of The Chronicles

In the "Gradual Interview" available on Stephen Donaldson's official website, the author has repeatedly commented on his attitude to religion and its impact on the religious aspects of *The Chronicles*. The author confirmed that he was raised by parents who were fundamentalist Christian missionaries, and because of that he possesses a strong background in fundamentalist Christianity. This background explains the series' multiple references to Christianity (present in the images of the numinous and in the structures of fictional religions) and the abundance of religious and Christian-oriented motifs and linguistic phrases that characterizes *The Chronicles*. Though Donaldson argues that the purpose of including Christian-related vocabulary was "to preserve the theoretical possibility that everything in the Land flows outward from the many layers of Covenant's consciousness—and later of Linden's" ("Gradual Interview," November 3, 2008), we could add that, after all, the Land and everything in it emerge from the writer's consciousness—and unconsciousness. Interestingly, while Donaldson does acknowledge that fundamentalist Christianity is deeply ingrained in his (un)consciousness ("Gradual Interview," June 8, 2006), he also claims that though Christianity was his starting point, he developed his work "in directions which would doubtless have horrified the missionaries of [his] childhood" ("Gradual Interview," May 27, 2004)—an example of this can be the ambiguous relationship between the Creator, the Despiser, and Covenant, which was inspired by the Christian concept of the Trinity and then realized as a theme of shared identity, i.e., both deities and white gold magic can be regarded as aspects of Covenant ("Gradual Interview," April 27, 2004).

It should be noted that in another part of the interview Donaldson stated that he is not a believer ("Gradual Interview," April 27, 2004), and then he voiced his objections to the theological distortions and several faults of organized religion as well as to "the evils which are practiced in the name of Christianity" ("Gradual Interview," April 11, 2007). It can be argued, therefore, that the series' distrust of institutional religion is rooted in Donaldson's personal experiences, and the corrupted Clave becomes an embodiment of the faults which Donaldson ascribes to religious institutions. On the topic of the Clave, Donaldson explains that though he would not say that it is based on the Christian Church, "there's no question that the Clave (intentionally) reflects my personal experience with specific churches, specific brands of fundamentalism" ("Gradual Interview," July 18, 2006). What is more, in *The Last Chronicles* Donaldson suddenly begins to use the word "magick" in relation to various powers, both good and evil. "Magick" spelled with "ck" is traditionally understood to refer to witchcraft practices and the occult. When Donaldson uses this word in reference to good powers which are not condemned in the series, his intentions become difficult to decipher. Interestingly, when he was asked by one reader about the position of "nature magick" in the story, he avoided a direct response and instead talked about his overall religious attitude ("Gradual Interview," October 15, 2007). In addition, the series' message—that through their dedication and love people can achieve redemption and forgiveness—also seems to stem from the author's own beliefs which could be defined as a combination of Humanism and practicality rather than Christian piety since, though Donaldson acknowledges the beneficial influence which the figure of Jesus can have on people's lives, he has also highlighted the importance of people's duty to bear responsibility for their actions and condemned their attempts at justifying their failure to do so with religion ("Gradual Interview," May 31, 2004). Finally, Donaldson has stated that he is against allegory, that he does not intend for his texts to be allegories of anything, and that he strongly believes in "selfless storytelling":

> the content of any communicative work arises from an interaction or synergy between the work and its audience. And (speaking now exclusively of books) in this interaction or synergy the author is conspicuously absent. Only the text is relevant to the reader. In other words, what you see is what you get ["Gradual Interview," February 28, 2006].

Thus, Donaldson implies that the writer's background (probably including the religious background) is irrelevant for the interaction between the reader and the text, and so he conveniently shifts the responsibility for a text's meaning from the writer to the reader.

If all of these claims about authorial intent and consciousness are taken into consideration and juxtaposed against *The Chronicles*, the series' religious background becomes ambiguous. After all, despite Donaldson's claims to neutrality, the series' multiple biblical references and religious language prove that the narrative is deeply embedded in the Christian tradition and the author's extensive knowledge of it. Moreover, the moral premises of the imaginary world correspond to Christian ethics. At the same time, however, the Land is infused with a kind of animism and nature worship of Earthpower, institutional religion is portrayed as ineffective, and the story promotes salvation by works. Thus, *The Chronicles of Thomas Covenant, the Unbeliever* are either an example of how the author's past knowledge unconsciously resurfaces in the text or of the author's deliberate manipulation so that the text will reflect his personal convictions. It is difficult, if not impossible, to determine how many (and which) of the references to Christianity appearing in the series are Donaldson's conscious allusions and artistic recreations, and how many of them slipped into the series unwittingly, seeping from the author's subconscious. Only Donaldson himself would be able to tell the difference and reveal to what extent Thomas Covenant the Unbeliever is perhaps his literary alter-ego—a man similarly dissatisfied with religious institutions who, therefore, establishes his own path to spiritual development that will allow him to achieve a meaningful relationship with the Holy, however he perceives and defines it. Regardless of whether the protagonist really is the author's alter-ego, Donaldson has managed to create a fantastic secondary world with multilaterally developed images of the numinous and religion. It is a world in which the heroes' religiousness, experiences of and responses to the divine prominently shape the entire narrative. Most importantly, it is a world richly suffused with elements of the biblical tradition and Christian ethics, which are skillfully integrated with the structures of the secondary world, and which retain much of their original connotations.

3

Christianity as a Constituent of Religious Pluralism in Guy Gavriel Kay's *The Fionavar Tapestry*

Introduction to The Fionavar Tapestry

Guy Gavriel Kay (b. 1954) is one of the leading contemporary Canadian fantasists. His debut work—*The Fionavar Tapestry*, comprising *The Summer Tree*, *The Wandering Fire*, and *The Darkest Road* (1984–1986)—has become internationally popular, thus giving impetus to the development of both Kay's literary career and Canadian fantasy fiction. Prior to the publication of *Fionavar*, Kay assisted Christopher Tolkien in editing the manuscript of *The Silmarillion* which Tolkien did not finish before his death in 1973. Though it would be incorrect to say that *Fionavar* is a completely derivative work, Tolkien's style of writing did have a profound influence on Kay's first series. Arguably, *The Fionavar Tapestry* is a compelling mixture of imitation, reconstruction, and creativity. On the one hand, it is fairly easy to spot the analogies between Kay's imaginary land of Fionavar and Tolkien's Middle-earth in terms of their fictional geography (a western coast bordered by an ocean), fantastic races (Kay's "lios alfar" and "svart alfar" are equivalents of Tolkien's elves and orcs both in appearance and behavior), and main themes (both deal with a cosmic battle against an Evil Lord). On the other hand, Kay and Tolkien are markedly different in their choice of heroes (*Fionavar*'s protagonists are citizens of modern Toronto who are magically transported to a fantastic realm), reconstruction of mythological borrowings (Kay's is more conspicuous since he includes Arthur, Lancelot, and Guinevere as major characters), and treatment of religion (while Tolkien was very careful to avoid any direct references to religion, Kay includes numerous). Still, Kay's subsequent publications have confirmed that he is not an imitator, but a gifted author who excels at writing historical fantasy, in which he interweaves fantastic plots with authentic historical settings and events. Consequently, critics of fantasy fiction have recognized Kay for his skill in worldbuilding (Clute and Grant 530–531), lyrical language (Ivison 139), and development of heroes who are not cardboard figures, but individuals with realistic personalities. Kay's most acclaimed works are *Tigana* (1990), *A Song for Arbonne* (1992), and *Sailing to Sarantium* (1998).

The Fionavar Tapestry chronicles the adventures of five young Torontonians—Paul Schafer, Kevin Laine, Dave Martyniuk, Jennifer Lowell, and Kimberley Ford—who are magically transported to the kingdom of Brennin located in the secondary world of Fionavar. Once there, they learn that a malevolent deity, Rakoth Maugrim, is threatening the realm's safety. If Fionavar is overtaken by evil, other worlds will suffer as well. Thus, the protagonists become involved in a cosmic battle, during which each of them discovers their unique role in the conflict. These roles allow them to directly experience the Fionavarian numinous and, in some cases, acquire divine powers and an intermediary status between mortality and divinity.

In contrast to Donaldson's *Chronicles of Thomas Covenant* in which the characters rarely faced gods, but frequently dealt with lesser divine beings, in Kay's *Fionavar Tapestry* people are constantly challenged by different embodiments of the numinous, which actively participate in the realm's affairs. The five protagonists learn that for the inhabitants of Fionavar deities are not a remote abstraction, but entities that can be encountered in the material world. Thus, to fully evaluate the trilogy's religion(s), it is essential to analyze Fionavar's cosmology, pantheon of gods, and divine beasts. Following other categories established by the phenomenology of religion, the analysis[1] focuses on the structure of the fantastic religious institutions and figures of divine intermediaries. It investigates both groups' relationship to gods, their access to divine powers and instruments of power, their religious practices, and sacred places. Moreover, it is essential to account for the protagonists' personal experiences of the divine, because they reveal their attitudes toward the numinous and, in general, the religious depth of human life.[2]

Images of the Numinous

First and foremost, the trilogy's cosmological vision revolves around the idea that the fantastic land of Fionavar is the first of all worlds, "the prime creation, which all the others imperfectly reflect" (*TST* 18). This implies that

Fionavar is both a matrix for other realms and an unattainable sacred ideal whose fate affects the well-being of those other realms. Though ordinary people from other worlds neither know about Fionavar nor are able to enter it, some wielders of power can nevertheless transgress the boundaries. Aside from constantly reminding readers that it is of paramount importance to protect the divine Fionavar and maintain a balance between the existing realms, the trilogy never delves into more detail about the nature of the parallel worlds or their dependency on the first world. It is only said that the worlds form a grand pattern (*TST* 69) and that they rarely intersect (*TST* 18). This shortage of information can be regarded as a component of the mystery—*mysterium*—surrounding the numinous, because it highlights both humanity's general lack of knowledge about the complexity and nature of divine creation, and its lack of access to such knowledge.

Second, the trilogy's portrayal of the numinous combines elements of monotheism and polytheism. Though there is a supreme sovereign deity who is challenged by a malevolent divine antagonist, there are also several lesser gods and goddesses who fulfill their own duties and mediate between humankind and the divine. The supreme god—known as the Weaver—is presented as a figure akin to a Heavenly Father, as the absolute creator who formed Fionavar and all of the subordinate worlds, and as a benevolent deity who constantly tends to his creation. Though he never directly manifests his powers in the material world, appears in a bodily form, or intervenes in the affairs of his land (which makes him another fantastic *Deus Absconditus*), Fionavarians generally acknowledge his existence and divine reign, universally laud him as an omniscient and omnipotent god, and believe that everything created by him is good. As there is neither formal worship of the deity (and apparently no need of his formal worship, which emphasizes the deity's *a priori* existence) nor official doctrines regulating people's knowledge about him, Fionavarians are left to experience the numinous according to their own intuition and emotional judgment. Unfortunately, since the protagonists never encounter the Weaver personally and the few secondary myths recounted in the trilogy do not reveal much about the genesis of the secondary world or the figure of its creator, it is impossible to discuss in more detail the characters' reactions to the numinous embodied by the Weaver. Given the few hints spread throughout the narrative, we can only speculate that such an encounter would inevitably inspire the mortal witness of divine majesty with reverential awe and humble submission, and perhaps also evoke a shudder of dread—though the Weaver is generally presented as a benevolent deity, his laws are observed partly for the fear of punishment awaiting the disobedient.

According to Fionavar's cosmology, evil was introduced into the realm (and subsequently into related worlds) through the arrival of Rakoth Maugrim, the Weaver's antagonist. Rakoth's pseudonym—"the Unraveller"—emphasizes his opposition to the supreme god and the destructive nature of his powers: he aims to unravel the divine tapestry, i.e., to take control over the worlds and refashion them to his liking. Kay's secondary creation myths explain that Fionavar and the entire material reality were formed by the Weaver on his Loom, and that Rakoth is a foreign entity that came from outside the Loom, bringing with him suffering and corruption (*TST* 366). The secondary myths provide various explanations as to why Rakoth was able to penetrate the divine creation. One version claims that the malevolent god took advantage of a conflict between the younger gods and slipped from their watch (*TST* 296). Another questions, perhaps inadvertently, the supreme god's omniscience by suggesting that Rakoth entered Fionavar when the Weaver was too preoccupied with the creation of his most beautiful children, the lios alfar (*TST* 296). Yet another speculates that the evil deity came after the first man killed his brother (*TST* 296), as if lured by human sin. Like in the case of Donaldson's *Chronicles*, the origins of the malevolent deity are a matter of speculation, which also points to the mystery (*mysterium*) of the numinous. Regardless of which version is true, it is generally accepted that Rakoth is not subjected to the reign of the supreme creator and is not a part of the divine plan (it is said that no thread in the pattern of the Tapestry bears his name). Consequently, he cannot be annihilated, but only imprisoned within the material world.

Though such a condition might seem to point to Rakoth's omnipotence, even to his superiority over the Weaver, his divine attributes of majesty and might are repeatedly negated. First of all, the very fact that the evil deity can be imprisoned by the mortal Fionavarians for a thousand years undermines his infinite divine power. Secondly, to escape from his prison, Rakoth severs his chained hand, which he is later unable to restore—his is only the limited power of corruption and destruction, not of creation or restoration. Thirdly, the deity is not only bound by a prophecy—if he begets a child with a mortal woman, he will become part of the Loom and susceptible to death—but his knowledge and foresight prove insufficient to avoid the prophecy's fulfillment. Thus, he is eventually killed by his own son, and good unquestionably triumphs over evil.

Though the Weaver never appears in the material world, Rakoth adopts a corporeal form and personally supervises the conquest of the fantastic world. Unlike Donaldson's Lord Foul, he is presented as a contemptuous and wrathful monstrosity (*TST* 368), and his abode, Starkadh, is similarly dreadful and gruesome (*TST* 210). On the one hand, such a portrayal of evil falls prey to one of the fantasy genre's clichés: that everything malevolent and destructive is necessarily ugly and degenerated. On the other, it emphasizes the frightening terribleness (*tremendum*) of divinity—in contrast to other forms of the numinous present in Fionavar, Rakoth and everything connected to him evokes in the heroes only the feelings of disgust, terror, and abasement rather than the worshipful awe and humble admiration which Otto also associates with the numinous experience (as part of the category *augustum*). Encounters with Rakoth are traumatic ordeals which arouse all the negative emotions hidden in Otto's definition of the creaturefeeling, i.e., "the emotion of a creature, abased and overwhelmed by its own nothingness in contrast to that which is supreme above all creatures" (10). Nonetheless, because of the nature of people's relationship with their god, the trilogy never questions the Weaver's absence or the necessity for human agents to save Fionavar in his stead. Instead, the series consistently reaffirms the freedom of human will and the god's trust in his children. That the protagonists must oppose evil out of their own choice and with their own strength is even set as a divine commandment (*TST* 367). Moreover, even though the Weaver constantly attends to his creation—the narrator frequently uses phrases such as: "For a moment the Weaver's hands were still at his Loom" (*TST* 325)—the trilogy insists that the heroes' future is not preordained, but shaped by their independent choices. When one of the protagonists morosely states: "I am the agent of the Weaver's will. For what should I hope?," another defiantly claims: "We are not slaves to the Loom" (*TWF* 279). Thus, like *The Chronicles*, *The Fionavar Tapestry* also acknowledges human freedom as a key element of divine creation and a gift from the benevolent creator.

The divine conflict between the Weaver and the Unraveller is portrayed as a clash between the contradictory forces of Light and Darkness. Yet though Kay argues for a balance between Fionavar and the subordinate worlds, he does not advocate in favor of a similar balance between these contradictory forces. Darkness is apparently unnecessary and has to be controlled or removed, because it only corrupts god's perfect work. Thus, Rakoth—the supreme embodiment of evil and Darkness—is eventually defeated and destroyed. Yet since Rakoth was not created by the Weaver in the first place, but lured into the fantastic world by conflict and/or human sin, readers may speculate about the purpose of his existence within the secondary universe and his possible return in the future.

The trilogy's monotheistic vision of a divine creator, his evil adversary, and their conflict over the material world is disrupted by a pantheon of lesser gods and goddesses. No explanation is given about their origins, only a hint that they received their "names and powers by grace of the Weaver's hand" (*TDR* 113); Rakoth mockingly calls them tamed (*TST* 366). These lesser deities can be encountered in specific regions of the imaginary realm, where they tend to their duties and function as intermediaries between humankind and the Weaver, whose commands restrict their actions: they cannot help people unless they are bound by a wielder of power and summoned to do so.

Otherwise, they will be punished for their transgression. Their divine omnipotence is, therefore, fragmentary or illusory.

In contrast to the Weaver and the Unraveller, the minor gods are associated with various elements of the natural world (and thus correspond to similar entities present in various mythological traditions). Chief among them are Mörnir and Dana, who are identified with heaven and earth, and represent the duality of a divine father and mother. Mörnir of the Thunder is a sky god particularly revered by the High Kings of Brennin, who are called "the Children of Mörnir" (*TST* 104) because of their bond with the deity. He is also respected by the Council of Mages, because he is the source of their mystical knowledge and power. Still, there are no temples or shrines dedicated to the god and no doctrines or scriptures that would regulate worship; his most sacred place is the eponymous Summer Tree situated in Godwood, where the Kings of Brennin perform their sacrificial offerings. Mörnir manifests his power through thunder and his divine animals are two ravens—Thought and Memory.

Dana is a mother-goddess identified with the earth and the moon.[3] Like Mörnir, she is worshipped throughout all of Fionavar (the banner of Brennin includes both the sacred Tree of Mörnir and the Moon of Dana), yet she is exclusively represented by a religious order of priestesses. The relationship between Mörnir and Dana is ambiguous and never clarified. On the one hand, their conversation rings with banter, flirtation, and affection (*TST* 236–237), which suggest an intimate relationship. On the other, their struggle for domination results in divine conflicts and is reflected in the animosity between the mages (or men in general) and the priestesses. Perhaps the relationship between the deities escapes human explanation; as one hero concludes about Dana: "Goddess of all the living in all the worlds; mother, sister, daughter, bride of the God. [...] it didn't matter which, all were true: that at this level of power, this absoluteness of degree, hierarchies ceased to signify" (*TST* 230). Mörnir's and Dana's superior position among the lesser deities is reinforced by a secondary myth explaining how the first men came to Fionavar: "there were men in Fionavar then, for Iorweth had come from oversea, in answer to a dream sent by Mörnir with sanction of the Mother" (*TST* 367). It is also said that Jaelle, the High Priestess of Dana, "seeks a return to the old ways of the Goddess ruling through her High Priestess, which is how it was before Iorweth came from oversea" (*TST* 71). This seems to suggest that before men came to Fionavar, the land was ruled by women on behalf of the goddess. But since this idea is never explored in the series, it might be an editorial mistake made by the author.

Apart from Mörnir and Dana, the protagonists occasionally encounter Cernan of the Beasts who is the antlered master of the wilderness, his twin sister Ceinwen of the Bow—goddess of the hunt, Liranan—god of the sea, and Macha and Nemain—the twin goddesses of war. Though powerful in their own domains, these deities are neither omniscient nor omnipotent (*TST* 325), and need to follow the laws established by the Weaver. While their divinity and superior status are acknowledged by the inhabitants of the realm, little is revealed in the trilogy about any specific religious practices pertaining to these deities. Also, these minor deities are allowed to have love affairs with mortals; the offspring of such union are the Andain, a race of semi-divine beings, that blurs the boundaries between mortal creation and the numinous (given that Rakoth also engages in a sexual intercourse with a mortal woman, it seems that the Weaver is the single deity that remains beyond human sexuality, which somehow elevates him above other divine entities). The Andain are privileged beings, because they take the best of both worlds: they possess divine powers and human freedom of will to act according to their own choices (*TWF* 260).

Whenever the protagonists are confronted by any of these minor deities, they are again exposed to the Fionavarian numinous in its various aspects. The minor gods, though not as mighty as the Weaver or Rakoth, are also an otherworldly mystery whose nature and existence escapes the heroes' fallible human reasoning, and any encounter with them is both a frightening and fascinating experience (*mysterium tremendum et fascinas*). When faced by these gods, the heroes become aware of the contrast between their puny mortality and the might and beauty of the immortals. This majesty and potency of the numinous (*majestas*) overwhelms them even when they face benevolent gods. When they encounter the malevolent Rakoth, the experience is one of sheer terror, because he represents the tremendous horror of the numinous (*TST* 366). Moreover, the deities' powers are unattainable if they are not willingly lent to a mortal. However, even when some of the protagonists temporarily acquire godlike powers or become earthly intermediaries to the minor gods, they hardly comprehend their new status and constantly struggle to control their new abilities. Thus, the protagonists' responses to Fionavarian numinous vary from awe and gratitude to humble obedience, insecurity, and mortal dread (*augustum*). Anxiety prevails, because though Rakoth is the only truly malevolent entity, the heroes learn that even the help of the benevolent gods is a double-edged gift which drastically changes the existence of its mortal recipient and can eventually prove destructive. In addition, some of the lesser deities (even though they presumably are subjected to the Weaver's will and cosmic plan) are entirely indifferent to humankind's well-being and do not even participate directly in the fight against Rakoth. Consequently, the heroes cannot judge these gods according to their human concepts of what is morally good or evil, which corresponds to Otto's claim that the numinous escapes such logic and rationalization. When encountering the Fionavarian deities, the protagonists need to forsake their assumptions and instead open their minds and hearts to the numinous experience.

Other Faces of the Numinous

Like in the case of Donaldson's *Chronicles*, Fionavarian numinous is linked to various creatures related to the gods, which to a different degree embody divine nature and potency. Consequently, encounters with these creatures also shape the inhabitants' perception of the numinous, and form another level of mediation between the human and the divine.[4] As far as the Weaver is concerned, his divine nature is best expressed through three of his creations: the Paraiko, the lios alfar, and the Wild Hunt. The Paraiko are a race of giants and the first among the Weaver's children (*TDR* 113), special for two reasons: their bloodcurse and "kanior." The former is a curse that will fall on anyone who sheds the Paraiko's blood, while the latter is a rite of lamentation for the dead which offers consolation and cleansing of guilt to the living. Both the curse and kanior are conditioned by the Paraiko's inborn innocence: they do not know hatred and restrain from violence even at the expense of their own safety. As the Weaver's first children, they are the embodiment of his gentleness and goodness. Given the spiritual dimensions of their existence, we could assume that the Paraiko should have developed some form of religious worship. Nonetheless, nothing is said of whether they possess any rites or practices which would honor their creator (even though it can be inferred that the Paraiko live in structured communities regulated by certain laws and customs).

The lios alfar (elves in traditional fantasy novels) are the epitome of the Light, beauty, and joy of life permeating the Weaver's creation (*TST* 167). To honor his beloved Children, the god formed a separate world to which they head after they are weary of earthly existence; to reach their promised land, the lios alfar embark on a sea journey and sail until they cross the boundaries of worlds (*TWF* 302). Because the lios alfar embody Light, the heroes are invariably mesmerized by their inborn grace, whereas Rakoth's perennial wish is to annihilate them. As in the case of the Paraiko, nothing is said about the lios alfar's religious practices; they acknowledge their creator only by occasionally referring to him in reverential speech.

The Wild Hunt is by far the most intriguing among the Weaver's creations, because it seems distinctly different from the god's nature. The Wild Hunt—a group of ghostly kings on ghostly horses, guided by a human child—began to roam the Fionavarian sky soon after the creation of the world. They are blood-thirsty and indifferent to humankind, yet they cannot ride without their human guide. When they had once lost their guide, they agreed to be bound by magical sleep (broken only by an item of power—Owein's Horn) until another child joined them on "the Longest Road." Apart from the loss of the child-guide, only divine intervention can curb the Hunt's killing. Yet though the Hunt is a source of chaos, it cannot be destroyed, because its presence conditions the existence of Fionavar and other worlds:

the Hunt was placed in the Tapestry to be wild in the truest sense, to lay down an uncontrolled thread for the freedom of the Children who came after. And so did the Weaver lay a constraint upon himself, that not even he, shuttling at the Loom of Worlds, may preordain and shape exactly what is to be. We who came after [...] we have such choices as we have, some freedom to shape our own destinies, because of that wild thread of Owein and the Hunt [*TDR* 113].

The creation of the Wild Hunt not only conditioned the existence of free will, but it also had a paramount impact on entire divine genesis. While the Hunt's unpredictable nature became the basis for individual human freedom, because of its presence the divine Loom ceased to be "sacrosanct" (*TDR* 114), and so Rakoth could enter the Weaver's worlds. The trilogy implies, therefore, that the existence of evil is the price that humanity has to pay for their gift of freedom. Interestingly, before the Wild Hunt is bound by sleep for the second time, it is promised its own freedom in all of the Weaver's worlds before the end of time (a kind of pre-apocalyptic vision). Since the Hunt is also one of the Weaver's creations, their readiness to kills and their disregard for humankind can point to the creator's own capacity for violence and indifference (the terribleness of the numinous).

While the beings created by the Weaver generally affirm his goodness and love for his Children, Rakoth's beast-servants, who are a caricature of the Weaver's work, are proof of his malice and corruption. Rakoth's svart alfar (orcs/goblins in conventional fantasy fiction) are foul and perverse creatures who find pleasure in tormenting and killing; they are the Darkness which symbolically opposes the Light embodied by the lios alfar. To destroy the lios, Rakoth hides a gruesome monster—the Soulmonger—in the sea, so that they will never reach the promised land. The monster's other role is to guard access to Cader Sedat (the Spiral Castle), a place situated on a remote island in the very center of creation (*TWF* 353). Cader Sedat is not only a place of power, but also a mystical place of death (*TWF* 282), where the mightiest men from all worlds lie dormant in an underground chamber symbolically lit by a single candle. Rakoth's other beast-servants are Avaia (a carnivorous black swan) and the gigantic Black Dragon (*TDR* 351–353). Like their master, all of these creatures evoke disgust and fear, and all are eventually killed by the protectors of Fionavar, which reaffirms the claim that instead of favoring a balance between the forces of Light and Darkness, Fionavar (and Kay) undeniably glorifies Light.

Among the lesser gods, only Dana is represented by a divine animal which she creates with her own power, thus confirming her superiority over other deities. In response to Rakoth's declaration of war, she gives life to Imraith-Nimphais—a flying unicorn. This female beast epitomizes the nature of the goddess (who can be both protective and destructive): vicious and lethally dangerous to her enemies, she is ready to sacrifice herself for her rider.

Imraith-Nimphais becomes the steed and totem animal of young Tabor from the Dalrei; their union resembles a spiritual marriage, since they call each other "beloved." However, such a direct experience of the numinous proves to be lethally dangerous for the boy's mortal existence, since the strong bond with a divine creature gradually "translates" Tabor into a transcendental state of being. The bond is broken only because Imraith-Nimphais saves her rider during their suicidal attack on the enemy.

In addition to the creatures that are directly ascribed to one of the gods, Fionavar is inhabited by beasts whose origins or affinity are not clear, which increases the sense of the mystery surrounding the numinous. For instance, the majestic Crystal Dragon might be one of the Weaver's prize creations (a spectacular embodiment of Light), but also a deity in its own right. The Dragon dwells in Calor Diman (Crystal Lake), a place revered by the race of dwarves. Recognizing the numinous power hidden in the Lake, one of the protagonists describes it as a terrifying place unfit for mortals (*TDR* 280–281), which reaffirms that the Fionavarian numinous is a great and fascinating, but also frightening mystery (even if the divine powers in question are generally acknowledged as benevolent toward a community). Any candidate for the King of the Dwarves must remain on the Lake's shore during the night of a full moon and retain his sanity. Afterward, the King is bound with the Lake—this union also resembles a spiritual marriage, since the candidate customarily offers to the Lake a crystal sculpture of his own fashioning and it is later said that the King is wedded to the Lake (*TDR* 228). In a way, the King becomes an intermediary between his people and the divine beast by which he is chosen worthy of kingship (though he is apparently not given any divine powers). Yet since the Crystal Dragon's existence is a secret revealed only to the chosen, the dwarves do not worship the beast in any way (or at least their religious practices are never presented in the trilogy).

Apart from the Crystal Dragon, there are several other creatures which add to the diversity of the Fionavarian numinous. Curdardh (called the Oldest One) is a shape-shifting earth monster whose duty is to protect a sacred glade in the Pendaran Wood (Pendaran is a forest filled with intelligent, ancient, but nameless forces which loathe humankind).[5] Since Curdardh embodies the primeval force of earth, he might be subjected to the Goddess who is also identified with that element. Still, the monster is apparently not involved in the grand conflict between the deities. The water spirit Eilathen also does not intend to assist the protagonists, though he has enough power to generate intricate visions thanks to which one of the heroes is introduced to the detailed history of Fionavar. Yet Eilathen creates these visions because he is compelled by external magic, and he never ceases to desire complete freedom. Flidais, a half-god and a wood spirit resembling a portly gnome (*TST* 319), can control the forces residing in the ominous Pendaran Wood, yet his greatest power is knowledge about matters related to the gods. Though he helps the heroes, he also resorts to blackmail to obtain from them the information he desires. Finally, Fordaetha of Rük, one of the oldest powers in Fionavar (*TWF* 90), is a malicious snow queen serving Rakoth. It is difficult to place these four beings—Curdardh, Eilathen, Flidais, Fordaetha—in Fionavar's pantheon. Rather than categorize them as lesser deities or divine creatures, it is perhaps better to see them as personifications of various forces of nature, whose divine powers mark them, nonetheless, as an extension of the Fionavarian numinous.

Religious Practices and Institutions in the World of Fionavar

Taking into consideration the multitude of gods, goddesses, and divine beasts inhabiting Fionavar, we could expect that the land's communities formed several congregations dedicated to the worship of particular deities, which would regulate their relationship with the numinous. Yet it is just the opposite. Apart from one religious and one pseudo-religious institution revering respectively Dana and Mörnir (which are rather exclusive in their admission of new members), Fionavarians have not formed any other religious gatherings. Instead, they respectfully acknowledge all of their gods and follow a set of customary practices (which are, unfortunately, introduced very briefly).

The cult of Dana is presumably the oldest (and the only) fully institutionalized religion in the imaginary world. The cult is a congregation of women schooled in a holy sanctuary, who dedicate their lives to worshiping and serving the Mother-Goddess. The cult is organized into a strict hierarchy: the acolytes (wearing brown), the priestesses (clothed in grey), the Mormae (in red) who form a higher echelon of power, and the High Priestess (clad in white). The High Priestess is the goddess's earthly representative and an intermediary to her divine power (drawn from avarlith—the "earthroot"). Because of her religious status, the Priestess is also granted political authority: she can designate and crown the High Kings of Brennin (*TST* 359), and speak on behalf of the deity in matters concerning the state. The cult of Dana is the only religious body in Fionavar which possesses temples, rituals, and sacred objects (a holy axe that rests near the altar, which can be handled only by the High Priestess).

Since Dana is a female deity identified with fertility, the cult's practices are focused on blood and earth. The priestesses are characterized by their distrust of men, who are required to offer their blood whenever they enter one of Dana's temples. The only described religious event—the annual festive celebration of Maidaladan (Midsummer's Eve)—is also called "blood magic" (*TST* 121). Maidaladan is a celebration of life and fertility, during which the priestesses commemorate Liadon, the Beloved of the Goddess, whose annual union with the deity and sacrificial death symbolize the death/rebirth cycle of nature. During the event, the congregation's sanctuary of Gwen Ystrat is permeated by sexual desire and the priestesses, save the High Priestess who must remain a virgin, are required to have intercourses with random men (*TWF* 227). Thus, apart from prayers and lamentations for Liadon, the rite of Maidaladan includes religious prostitution. It was perhaps because of its chthonic nature that the rite was forbidden by one of the first Kings of Brennin; nonetheless, it is still symbolically reenacted every year (*TST* 121). One of Fionavar's mages makes an interesting remark in relation to Maidaladan: "He thought of the flowers strewn by the maidens chanting his [Liadon's] death and return as the spring: *Rahod hedai Liadon*. In every world, the mage knew; but his soul rebelled against the darkness of this power" (*TST* 121). This comment both suggests that even Fionavar's religious practices are reflected in other worlds, and highlights the animosity and lack of understanding between the priestesses and the mages.

This animosity is a result of a centuries' long conflict which has prominently shaped people's relation to the divine. Men were dependent upon the power drawn by the priestesses until Amairgen, the first mage (and a prominent figure in Fionavarian mythology, known also because of his tragic affair with a wood spirit, Lisen), rebelled against the female domination, and spent a night in the holy glade of Pendaran Wood. Amairgen's victory over the glade's guardian (Curdardh) was both proof of his strength and an indirect male triumph over the Mother-Goddess (since Curdardh is an earth-demon). Consequently, the god Mörnir granted him the runes of skylore, which gave mages access to their own power. However, this other form of magic is also not cost-free, since the mage must form a bond with another person, called "the source"—any abuse of power may result in the source's death. To further separate themselves from the priestesses, the mages established their own Council of the Mages which trains potential candidates and functions as an advisory body to the Kings of Brennin (in this respect, the Council competes for political authority with the High Priestess). Yet in contrast to the women in the cult of Dana, the mages do not have any temples or religious-like practices connected to the god that is the source of their power, so their gathering can hardly be seen as a fully established religious institution.

Into this clear-cut distinction between male and female power, Kay introduced yet a third form of magic called "wild magic" and "blood magic." This force can be temporarily evoked by chosen mortals, not through learning and skill, but through self-sacrifice to a god or goddess, or thanks to a particularly strong instrument of power.[6] Out of the five protagonists, three—Paul,

Kim, and Kevin—sacrifice themselves in the course of the trilogy and become vessels of divine power. Their individual experiences of the numinous are investigated in a separate part of this chapter.

The cult of Dana and the Council of the Mages are self-contained gatherings in whose practices average Fionavarians seldom participate to share their closeness to divinity and divine powers. Surprisingly or not, there is no organized worship of the Weaver in which all of the land's communities could participate (which might be another inspiration from Tolkien, because in Tolkien's texts the divine creator—Eru Ilúvatar described in *The Silmarillion*—was also not represented by institutionalized religion). The lack of a formalized religion dedicated to the Weaver does not mean, however, that the people of Fionavar ignore their creator. On the contrary, Kay's imaginary world is different from the protagonists' modern Toronto in that it is a world not affected by desacralization. The inhabitants of Fionavar are well aware of the divine which permeates their material reality. They acknowledge the Weaver's authority as the supreme creator and his benevolence by saying that something is "brightly woven" if it is good, by invoking the god's protection with phrases such as *"The Weaver hold your thread fast in his hand"* (*TDR* 77; italics in the original), and by sending "heartfelt prayer to the Weaver at the Loom" (*TWF* 188). Even the semi-divine Andain acknowledge the Weaver's reign: "It is in the Weaver's hands," says Flidais (*TDR* 267)—to which Lancelot responds: "Half a truth, little one. It is in our own hands as well, however maimed they are. Our own choices matter" (*TDR* 268), thus affirming human freedom. What is more, the denizens of Fionavar realize that evil in the embodiment of Rakoth is a genuine threat to their world; whenever they see Mount Rangat (his prison), they remember that one day the malevolent god may attack again.

As far as other lesser deities are concerned, separate communities may revere those with whom they feel particularly bonded. The Kings of Brennin sacrifice their lives to the father-god, Mörnir, whenever the kingdom requires divine intervention; they are therefore called "the Children of Mörnir." The wandering tribes of the Dalrei are particularly respectful toward the deities Cernan and Ceinwen, who represent wilderness and hunting. According to the tribes' tradition, boys need to participate in a ceremonial fast and experience a union with their holy animal before they are accepted as men by their community. The life of adult men revolves around hunting, which is regulated by a strict and unbreakable code of rules (taboos) whose fulfillment brings glory to the tribe. After the hunt, women and younger boys recreate its events by performing elaborate dances around the bonfire. The head of the Dalrei's spiritual life are shamans—holy men ritually blinded so that they can see hidden truths and contact the gods; a shaman's authority is comparable, if not superior, to that of a chieftain. Regrettably, the descriptions of

Fionavarian religious practices are fragmentary and nothing is said about the customs of other communities (Cathal, Eridu) or the worship of other gods (Macha and Nemain, Liranan). As a result, Kay's imaginary religions and religious institutions only partially reflect the diversified pantheon of Fionavarian gods.

The Protagonists' Experiences of the Numinous

To complete the phenomenological analysis of *The Fionavar Tapestry* it is essential to take into account the protagonists' individual experiences of the numinous. During their adventures, the protagonists are exposed to various otherworldly powers and become intermediaries to gods, which is probably a terrifying experience for people who do not seem particularly religious and whose modern world has been significantly desacralized by science and technology. For Kim, Jennifer, Paul, Kevin, and Dave, Fionavar is a world which radically changes their perception of the divine, because it is a world of active gods who demand something from humankind, and subsequently reward or punish people for their deeds. In the face of the Fionavarian numinous, Kay's protagonists are forced to adopt new attitudes toward the divine and reestablish their identities. Their individual cases are worthy of investigation, because they reveal crucial details about Fionavar's imaginary deities and present an array of human responses to the divine.

Kim becomes entangled in the matters of gods when she is appointed as the new Seer of Brennin—an oracle figure whose dreams allow her to glimpse the future (the archetypal Wise Woman). Such oracles are apparently present in every world and form a connection between their world and the sacred Fionavar (*TST* 33). Though as an oracle Kim is granted immense knowledge, it is clearly stated that she is still a mortal, and therefore not omniscient (*TST* 103). Apart from knowledge, Kim "receives" the soul of the previous Seer[7] and the magical ring Baelrath which establishes her as an intermediary to the goddesses of war (Macha and Nemain) and grants her some divine powers. Thus, in spite of her mortality, Kim temporarily experiences a state of existence akin to godhood (*TDR* 211)—her newly acquired majesty and potency both fascinate her and humble her, because she becomes all the more aware of the constraints of mortality. Both gifts (the soul and the ring) represent the trilogy's recurring theme: power is received through sacrifice and is a great burden on the receiver. Kim is soon tormented by her role as the herald of war who has to disrupt peace. She eventually rebels against her role when the ring demands that she should summon the Crystal Dragon to war. Reflecting on her actions, Kim independently decides that she does not want to ruin such a beautiful creature and the dwarves' community, so she neglects her obligations. Even though the woman's decision results in her loss of power and status as a divine intermediary, her refusal is a bold proclamation of human autonomy.

Jennifer, the second female protagonist, has an entirely different experience with the Fionavarian numinous. Kidnapped and then violated by the evil Rakoth, Jennifer experiences the horror of utter weakness and insignificance in the face of a god. The woman's only consolation is her determination not to yield to her tormentor, which is another audacious proclamation of human autonomy. That the tragic events do not break Jennifer is later evident in her decision to give birth to the child begotten in rape, Darien. Afterward, Jennifer is recognized as another reincarnation of Guinevere who, together with Arthur and Lancelot du Lac, is repeatedly reborn (in a centuries' long cycle of reincarnation) to atone for sins: Arthur is guilty of killing newborn babies in a desperate attempt to eliminate his future rival, whereas Guinevere and Lancelot are punished for their adulterous love. All three are eventually graced with redemption and allowed to go to a mystical place beyond time (a form of afterlife). Though Jennifer does not become an intermediary to any divine power and hence does not partake of the potency of the numinous, her fate illustrates the strength of human will and offers hope that humble penance for one's sins will eventually result in forgiveness.

Paul becomes an earthly representative of the sky-god, Mörnir, when he willingly sacrifices himself on the sacred Summer Tree. Traditionally, it is the High King of Brennin that should offer his life in order to placate the god and win his favor. Yet since King Ailell rejects his royal duty and Paul wishes for a meaningful death, the monarch allows him to appropriate the role. When the men delve into Godwood, there is no doubt that they are entering sacred grounds filled with numinous powers (*TST* 164–165). The ancient Summer Tree is an Axis Mundi, i.e., a link between the sky and earth, between divinity and humanity. Left on the Tree—in hunger, thirst, and pain—for three days and nights, Paul experiences spiritual catharsis. The man is tormented by the death of his girlfriend, Rachel, because he feels he could have prevented the accident in which she died, if he had not been so devastated by her decision to end their relationship. His time on the Summer Tree forces Paul to relive his memories, as if stripping him of layers of identity, until he is "so open the wind could pass through him, light shine, shadow fall" (*TST* 222). At some point, the man even experiences a mystical union with the sacred Tree: "He was becoming root, branch. He was naked there, skin to bark; naked in all the ways there were, it seemed, because the dark was coming down inside again, the door unbolting" (*TST* 222). In a moment of enlightenment, Paul understands that a person's soul has to be completely exposed for the coming of God, but that he can still choose death if the process of cleansing and transmogrification is too painful (*TST* 223). His freedom to choose is never denied, and it is the man's willingness to endure the entire ordeal that makes his actions meaningful. Eventually, Paul begins to feel powers surging through the holy tree and anticipates Mörnir's arrival; this newly formed awareness is the threshold of the approaching union with a god. Even Galadan—Lord of the semi-divine Andain—confirms Paul's transubstantiation (*TST* 187).

When Paul is ready to die and fulfill his role, he receives an unexpected grace from the Goddess Dana: he is told that he failed to avoid the fatal accident because he is only human and human fallibility can be absolved. Thus, the man finally forgives himself and sheds tears for his beloved. His tears, the symbol of redemption and cleansing, bring rain to the withering kingdom. Yet instead of claiming Paul's soul, Mörnir fills the man with his divine power. Called Pwyll Twiceborn and Lord of the Summer Tree, Paul becomes the sky-god's representative in the material world. It is interesting how after the events Paul—a modern man from Toronto—sees himself as part of Fionavar. He proclaims that he is one of Dana's children (*TST* 337), recognizes himself as an "Arrow of the God" and "Spear of the God" (*TST* 339), and feels "the stillness within his blood that marked the presence of Mörnir" (*TDR* 88). Granted knowledge inaccessible to mortals and control over lesser gods, Paul can wield divine power to protect and cleanse the world (yet he does not immediately understand the nature of his new abilities, because even after his transubstantiation the numinous remains a mystery). The man never renounces his status as a divine intermediary and decides to remain in Fionavar even after evil is defeated.

Though Kevin also sacrifices his life to a deity, his ordeal is entirely different from Paul's. Kevin is a man for whom the act of love-making is a deeply spiritual experience, though he is never able to find sexual fulfillment. In Fionavar, he discovers his role as Dana's divine lover. Before the onset of the fertility rite (Maidaladan), Kevin is symbolically wounded in the groin by an enormous white boar. Then, enticed by strange sensations evoked by the name "Liadon," he surrenders to his instincts and travels to Dun Maura, the goddess's underground chamber. By wandering through the narrow corridors that lead to the chamber, Kevin-Liadon (also called "the Beloved"), recreates a symbolic return to the womb of the Mother-Goddess. The entrance to the chamber is guarded by a crone, who is restored to youth and beauty when the man confirms his identity as Liadon and offers blood at an ancient altar. After summoning Dana with another offer of his blood, Kevin-Liadon finds fulfillment of his deepest desire—and death—in his union with the goddess. Nonetheless, his willing sacrifice completes the rites of Maidaladan and enforces the coming of a much awaited spring.

Dave's experience of Fionavar's numinous is not as spectacular or dramatic. After joining the tribes of the Dalrei, Dave breaks a divine taboo by seeing the goddess Ceinwen during her hunt. Exposed to her divine beauty and majesty, the man feels utterly diminished and humbled (*TST* 284). Since he promises to pay for his transgression, the goddess, in recognition of his courage, not only spares his life, but later gives him the magical Owein's Horn and accepts him as her lover. Their union is another example of how in Fionavar the gap between humankind and the divine may be bridged by sexuality.

The phenomenological analysis of *The Fionavar Tapestry* reveals that though Kay's development of the secondary numinous and religion is not outstandingly intricate (in comparison to Donaldson's creation), the heroes' varied experiences of and responses to the divine are a major part of the narrative. Of course, the lack of detail in the descriptions of Fionavar's religious dimension is conditioned by the length of the series. Since there are only three volumes (in comparison to Donaldson's ten installments), Fionavar's cosmology, pantheon of gods, religious institutions and practices are but briefly sketched. Instead of dwelling on the details of Fionavarian temples and rites, Kay focuses on the dynamic, very intimate, and constantly changing relationship between people and their deities. His heroes are not allowed to be indifferent to the numinous, because the numinous repeatedly enters into and disturbs their everyday lives. The deities and divine powers constantly manifest their presence in the material world, and the heroes need to actively decide how to deal with divine commandments and demands, accept their roles as intermediaries to divine beings, and face the consequences of their decision and actions. Fionavar is a world in which people co-exist with gods, a world in which the limits and virtues of humankind are tested by the divine. In other words, in Fionavar there is no room for the desacralization of human life.

Diversity in the Structures of Fionavar's Secondary Religions

The phenomenological analysis of the trilogy highlights the diversity of elements which Kay utilizes to create the secondary numinous and religions of his fantastic world. Apart from the multitude of references to biblical tradition and Christian theology, there are concepts borrowed from Eastern spirituality, as well as several figures, beasts, and motifs inspired by various world mythologies. This observation is of paramount importance in relation to the trilogy's claim that Fionavar is the first of all existing worlds. At various points, readers are reminded that other worlds are but a reflection of Fionavar. For instance, when the protagonists wonder about Fionavar's magic and fantastic races, they are told: "Your own world, too, was once like his, though it has been drifting from the pattern for a long time now" (*TST* 20–21). Later, the narrator talks about "the twin goddesses of war, who are named in all the worlds as Macha and Nemain" (*TST* 188). These and other comments accentuate both the correlation between the subordinate worlds and Fionavar's supreme position among them. Yet if other worlds are but reflections of Fionavar, then the religions and gods present in those lesser worlds are also merely reflections of Fionavar's divine pantheon. Consequently, Kay had to design the Fionavarian numinous as a blend of monotheism and polytheism since these varieties are to be found in the subordinate worlds (under the separate names of Christianity, Eastern spirituality, ancient mythologies, etc.). Though *The Fionavar Tapestry* never tries to convince its readers that this theory of reflection is a valid explanation for the religious diversity existing in our world, the implication itself might possibly be disturbing for some Christian readers.

To fully evaluate the position of Christianity in the structures of Fionavar's religious dimension, it is necessary to acknowledge the series' other religious components which are combined with references to the biblical tradition and Christian theology. As far as Eastern spirituality is concerned, Kay enriches his world with three main concepts found in Taoism and Buddhism: the dualism of *yin* and *yang*, the necessity of harmony and balance, and the notion of reincarnation. *Yin* and *yang*—explained respectively as the dark/negative/female side and the light/positive/male side (other extensions of these pairings are possible)—are key concepts of Taoism, which treats them as complementary and interdependent entities (*Britannica...* 1066). They are regarded both as cosmic powers and mental categories, i.e., they allow to recognize the order and function of different phenomena and entities in the surrounding world and human life, but they should also be acknowledged as powers that permeate that world and human life, which highlights the interconnectedness of existence (Pas 5, 370–372). Kay's world operates with complementary pairings which mirror the polarity of *yin* and *yang*, e.g., Light is counterbalanced by Darkness, the female power granted by Dana—by the male power coming from Mörnir, the Crystal Dragon—by the Black Dragon, and the mythic white swan (Lauriel)—by the black swan (Avaia). Yet while Taoism advocates in favor of harmony and balance between such forces (*Britannica...* 1111; Pas 370), in Kay's imaginary world Light is generally elevated over the embodiments of Darkness, and the latter's presence in Fionavar is inarguably presented as harmful and unwanted. Nonetheless, Taoist teachings about the necessity of harmony and balance between powers and elements of creation reverberate both in the narrator's insistence that a balance between the existing worlds is of paramount importance (a priority objective) and in the eventual reconciliation of male and female powers through the union of Paul (the intermediary to Mörnir) and Jaelle (the High Priestess of Dana).

What is more, Kay enriches his fictional world the motif of rebirth/reincarnation in order to reconstruct the fate of Arthur, Guinevere, and Lancelot. This idea is also clearly indebted to Buddhism and Eastern spirituality rather than to Christian thought. Unfortunately, in popular thought the Buddhist understanding of reincarnation is often simplified to the notion of a repeated death-rebirth experience (in different bodily forms) until one achieves the state of nirvana. In reality, the concept or reincarnation (transmigration) is much more complex and nuanced:

> There is merely a continuity of a particular lifeflux; just that and nothing more. Buddhists employ various similes to explain this idea that nothing transmigrates from one life to another. For example, rebirth is said to be like the transmission of a flame from one thing to another: The first flame is not identical to the last flame, but they are clearly related. The flame of life is continuous, although there is an apparent break at so-called death [Buswell 19].

Given this explanation of transmigration, it seems that Kay's version of reincarnation (with heroes who regain their past experiences and identities) is nevertheless more akin to the popular belief that a person's soul will be reborn until the person in question learns a particular lesson or repents for their bad deeds. Interestingly, none of the heroes ever questions the possibility that sinners might be forced into a seemingly unending cycle of death and rebirth to atone for their transgressions (regardless of the assumed benevolence of the supreme creator), and at no point in the series is the idea of reincarnation dismissed as not fit for Fionavarian religions. This emphasizes the claim that the religious dimension of Fionavar is composed of several units, and none of those units—Christianity including—is elevated over another. Thus, it seems that the balance advocated in reference to all worlds extends also to the coexistence of various religious traditions.

What is more, Fionavarian numinous consists also of bits and pieces borrowed from various world mythologies. As far as deities are concerned, Rakoth's imprisonment under a mountain is similar to the fate of Loki, the trickster god from Norse mythology, who was bound with chains in a dark cave (Daly and Rengel 65). Next, Kay's Mörnir of the Thunder is a fusion of two Norse gods: Odin and Thor. To obtain wisdom and magic runes, Odin sacrificed his life on the sacred tree Yggdrasil, and Kay's Mörnir, who gave the runes of skylore to the mages, is venerated by Kings who offer themselves on his sacred Summer Tree. Both the mythological and the fantastic deity are accompanied by two ravens: Odin by Hugin and Munin (Lindow 186), and Mörnir by Thought and Memory. On the other hand, Mörnir's title "of the Thunder" suggests an affinity with Thor, the god of storm and thunder, who bears the lightning-invoking hammer, Mjöllnir. Three Fionavarian gods are derived from Celtic mythology: the Celtic goddess, Ana (Matson and Roberts 4), seems to be the prototype for Kay's Dana, the goddess of earth and fertility;

Cernan of the Beasts, the antlered lord of woods, resembles the antlered god Cernunnos (Matson and Roberts 28); Kay's "Liranan" is probably derived from the sea god named Manannán Mac Lir (Matson and Roberts 80); and "Flidais" is the name of a Celtic woodland goddess (Matson and Roberts 59). The Fionavarian twin goddesses of war, Macha and Nemain, resemble the Irish war goddesses, Macha and Nemai (Matson and Roberts 79, 88). Moreover, there are some references to classical mythology: Ceinwen of the Bow, who would punish with death those that see her during hunting or bathing, is similar to the Greek goddess Artemis (Cotterell 23), whereas the earth-demon Curdardh, with his crippled leg and a hammer, resembles the Greek Hephaistos, the lame blacksmith god (Cotterell 46–47).

Aside from deriving his imaginary pantheon from existing mythologies, Kay filled his trilogy with a handful of beasts and items based on classical, Norse, and Celtic myths. Imraith-Nimphais is a combination of two mythical creatures appearing in Greco-Roman mythology: Pegasus and the unicorn. The monstrous Black Dragon, raised by Fionavar's equivalent of a fairy-tale Snow Queen, is similar to Nidhogg, the dragon from Norse legends that lived in Nifelheim—the land of the dead (Eason 47). Other references to Norse tales include the name "svart alfar" which is a derivation from Nordic Svartalfheim—the realm of dark elves (Daly and Rengel 63), and the motif of the Wild Hunt (Eason 105–108). As far as Celtic mythology is concerned, the fictional Cauldron of Khath Meigol, which resurrects the dead, has a counterpart in Celtic myths (Matson and Roberts 26). Likewise, the white boar that wounds Kevin is a Celtic symbol of strength and sexual potency (Monaghan 50). In fact, in Celtic tradition it is a man called Diarmuid who is lethally wounded by a boar (Cotterell 123), but Kay reserved that name for another one of his heroes. Kevin's sacrifice as Liadon is a blend of the Celtic story of Diarmuid with the classical tale of Adonis who, killed by a boar, is adored by both Aphrodite and Persephone (Cotterell 19).[8] What is more, the story of the old King Ailell, who does not wish to save his withering kingdom struck by drought, is reminiscent of the Arthurian tale of the wounded Fisher King and his barren land (Monaghan 196). In addition, Kay borrowed some concepts from Native American religious practices (the concept of totem animals obtained during a ritualistic fast, the figure of a shaman), and from pagan rites of fertility (the sacrifice performed during Maidaladan—Midsummer's Eve).

Into this plurality of traditions Kay introduced also Christianity. On the one hand, the author treats biblical tradition as any other source of inspiration, whose motifs and figures might enrich the structure of his imaginary world. Thus, the trilogy contains numerous references to the Old and the New Testament, which are then freely interwoven with elements borrowed from various myths and Eastern spirituality. These biblical references emerge in the attributes of the fantastic gods, in the character and functions of the divine beings, and in the fate of the protagonists. On the other hand, the existence and the moral premises of Fionavar seem to be embedded not in any mythological tradition or Eastern spirituality, but in Christian ethics and theology, which is confirmed by the way in which Kay develops such themes as the freedom of human will, sin, redemption, divine grace, and salvation. When both levels of Kay's inspiration with Christianity are taken into consideration, the position of Christianity within the structures of his fictional world is revealed to be rather ambiguous.

Christianity and the Fionavarian Numinous

First and foremost, references to Christianity appear in the portrayal of the fictional deities—the Weaver and the Unraveller—whose attributes respectively correspond to those of the Christian God and Lucifer/Satan. As far as the Weaver is concerned, he is presented as the supreme god and creator of life, whose reign extends over the entire universe and the lesser divine beings. It was said in the previous chapter that the descriptions of Donaldson's Creator and his divine work correspond to imagery from Genesis 2 in which God "works with his hand, taking pride in his creations. Like a potter, he shapes man from dust. Like a gardener, he plants trees" (Ward et al. 17). A similar parallel appears in *The Fionavar Tapestry*, which presents the Weaver as a meticulous artisan devoted to the slightest detail of his divine work: "the shuttle of the Worldloom slowed and then was still, and the Weaver, too, watched to see what would come back into the Tapestry" (*TWF* 156); "the Weaver's hands moved to reclaim a long-still weft of thread for the web of the Tapestry" (*TWF* 158). It is worth noting that while these passages confirm the god's divine supremacy, they also affirm the importance of human freedom: though it is the Weaver that attends to the Loom, human actions have influence over whether a particular thread will be included or altered.

The genesis myths of Fionavar generally assume that everything created by the Weaver is inherently good and that it was the arrival of the Unraveller that brought corruption. In this respect, Kay's vision corresponds to Christian theology which declares that despite being ruined by human sin, God's creation is innately good and can still be redeemed (McGrath 130). Moreover, though it is universally affirmed that the Weaver is a benevolent deity, his punishment for Arthur suggests that he is a just, but severe judge: "the Weaver had marked him down for a long unwinding doom. A cycle of war and expiation under many names, and in many worlds, that redress be made for the children and for love" (*TWF* 40). These attributes correspond to the Old Testament portrayal of Yahweh as an uncompromising judge who expels Adam and Eve from Eden for their disobedience, sends a deluge to punish sinful humankind, diversifies people's languages when they attempt to build the Tower of Babel, and punishes the Egyptians for prolonging the Israelites' captivity. Since in the course of the trilogy the Weaver never manifests his presence or is given a voice, his image must be reconstructed from the available bits of information. Still, the attributes of omnipotence, omniscience, benevolence, justice, and authority ascribed to this fictional deity do parallel the image associated with the Christian God.

If the Weaver is a Fionavarian equivalent of the Christian God, then the evil Rakoth functions in the role of Lucifer/Satan who wishes to supplant the supreme deity and reign over his divine creation. Rakoth is a Luciferian figure in the world of Fionavar, because he rebels against the rightful creator driven by his own ambitions; at one point, he is even explicitly called "the first and fallen god" (*TST* 208), which resembles Lucifer's description as the mightiest among God's angels, whose disobedience resulted in his downfall (Ryken et al. 205). Rakoth's similarity to Satan is present in his names and identification with sin. The evil deity's different titles—Maugrim, the Unraveller, and Sathain (the reference is obvious)—correspond to the biblical idea that Satan is known under many names (Ward et al. 223). It is then implied that Rakoth is the personification of sin, because his demise spiritually liberates humanity: shortly after the malevolent deity is annihilated, Paul feels "as if a weight had been stripped away from him, a weight he hadn't even known he was bearing—a burden he seemed to have carried from the moment he'd been born into time. He, and everyone else, cast forth into worlds that lay under the shadow of the Dark" (*TDR* 370). This burden carried since birth can be interpreted as a veiled reference to the Christian concept of the original sin with which every human being is born after Eve was tempted by the serpent. If the defeat of Rakoth is perceived as humankind's liberation from sin and complete destruction of Darkness/Evil, then this triumph should be equivalent to the Christian concept of the coming of the Kingdom of God after the Apocalypse. However, this is only a far-fetched speculation, since the last pages of the trilogy focus on each protagonist's choice of whether to stay in Fionavar or not, and nothing is said about the fate of the worlds now that Darkness has been defeated.

The appearance of a Christ figure also reinforces the Christian dimension of the cosmic conflict. Russell W. Dalton argues that a Christ figure in fantasy fiction is a hero who displays similarities with Jesus, but who "can be most thought provoking when some aspects of the character are quite different from Jesus Christ" (138–139). Since Kay's rendering of the Fionavarian Christ figure, Paul, is indebted both to Christianity and Norse mythology, it reflects the diversity of the Fionavarian pantheon, and follows Dalton's definition by partially diverging from the scriptural image of the Savior. On the one hand, the imagery surrounding Paul's self-sacrifice on the Summer Tree in order to save the withering kingdom, as well as his subsequent miraculous resurrection, inarguably evoke the images of Christ's death on the cross to redeem humankind. It is significant that Paul has to spend three days and nights on the Tree. In Christianity, the number three pertains to divinity as it symbolizes the Holy Trinity and the three days that Jesus lay in the tomb after crucifixion (Steffler 133).⁹ What is more, Paul's last night on the tree is illuminated by a red moon. Though the moon is clearly identified with the Fionavarian Goddess, a red moon is present also in the Bible's apocalyptic visions (Ryken et al. 566) and recognized as the sign of Resurrection (Steffler 116). Though after his return from the Summer Tree Paul sees himself as "the Arrow of Mörnir," i.e., as a representative of one of the lesser fictional gods, Christianity operates with a similar symbolism of the arrow as "God's instrument of discipline" (Steffler 104). Paul's role as a Christ figure is then further strengthened by a scene in which the man walks on water to reach a sailing ship (*TDR* 184). This scene is reminiscent of a memorable episode from the New Testament, in which Jesus walks on water to reach his disciples' boat and then calms a raging storm, thus confirming his divine status. If all of the abovementioned elements are combined, they clearly embed Paul's fate in a messianic context. Nonetheless, the man's ordeal on the Summer Tree is also strongly related to Norse mythology. According to Norse myths, the god Odin spent several days and nights on Yggdrasil to gain wisdom and magical runes. It should also be noted that Paul's sacrifice is acknowledged not by the Weaver (the ultimate creator), but by one of the lesser gods, Mörnir, who is also derived from Norse myths. It is, therefore, impossible to view Paul's agony as inspired exclusively by Christianity.

Biblical Motifs and Christian Ethics in The Fionavar Tapestry

The Fionavar Tapestry includes a handful of other references to biblical figures and events. The fate of the Paraiko (the name could be derived from the Greek word *paroikos* which means "alien resident" or "stranger," and appears also in the Bible) is a reconstruction of the story of humankind's creation, temptation, and fall. Kay writes: "in the forests and the valleys and across rivers and up the mountain slopes there walked the Paraiko in the young years of the world, naming what they saw" (*TDR* 113). This fragment suggests that as the Weaver's first children, the Paraiko were offered the same role as Adam, whom God told to bestow names on the animals. What is more, not knowing the feeling of hatred, the Paraiko lived in an Edenic state of innocence, and their existence was even described as sacrosanct (*TDR* 71).

When Kim comes to summon them to war, she plays the role of the biblical serpent that tempted Eve to learn the difference between good and evil. The woman similarly forces the Paraiko to learn about hatred, which puts an end to their original innocence.

Another reference to the Old Testament is hidden in the suggestion that evil originally appeared in Fionavar after the first man killed his brother (*TST* 296)—this remark is reminiscent of the first biblical tale of murder in which Cain kills his brother, Abel. Next, at the end of the trilogy, Paul—drawing on divine power—summons the sea god, and the incoming sea waters cleanse the plain which served as battlefield; afterward, the plain miraculously regains its lost fertility (*TDR* 401). This scene reflects the Old Testament episode of the great deluge and the cleansing of earth. In addition, two of Rakoth's beast-servants resemble biblical monsters. The gigantic Soulmonger is comparable to the sea-beast Leviathan, whereas Rakoth's Black Dragon, defeated during the final battle, is like the great dragon—the symbol of evil in the Book of Revelation—ultimately defeated by God. The Bible affirms that after the demise of the dragon God's creation will be restored to greatness and goodness (Ryken et al. 565). Likewise, the death of Rakoth's Dragon is a prelude to the deity's downfall which eventually liberates the Weaver's worlds from the threat of evil. Finally, two symbols appearing in the trilogy—the candle and the owl—become more meaningful if they are explained according to Christian interpretation. The candle is mentioned as the sole light in the chamber of the dead situated in Cader Sedat. In the Christian tradition, both light and a source of light represent God (Sill 30; Steffler 8). Thus, the candle in Cader Sedat, in the center of all creation, might denote divine presence—the resting warriors are not left to Darkness and oblivion. As for the owl, it is the animal-form adopted by the half-god child, Darien, who is poised between Light and Darkness. Key's choice of an owl might not have been accidental. Since in the Christian tradition an owl represents spiritual darkness (Steffler 117) and solitude (Sill 24), the bird is a fitting choice to illustrate Darien's poignant loneliness and his inability to decide about his allegiance.

As far as the trilogy's ethical premises are concerned, Kay invariably praises and eventually rewards his protagonists for their perseverance and goodness. These, however, are not exclusively Christian virtues. Christian ethics and theology are for the most part present in the trilogy's treatment of such motifs as personal freedom and redemption from sin. *The Fionavar Tapestry* consistently reminds its heroes that they possess individual human freedom which makes them responsible for their self-improvement and a conscious choice between good and evil. Thus, the protagonists Kim and Jennifer exercise their freedom to do what seems morally appropriate (Kim rejects her magical ring) or what defies the power of Darkness (Jennifer gives birth to the child begotten in rape), even if their decisions endanger their own well-being. Similar choices are made by two other characters: Diarmuid and Darien. Diarmuid, the carefree prince of Brennin, insists that Arthur, Guinevere, and Lancelot have already suffered enough for their sins. Thus, to end their cycle of reincarnation, Diarmuid appropriates a challenge to a fight which would have surely killed one of the two men (and perpetuate their punishment). Though the prince dies, thanks to his sacrifice the cursed trio is offered forgiveness and eternal rest. Diarmuid's brilliant victory over the enemy is his rebellion against a fate he deems unjust. It proves that in spite of divine omnipotence and omniscience, personal choices stemming from human freedom do matter in the world of Fionavar: "Diarmuid chose otherwise. He made it *become* otherwise. We are not slaves to the Loom, not bound forever to our fate" (*TDR* 393).

Darien's case also illustrates the importance of an individual's rejection of evil. Begotten in rape by the malevolent Rakoth, Darien is a half-god child unsure of his identity. His mother, Jennifer, insists that the boy must be given liberty to choose his allegiance; therefore, she refuses to offer him consolation and protection. Rejected by her, Darien hopes to be accepted by his father. The confrontation with Rakoth's malice allows him to fully comprehend the difference between Light and Darkness—between good and evil. Therefore, the boy consciously decides to sacrifice his life to destroy the evil deity (and to save the people he cares about). It is clear that Kay's heroes exercise their freedom to renounce injustice and Darkness even if they have to sacrifice their own safety and happiness in the process. Such behavior remains in accordance with the model of Christian life, which advocates selfless love for fellow men and women, and unyielding rejection of evil. It is worth noting that the heroes' decisions do not undermine the Weaver's divine plan. For instance, though Paul had no idea about the Summer Tree before he came to Fionavar, his independently made decision about self-sacrifice seems "to have been written a very long time ago" (*TST* 164). Paradoxically, though certain events might have been preordained by the creator, they are also dependent on human will.

Elements of Christian theology are present also in the trilogy's treatment of sin, redemption, and divine grace. One the one hand, Christianity defines sin as any deed that violates God's commandments and requirements of morality. On the other, it perceives sin as "a theological category, not a legal or even moral one. Sin, in the end, means not knowing who we are in relation to our Maker; it means either thinking that I am God or that there is no God and no meaning to life" (Jonas 250). Both variants appear in *The Fionavar Tapestry*, because the characters' deeds—murder, adultery, and vengeful jealousy—are presented not only as a violation of the Christian commandments, but also a breach of their relationship with the Holy and a disruption in their spiritual lives. Arthur sinned by killing innocent children, whereas Guinevere and Lancelot committed adultery; all three are punished by a cycle of rebirth in which they relive their tragedy. Because he did not win the love of his chosen woman, Galadan (the lord of half-gods) allied with evil and brought death to thousands of Fionavarians. Afterward, he suffers centuries of banishment and emotional torment. Paul accuses himself that out of jealousy and spite he caused the car accident in which his girlfriend, Rachel, died; as if feeling guilty of murder, he inflicts self-punishment by refusing to mourn his loss. All of these characters are eventually forgiven and their relationship with the divine is, in a way, restored.

Yet their redemption is not earned, but offered as divine grace. Therefore, in spite of its elevation of human freedom, the trilogy is closer to Augustine's theory of salvation by grace than Pelagius's salvation by works (McGrath 150). Arthur, Guinevere, and Lancelot are mercifully allowed to move together to the afterlife. Though it is said that they have fulfilled their penance, the trilogy also makes it clear that their salvation is a divine gift: "the dimensions of the miracle were made manifest. It was then that grace descended" (*TDR* 396). Galadan learns that despite all his evil deeds, there is still Light in him and he can be healed (*TDR* 390–391). And when Paul suffers on the Summer Tree, the Goddess mercifully makes him realize that he missed his chance to stop the accident, because he is only human (*TST* 231). Christianity similarly does not perceive human fallibility as a sin, because perfection and omnipotence are the domain of God alone (Jonas 253). Nonetheless, the trilogy's vision of salvation by grace is not entirely in accordance with Christian theology, because in the aftermath of their redemption, the heroes neither rediscover their faith nor reestablish their relationship with the supreme god. The cursed trio moves to the afterlife, Galadan converts to Light in general, and Paul becomes an intermediary to one of the lesser gods. Thus, the Christian vision of a sinner restored to a life in God by divine grace is diluted by the Fionavarian multilayered numinous.

In fact, it is impossible to say that the experience of Fionavar, a world filled with the numinous, has had a striking impact on the protagonists' religiosity. To start with, hardly anything is said about the heroes' attitude to religion before their arrival to the fantastic realm; it is only mentioned that Jennifer is Catholic and that she has always relied on Father Laughlin (*TST* 369), and that Kevin was raised by his orthodox Jewish father (*TST* 27). The protagonists do call on divine names: Jennifer—"oh, Mary Mother" (*TST* 369), Kevin—"Almighty God" (*TST* 17), Dave—"Jesus" (*TST* 25) and "Holy Mother" (*TST* 242), Kim—"Dear God" (*TST* 213). These outcries, however, are not pleas for divine intervention, but meaningless exclamations in times of emotional strife. The heroes never resort to faith in God's benevolence to deliver them from harm. Moreover, even after they are told that Fionavar is the first of all worlds and they discover the Fionavarian pantheon of very active gods, little is changed in their perception of religion. They never debate the nature of the divine or question the veracity of the religious doctrines which they have come to know in their own world. Instead, they easily accept the idea that their religious knowledge might be just a distortion of the religions and gods of Fionavar, which the subordinate worlds reflect. Perhaps they just never realize that their discovery of Fionavar contests everything they have known about religion so far (which, in a way, undermines their psychological plausibility). Consequently, even when the protagonists assume new roles and identities, they do so without considering what this role or identity means for their spirituality or religiosity. For instance, Paul is more worried about his inability to summon divine power, than by his status as an intermediary to a god of the thunder. Kevin is relieved to solve the dilemma of his troublesome sexuality and never objects to his role as a sacrifice in a pagan celebration of fertility upheld by the matriarchal institution. Dave displays the type of mentality that appears in classical mythology: though he is awed by the goddess's beauty and might, he does not seem particularly surprised by meeting her in a forest or by her wish to take him as her lover. Therefore, even though the protagonists become immersed in Fionavarian sacred, their experiences do not seem to deepen their understating of religion or their faith in god/God.

Guy Gavriel Kay and the Religious Dimensions of The Fionavar Tapestry

The Fionavar Tapestry truly is a Tapestry, since the author interwove multiple threads taken from biblical tradition, Eastern spirituality, Native American shamanistic practices, pagan nature worship, and diverse mythologies in order to shape his imaginary world. In several interviews, Kay has confirmed that such a representation of religion was his deliberate aim. Instead of advocating in favor of a particular religion or promoting the religious depth of life, as a fantasist he was primarily interested in exploring the implications of the theory that one world—and its deities—are reflected by all the other worlds, including their beliefs and myths (Kay, n.p.). Thus, the writer consciously interwove fragments of various traditions and embedded them in a "Homeric world," i.e., a world in which people frequently interact with gods ("Interview with Solaris," n.p.). Moreover, though Kay says about himself: "I am not a religious man, what I think I am is a person keenly interested in history" ("Interview with Solaris," n.p.), he does recognize the social importance of religion as a means to rationalize the world and impose a code of morality on a community ("Interview with Solaris," n.p.)—hence he did not forget about the religious dimensions of his own fictional societies.

Yet though Kay frequently comments on the mythological aspects of Fionavar's background, he almost never discusses the series' Christian undertones. One of the rare exceptions is when he describes the trilogy's language: "In *Fionavar* I did (as I said before) think in terms of operatic rhythms, the tale rising to and moving away from major arias, duets … and I used mythic, Biblical cadences to try to achieve that (lacking, obviously, music!) in such scenes" ("An Interview with Richard Marcus," n.p.). Yet there are no comments about other Christian elements of the trilogy such as the Weaver's and the Unraveller's parallels to God and Satan, Paul's role as a Christ figure, the nature of sin, the idea of salvation through divine grace, and the consequences of human freedom to choose.[10] Perhaps Kay does not perceive these parallels to Christianity as particularly significant because of their ambiguity (e.g., Paul is both a Christ figure and Odin's double) or because they represent just one tradition among many other that shape Fionavar's religious dimension.

Thus, the position of Christianity in Fionavar's amalgam of traditions is rather ambiguous. On the one hand, the moral premises of Kay's imaginary world are clearly more indebted to certain aspects of Christian ethics and theology rather than to Eastern spirituality or any other tradition. On the other hand, though the Christian components and biblical references are inarguably prominent, they do not dominate in Fionavar's fictional numinous, and Kay does not seem to favor Christianity over any other traditions. While Stephen Donaldson's *Chronicles* were an example of how the author's Christian upbringing resurfaces in his work, thus producing a fantastic reality steeped in Christian history and theology (perhaps even against Donaldson's wish), *The Fionavar Tapestry* treats the contents of the Old and New Testament like any other source material whose motifs and figures can potentially enrich a writer's creation. The references to the Old and the New Testament which have been identified in this chapter are, therefore, neither more nor less prominent than borrowings from other sources. In this respect, Kay's work might illustrate Attebery's claim that fantasy fiction "shamefully exploits mythic traditions" (2007, 109), because the trilogy reconstructs various myths and melds them into one fantastic universe with little regard for their original cultural and social contexts. Or perhaps the trilogy should be recognized as a literary experiment which indirectly advocates in favor of religious pluralism. One of the most influential contemporary proponents of religious pluralism was the British philosopher John Hick. Following Immanuel Kant's claims that perception of the Real is always affected by the human subject, Hick argued that a person's perception of divinity is also structured by a particular religious tradition and experience. In other words, different individuals and groups present their own claims about the nature of the divine, and problems arise when one of the groups declares that its vision/truth is the absolute one, without acknowledging that other approaches are equally valid (simply different). Thus, by acknowledging religious diversity, Hick advocated in favor of an inclusive rather than exclusive approach to religion, and postulated inter-faith dialogue (27–30).

Since at no point in the trilogy does Kay seem particularly interested in promoting or criticizing Christianity (or any other religion for that matter), or in questioning Christian theology and institutions as Donaldson does in *The Chronicles*, his works should be perhaps treated as an exercise in religious pluralism in which no tradition is diminished so that another is elevated. Also, rather than as a religious manifesto, his work can be regarded as an exploration of a riddle: what does it mean that one supreme world is reflected by an unspecified number of subordinate worlds?[11] Kay's extrapolation from this idea produced *The Fionavar Tapestry*, a compelling and intensely emotional work, rooted in various traditions and beliefs, whose role in the trilogy and degree of reconstruction are worth exploring. And though Kay does not use *The Fionavar Tapestry* as his means to advocate in favor of a particular religion, he does offer his readers a detailed vision of the sacred—and of a life immersed in the sacred—which they might want to reconsider. Yet it also becomes the readers' task to disentangle the various threads creating Fionavar's secondary religions, and to decide whether Christian elements used by the author retain their original value even when they are embedded in a world which has its supreme Heavenly Father—the Weaver—command a whole pantheon of lesser deities who possess their own worshippers.

4

The Fantastic (De-)Evolution of Christianity in Celia S. Friedman's *The Coldfire Trilogy*

Introduction to The Coldfire Trilogy

Celia S. Friedman (b. 1957) is a contemporary American writer of science fiction and fantasy literature who debuted in 1986 with the novel *In Conquest Born*. Her next major work was *The Coldfire Trilogy*—consisting of *Black Sun Rising* (1991), *When True Night Falls* (1993), and *Crown of Shadows* (1995)[1]— which secured her position as a talented fantasist. Friedman's other notable novels are *This Alien Shore* (1998) and *The Magister Trilogy* (2007–2011). In 2011, she published *Dominion*, an e-book prequel to *The Coldfire Trilogy*, which provides a background for the main story.

Though Friedman's works are dominated by themes of space travel and extraterrestrial human civilizations, it is incorrect to categorize them all as purely science fiction novels. *The Coldfire Trilogy* is a case in point. On the one hand, the trilogy is set on a distant planet, Erna, which was colonized by humans hundreds of years ago; space travel, alien species, and heritage from Earth are inherent elements of the trilogy's imaginary world. On the other hand, these science fiction elements are by far less conspicuous than "fae"— a magic-like force wielded by a few individuals akin to sorcerers. While people's relationship with fae is one of the trilogy's driving themes, objects and technology from Earth are nothing but nostalgic memorabilia which few can use or understand. In addition, the technology of space travel has been mostly forgotten, and the alien power which appears at the end of the trilogy is more of a divine entity than some bizarre creature from outer space. If all of these points are taken into consideration, *The Coldfire Trilogy*, which follows the quest/adventure narrative pattern of high/epic fantasy with its motif of a grand fight against an evil force, is clearly closer to fantasy literature than to science fiction (and perhaps it should be categorized as science fantasy—a sub-genre that lacks a clear definition). Dickerson and O'Hara make a similar claim about C.S. Lewis's *Space Trilogy* (1938–1945), arguing that space travel and technological innovations are less significant for the trilogy than its fantastic elements (47). If *The Coldfire Trilogy* remains on the borders of fantasy fiction, it is worth including it in this study, because it is yet another thought-provoking example of how biblical tradition and Christian morality are incorporated into and reconstructed by an imaginary world.

Coldfire follows the adventures of Damien Vryce and Gerald Tarrant—a priest and an ex-human feeding on fear and blood—who form a temporary alliance to help a person they both know. When the protagonists discover that human civilization on Erna is threatened by a malicious demonic creature, Calesta, they decide to cooperate in order to thwart his schemes. Damien's and Gerald's shared goal and journeys across distant lands eventually turn their alliance into an uneasy friendship, which forces both men to reevaluate their morality and relationship with the Church on Erna.

The phenomenological analysis of *Coldfire* is different from the analysis of Donaldson's *Chronicles* and Kay's *Fionavar* for two reasons. First, while in the latter works deities frequently interact with people and divine creatures intercede between divinity and humankind, in *Coldfire* there are no active gods, but only an immaterial power of nature (fae), a being from outer space (the Mother of Iezu), entities that pretend to be gods (the Iezu), and a chaotic force of evil. Second, while the fictional religions of *The Chronicles* and *Fionavar* are autonomous systems of belief with more or less prominent borrowings from the biblical tradition, the secondary religion of *Coldfire* is explicitly rooted in Christianity. It is pointless to ignore the connection and "discover" *Coldfire*'s Christian background only in the conclusion. This chapter, therefore, employs the categories of phenomenology of religion to investigate the structure of *Coldfire*'s Christianity-inspired religion—the Church on Erna—and then juxtapose it against "original" Christianity to evaluate their similarities and differences. The Church on Erna is analyzed in terms of its historical development, internal hierarchy, worship of the One God, doctrines, practices, and goals. The analysis further encompasses the examination of the aforementioned divine and pseudo-divine powers appearing in *Coldfire*'s world, and of minor religious cults which compete with the Church. This chapter also investigates whether the morality of the secondary world corresponds to Christian ethics and evaluates the extent to which Friedman reconstructs some biblical motifs, figures, and events in the adventures of her protagonists.

Images of the Numinous

In *The Coldfire Trilogy* people encounter the numinous not when they are approached by gods or divine beasts, but mostly when they experience the power of fae. On the one hand, there is nothing divine about fae: it is a natural energy field encompassing the planet in uneven layers.[2] On the other, even though fae is not a personified deity and is never directly worshipped (there is no organized religion that would professionally address fae as a personified deity), its magnitude and creative powers elevate it to the position of Erna's impersonal, insentient divine entity. Fae is immensely dangerous to people, because it responds to their (un)conscious desires and fears, which are then incarnated in the real world—thus, this alien power can fulfill people's dreams and save lives, but it can also create nightmares and kill. Since their arrival on Erna, the colonists have striven to manipulate or suppress the force, yet they have never entirely comprehended or controlled it, because fae surpasses human comprehension and control. Thus, for the majority of Erna's inhabitants fae is an inexplicable mystery, and their attitudes toward it are divided between utter fascination and fear. Also, fae is an entirely amoral entity responding to the consciousness with which it interacts; thus, the results of its terrible potency can be both wonderful and horrible. For these reasons, any contact with fae should be recognized as *Coldfire*'s equivalent to an encounter with the phenomenological numinous—Otto's *mysterium tremendum et fascinas*—whose potency overwhelms the mortal witness of its manifestation (*majestas*), and evokes both worshipful awe and a shudder of dread which can quickly become an experience of terror (*augustum*).

Fae can be regarded as a creative force not only because it interacts with human consciousness, but also because it affects the evolution of species on Erna. The rakh, for instance, are a race of feline humanoids that evolved due to a complex interaction between fae, an indigenous animal species, and human consciousness. Also Erna's humankind changed after being exposed to the alien power: some descendants of the original colonists can learn to wield it, whereas people known as Adepts possess inborn abilities to "Work" fae. The Adepts can be perceived as a new echelon of humanity, because their perception of the material world and skills are greatly altered by their affinity with the force (though, of course, their existence cannot be compared to divine omniscience and omnipotence). One of the Adepts, Ciani, describes her experience of fae in the following way:

> "It's everywhere. In everything. [...] When I touch a stone, what I feel isn't hard rock—I feel everything that the stone has been, everything it might become, I feel how it channels the earth-fae and how it interacts with the tidal-fae and how the power of the sun will affect it, and what it will be when true night falls ... [...]. That bit of rock is alive *alive—everything* is alive to us, even the air we breathe" [*BSR* 85–86].

Ciani's explanation echoes the tenets of animism, i.e., that every element of the natural world is permeated by a spiritual essence which unites all parts of creation. If all Adepts, exalted by their special abilities, perceive fae as a divine force that animates the entire material world, then it is not surprising that the Church on Erna—largely based on Christian doctrine—strongly objects to any interaction with this alien entity.

While fae is an insentient force permeating the natural world, a being known as the Mother of Iezu is closer to the figure of a personified deity (though much ambiguity is still present). The Mother of Iezu is absent for most of the story and the protagonists are completely unaware of her existence. Eventually, it is revealed that she came to Erna from an unknown place long before the colonists, that she resides in some otherworldly sanctuary (*COS* 284), and that her bodily form escapes logical description in human terms (*COS* 431). Her children, the Iezu, are a race of pseudo-human immaterial beings, created by the female entity when she attempted to communicate with people: she "extracted" various emotions and desires from human men, hoping that the children created in such a manner would be able to communicate with both her and humankind. All of her attempts failed—though powerful, the Mother of Iezu is neither omniscient nor omnipotent—and it is only due to one of the protagonist's sacrifice that some contact is miraculously established. Nonetheless, the inexplicability of the Mother of Iezu's nature and the humbling magnitude of her powers also reflect the mystery and majesty of the numinous, even if it is impossible to determine whether she should be categorized as an alien, a deity, or an alien deity.

Whereas the Mother of Iezu remains unknown for most of the story, her children become pseudo-deities worshipped by numerous cults established by Erna's inhabitants. Yet though the Iezu possess godlike powers (they can create vivid illusions and assume any shape they wish), they are not true gods attributed with omniscience or omnipotence. On the contrary, they need to sustain their existence by feeding on human emotions, and that is why they appropriate the roles of deities. Karril, who feeds on pleasure, confesses: "All I am [...] is the hunger for pleasure that resides in your own soul, given a face and a voice and enough knowledge of etiquette to mimic human interaction" (*COS* 177). Thus, from the Iezu's point of view, the relationship between them and their "worshippers" is a mutually beneficial biological symbiosis dressed in the convenient guise of organized religion: in exchange for sustenance, the Iezu offer instant, though often fleeting and illusory, fulfillment of one's desire. The only constraint on their freedom is a law established by their Mother that they cannot openly fight one another or kill humans (*COS* 99). Though allegedly they are emotionally indifferent to humankind, some of them do care for people or try to act as benevolent deities. Others, like Calesta who feeds on sadism, are a threat to humanity. Even though the Iezu are not true deities, many inhabitants of Erna treat them as such and, consequently, any encounter with them or any experience of their powers becomes the denizens' experience of the (fascinating and frightening) numinous.

In addition to the all-encompassing fae, an alien Mother, and a group of pseudo-deities, Friedman introduces a power of evil which is the source of Gerald Tarrant's unnaturally prolonged existence. The power is at first vaguely described as "an amalgamation of those forces which on Earth were mere negatives" (*BSR* 314–315). On Erna, these minor forces are occasionally able to coalesce into a sentient and utterly malevolent entity known as "the Devourer" and "the Unnamed One" (*WTNF* 614). This fearsome, monstrous being is also called "Erna's great devil," and Gerald suggests that it did not exist before the arrival of the colonists whose interaction with fae incarnated various forms of evil (*COS* 224). However, the threat with which the protagonists need to deal in the course of the trilogy is not posed by this ultimate evil entity, but by a demonic Iezu. Though the Unnamed One is a sentient force that delights in corruption, it is not shown to be actively plotting against humankind. Instead, it is chiefly interested in having Gerald succumb to its domination. Perhaps that is why the Church on Erna hardly treats it as an enemy (at least in the trilogy), and instead perceives fae as the greatest threat to humankind's salvation and reunion with the One God. All in all, the fictional numinous of Friedman's world is clearly not as intricate and diversified as the numinous portrayed in Donaldson's *Chronicles* and Kay's *Fionavar*. This does not mean, however, that the entire religious dimension of Friedman's work lacks complexity. Rather than to images of deities and divine beasts, *The Coldfire Trilogy* pays more attention to other aspects of secondary religions (which, in turn, did not receive that much attention in the previous two series).

The Church on Erna and Other Religious Institutions

The One God mentioned throughout the trilogy never makes a direct appearance; he is an abstract and absent deity whose image is available only through the Church on Erna's doctrines. The Church of the Unification of Human Faith on Erna is the primary religious institution on the planet. Though there are numerous pagan cults (in the city of Jaggonath alone there exist ninety-six pagan churches) and though some people call upon "Gods!" (*BSR* 91) or "Gods of Earth 'n' Erna" (*BSR* 135) instead of the One God, there is no other institution with such a number of followers and such a rich history as the Church on Erna.

The historical development of the fictional Church is never entirely described, but it can be reconstructed from bits of information left by Friedman throughout the three volumes. The Church arose out of the colonists' desperate attempts to deal with fae which reacted not only to human dreams and fears, but also to their religious needs by generating numerous incarnations of gods and messiahs (*WTNF* 98–99). In response to that religious chaos, a group of men and women formed a movement known as the Revivalism which established the united Church and instructed the colonists to worship the God of Earth. The Revivalists hoped that God's inexplicable nature, which evaded human cognition (*mysterium* of the numinous), would not be mirrored by fae (*WTNF* 98–99). Their faith in God's potency and magnitude gave birth to Erna's leading Church.

Gerald Tarrant (one of the two protagonists) was initially the Prophet of Revivalism, a charismatic religious leader whose greatest ambition was to manipulate human collective consciousness in a way that would make a lasting impression on fae and thus allow people to create their ideal civilization. To reach that goal, the Prophet harnessed the power of religion and redesigned every prayer, ritual, and symbol so that they would serve his purposes (*WTNF* 99). Two documents which lie at the foundation of the Church are the "Church's Manifesto" (*BSR* 87) and "the Book of Law" (*BSR* 94); Damien later says that the Prophet "wrote half our bible. More than half! His signature is on nearly every holy book we have" (*BSR* 203). As the Prophet, Tarrant had a clear vision of what he wanted to achieve:

> One: To unify man's faith, so that millions of souls might impress the fae with the same image in unison. Two: To alter man's perception of the fae—to distance him from that power—thus weakening the link which permitted it to respond to him so easily. This meant a god who wouldn't make appearances on demand, nor provide easy miracles. It meant hardship and it meant sacrifice. But he believed that in the end it would save us, and permit us to regain our technological heritage. Three: To safeguard man's spirit [*WTNF* 100].

To obtain the last goal—the sanctity of man's spirit—the Church established by the Revivalists could not be lenient with its followers, like the false religions whose "godlings" immediately fulfilled people's desires, in return feeding on their emotions. Yet it was because of the instant gratification offered by the cults of Iezu that people were not keen on rejecting them. This eventually compelled the Church to wage war against them, which lasted three centuries and ended in the Church's defeat, because the institution could not win against fae (*WTNF* 100–101). Naturally, the defeat only further exacerbated the animosity between the Church and users of fae. Even the Prophet was forced to abandon the institution because of his idea to use fae for religious purposes. However, his desire for knowledge did not disappear after his expulsion, and due to a compact with the evil Unnamed One, the man was transformed into an almost immortal creature feeding on blood and fear (the Hunter).

Presumably, Gerald's metamorphosis should have had striking consequences for the Church on Erna: the corruption of the Prophet—the man who had established the Church and fashioned its doctrines and scriptures—could have questioned the validity of his religious teachings and, consequently, the validity of the Church itself. Friedman never explores this idea, probably because if the Prophet and his work were to be completely rejected by the Church, than the institution would destroy its own image. To avoid such a crisis and any ensuing schisms, the Church seems to have made a distinction between Gerald Tarrant—the Prophet and Gerald Tarrant—a man. Thus, the institution could both preserve Tarrant's work from the time when he was a divinely inspired Prophet, and treat him as a fallible human being prone to temptation. In fact, after Tarrant's expulsion from the Church, most people seem to have lost interest in him and no one identifies the fearsome Hunter with the ex–Prophet. As a result, no one questions the validity of the Church's teachings (and such a turn of events allows Friedman to sustain her secondary Church). Still, centuries later Tarrant did cause a crisis within the institution. Not knowing that the malicious Hunter is their ex–Prophet, Church authorities declared a Holy War against him—and again lost, overwhelmed by his power. That defeat not only weakened the Church's morale, but also publicly manifested its inferiority to the all-powerful Hunter.

The events of *Coldfire* take place hundreds of years after the era of Revivalism; the Church on Erna is a strong, though not homogenous institution divided into an eastern and western branch, ruled respectively by the Patriarch (Holy Father) and the Matriarch (Holy Mother)—the Church had one leader until late in the third century, when religious reign was eventually divided because the realm was too vast to be managed by one person (*WTNF* 120). Regrettably, the trilogy focuses solely on the male leader and never follows the female one (it also does not introduce any female priestesses; a female knight of the Church appears briefly in the e-book prequel, *Dominion*: her name is Faith and she possesses "Earth's blessing," i.e., her mind does not interact with fae). It is only revealed that the Matriarch is a woman of great faith and authority, whom the other leader respects as his equal. The elderly Patriarch is presented as a devout man who has never lost faith in the Church's goal: to enable humankind to find salvation through faith in the One God (*BSR* 25). The humble Patriarch constantly worries whether he will be able to protect the Church's followers from moral and spiritual corruption.[3] Though he does not agree with the Matriarch's every decision—the Matriarch allows an order of Warrior Priests to use fae for the benefit of the Church, whereas the Patriarch loathes even the mere idea of doing so—he disregards his personal feelings to avoid an internal schism. Eventually, he does not hesitate to sacrifice his own life to redeem the faithful from sin and to strengthen their unity with the Church.

4. The Fantastic (De-)Evolution of Christianity

Members of the Church on Erna worship the One God by attending church service held by priests, but the ceremonies are never described in detail. The interior of church buildings consists of pews and an altar, and the walls are adorned with murals and stained-glass windows (*BSR* 22). To mold people's faith appropriately, Church art is based on symbolism, so the One God or human subjects are seldom depicted (*COS* 143); on one altar, the One God is symbolically represented by an interlocked double circle (*COS* 136). The church buildings are permeated by an atmosphere of sanctity and otherworldly presence, which invites people to meditate on their relationship with God—at least as far as Damien is concerned (*WTNF* 128). The Church on Erna believes that only through unfaltering faith and a complete rejection of fae (which facilitates corruption of the spirit) can humankind thrive on its new planet. To secure both the prosperity of Erna's civilization and humanity's ultimate salvation through faith in the One God are the Church's ultimate goals.

Though Friedman produces a very positive image of the Church on Erna, she does not intend to glorify institutionalized religion in general. Another faction of the Church, located on a different continent (in a region called Mercia), is an example of how religious power may be usurped for personal gains. Initially, it seems that the faction in Mercia has achieved the goals of the entire institution: people whole-heartedly worship the One God and local fae is almost entirely suppressed. The supreme religious authority belongs to the Matria, female visionaries and oracles who "hear and interpret the Voice of the One God, and live eternally Sanctified in His Name" (*WTNF* 120). Every Matria is supported by a Lord Regent of a given province, who helps her rule the country according to the laws of faith established by the Prophet. Thus, holy dictates are combined with administration, which results in a country subjected to religious ideals. However, it soon becomes clear that the faction has fallen to corruption and its achievement is but a religious utopia. Gerald notices that the Church in Mercia has diverged from many of the doctrines of the central Church (which he himself established). While the central Church is not very strict on the point of celibacy, the local Order of the Sanctified vows chastity, because it believes that natural urges of the body are destructive to the soul. While the Prophet promoted gender equality in power, Mercia's Church is ruled by women. To minimize the influence of fae, the communities kill people with inborn skills to manipulate the power. Finally, hunting for fae-born monsters has become a bloody ritual devoted to the One God. Thus, the religious paradise of Mercia proves to be a façade supported by a corrupted faith. When the truth is exposed, Mercia is almost destroyed by internal power struggles within the Church.

As far as the minor religious cults are concerned, their "godlings" are either fae-born creatures whose images stem from the human psyche or the

Iezu who appropriate the roles of deities, in return feeding on human emotions. The law of the land ascertains people's freedom to worship whom they wish to (*COS* 67). As a result, from the city of Jaggonath's ninety-six pagan churches more than forty are dedicated to the Iezu (*WTNF* 341). Some of these minor cults are mentioned only once, e.g., the Temple of Bakshi (*COS* 100), Yoshti's house of worship (*COS* 173), and the Maidens of Pelea Temple (*COS* 199). The Temple of Davarti is only briefly described when it is attacked by worshippers of the One God; the temple's idol is a monstrous figure with eight sets of arms and four pairs of male and female genitals, a face set in the crotch, and a human body thrust into its mouth (*COS* 69).

Some of these pagan cults are presented with more detail, though they never achieve the complexity of the Church on Erna (and so it is impossible to trace their historical development or define their beliefs beyond the most basic tenets). For instance, in the Temple of Pleasure—which is dedicated to the pleasure-god, Karril—people perform worship by indulging all sorts of stimulants and sexual activities. In the center of the decadent temple there is a fountain embellished with erotic carvings, which functions as the altar (*BSR* 75). The deity's priests wear a silver neckpiece with a phallic symbol (*COS* 173). Karril, a secondary character in *Coldfire*, wonders whether fae, reinforced by people's faith, will someday transform him into a true god. Another religious institution, the Temple of Saris, is dedicated to the goddess of beauty and art. Saris's priests wear silver masks and loose robes which obscure their gender. This reflects the image adopted by the Iezu-goddess who materializes in an androgynous silvery body. When Narilka, another of the secondary characters, asks for a "communion" with the goddess, she needs first to symbolically purify herself: she changes her clothing and washes her face and hands. Only then is she led to a separate room where she burns herbs to receive visions. Surprisingly, Saris offers the girl her protection. It is not clear whether the Iezu-goddess does that because she sympathizes with Narilka or because she intends to convincingly play the role of a benevolent deity.

Other cults dedicated to Iezu are not so pleasant and rewarding for the faithful. The evil Calesta is worshipped by a group of physically deformed and mentally unstable people living in the wilderness. They venerate a statue representing Calesta (a human form with bug-like eyes) and ceremonially surround it with offerings to express their gratitude for his alleged protection. Afterward, they dance around their idol and offer themselves to it, until one of them is "chosen" by the deity and ritually killed by the group (*WTNF* 318-319). Calesta feeds on sadism, so this ersatz religion which promotes violence and death provides him with his desired nourishment. Since he is destroyed by the protagonists, his cult may eventually be dissolved, because the faithful will no longer receive any gratification from their god.

As for the rakh (Erna's indigenous humanoid species), Friedman indicates that their spiritual needs are satisfied by their experience of union with the natural world, so they do not need organized religion. In fact, they have a rather poor opinion of religion in general. Hesseth, a representative of the rakh, claims that human religions fulfill humanity's need to perceive itself as the center of the world, to control life, and to have the promise of an afterlife. In contrast, the rakh feel that they are but

> one small part of a very complex world, and we sense—and accept—our natural place in it. We see this planet as a living, breathing thing and we know ourselves an element of it. We understand what birth and death are to us, and we're at peace with that understanding. How can I explain? So many of these things have no words, because we never had a need to describe them. The world is. The rakh *are*. That's enough for us [*WTNF* 97].

Her words suggest that humankind needs religion to compensate for its various insecurities, whereas the rakh, by retaining their spiritual bond with the natural world, are able to live without such compensation. Readers can only speculate what will happen to the indigenous community once human civilization completely dominates Erna.

The Church on Erna and Christianity

In contrast to Donaldson's *Chronicles* and Kay's *Fionavar*, *The Coldfire Trilogy* does not showcase an array of fantastic deities or a diversified set of religious practices; in fact, few religious events, places, and objects are mentioned or described in detail, and there are hardly any secondary myths available. Yet this does not mean that *Coldfire*'s concepts of the numinous and secondary religion are inferior to Donaldson's or Kay's creations. On the contrary, *Coldfire*'s religious vision is as intricate and compelling, but simply founded on a different approach. Firstly, it is clearly indebted to the Christian tradition, with hardly any borrowings from world mythologies. Secondly, Friedman pays a lot of attention to the historical development of the Church on Erna and its "reconstruction" of Earth's religion. This focus on religious history does not appear in Kay's *Fionavar* and appears only partially in Donaldson's *Chronicles*. Thirdly, since one of *Coldfire*'s protagonists is a priest and the other an ex–Prophet of the Church, the series is strongly focused on exploring different dimensions of a person's faith in God and dedication to Church service (these levels of religious self-awareness are distinctly lower in *The Chronicles* and *Fionavar*). The gradual transformation of the protagonists' faith adds to their psychological plausibility, and becomes a sub-plot whose development readers might follow with much interest. The analysis of the protagonists' moral choices and attitudes toward religion clarifies what kind of morality is upheld by the series. Thus, this chapter first juxtaposes the Church on Erna against Christianity, and then investigates the fate of the protagonists in order to determine which biblical motifs and symbols are reconstructed in their adventures, and to decide whether the moral message of *Coldfire* can be reconciled with Christian principles and ethics.

From the Prologue of the second volume we learn that the colonists brought to Erna at least one copy of the Bible, and it can be assumed that some of the original colonists might have been Christians. Yet the trilogy never clarifies whether other religions, e.g., Buddhism or Islam, were also brought to the new planet—if they were, they were probably represented only by a few colonists, so their heritage was gradually lost to the denizens of Erna. Friedman's comments about the colonists reveal that she did consider their profile, so the presence of a particular religion and the absence of others is not coincidental:

> The Ernan expedition was not meant to represent the whole spectrum of human experience; it was merely one ship among many. Its unifying concept can be summed up in one sentence: Maximum genetic diversity with minimum cultural conflict. Colonists were chosen mostly from English-speaking, European-descended cultures: The US, Canada, Britain, Australia, etc. ["The Coldfire Trilogy: Author's Notes," n.p.].

Though the colonists possessed at least one copy of the Bible, this and any other copy must have somehow got lost or seemed "inadequate," since the Prophet of the Church undertook the task of writing the Bible anew. This new version of the Bible is never described or quoted, so it remains unknown how much of the original Christian Scriptures was actually preserved. At one occasion, Damien ironically asks Gerald: "How are you at parting the waters?" (*BSR* 266), which is an obvious reference to the Old Testament episode in which Moses' parted the Red Sea to allow the Israelites to escape from Egypt. Damien's ironic comment not only suggests that at least this part of the original Scriptures was preserved, but it also compares Gerald Tarrant, the Prophet of the Church on Erna, to an Old Testament prophet, the chosen of God. This is one of the many hints suggesting that the Church on Erna is both a continuation and a reconstruction of Christianity.

This ambiguous identity is visible, first of all, in the structure of the fictional Church, which reflects parts of Christian hierarchy, but also adds its own echelons of power. The Patriarch, considered the supreme religious authority of the Church on Erna and titled "His Holiness the Holy Father," is a papal figure whose life goal is to secure the Church's position and people's salvation through faith. The lower echelons of the institution consist of holy orders with their own particular vocations (e.g., Damien is a Warrior-Priest) and regular priests who serve in churches. Such a hierarchy corresponds to the internal structure within Christianity, in which religious orders are dedicated to particular tasks, while stationary priests attend to the needs of local communities. It is also significant that the fantastic institution is defined as the *Church* on Erna (not a synagogue or mosque), with the Patriarch located at a central cathedral—the name of Erna's religious institution and its hierarchy clearly indicate its roots in Christianity.

A major point of difference is the fictional church's internal division into the eastern and western faction, with the latter being supervised by a woman. While it could be argued that the division alone mirrors the internal division within Christianity—the Eastern Orthodox Church is prevalent in Russia and eastern Europe, whereas Catholicism and Protestantism dominate in different parts of Europe, Africa, and Americas—the issue of female empowerment within the Church on Erna is more controversial. Though women can be ordained to ministerial and priestly offices in Anglicanism and Protestantism, there is still no equivalent of Friedman's Matriarch—a female leader whose position would be equal to, for instance, that of the Pope. Thus, the figure of the Matriarch supports the claim that Friedman's Church is a reconstruction, not simply a continuation, of Christian institutions.

As far as religious doctrines are concerned, most of the tenets professed by the Church on Erna reflect Christian tradition though, like in the case of the institution's internal hierarchy, some ambiguity is also present. The core belief of the fictional Church—or at least the only one consistently mentioned—is the worship of the One God: the single, almighty, and supreme creator of humankind and the worlds, whom people should venerate and please by living according to the requirements of faith. Aside from omnipotence and omniscience, the One God is attributed both with severe justice and infinite mercy, so though it is assumed that he will punish sinners for their earthly transgressions, the sinners may pray for forgiveness and redemption from sin; the Church on Erna believes that only faith in the One God may protect people from spiritual corruption and grant them salvation after death. The scriptures of the fantastic Church profess: "*The nature of the One God is Mercy, and His Word is forgiveness*" (*WTNF* 353; italics in the original). Thus, *Coldfire*'s One God is described in very Christian terms: Christianity worships the Lord God as the absolute creator of life, who may become wroth with sinful humankind and mete out divine punishment (as it is often the case in the Old Testament, in which God severely punishes not only the oppressors of his chosen nation—the Israelites, but also the Israelites whenever they breach his commandments), but who nevertheless sent His Son to suffer on the cross in order to redeem humanity and offer it the promise of eternal salvation. However, the worship of the One God appears to be the only part of the original Christian doctrine that was preserved on Erna; angels are acknowledged only once or twice (*COS* 134), whereas Jesus Christ, the Holy Spirit, and Virgin Mary are never mentioned or addressed in worship. There are also no allusions to devil/Satan, i.e., God's personified adversary.

Perhaps it is the Unnamed One—the amalgamation of evil forces whose domain is Hell—that should be perceived as Erna's equivalent of the Christian God's ultimate adversary, since, similarly to Satan, the Unnamed One seeks to corrupt human souls and wreak havoc in the material world. Yet since the Church on Erna and its priests hardly ever mention the Unnamed One, its similarity or parallel to the biblical adversary remain unclear.

As it has been already mentioned, the major goal of the Church of the Unification of Human Faith on Erna is to unite humankind in worship of the One God, so that a universal faith will overpower the alien force of fae and allow human civilization to thrive on the new planet. Such a goal is a distant echo of Christianity's ecumenical movement, which aims at fostering and strengthening cooperation between various Christian denominations that are separated by theological and liturgical discrepancies, but united by their faith in the Lord God (*Britannica...* 313). In Friedman's world, the ability to unite in one faith is treated as a prerequisite for humanity's survival and further development.

In view of that goal, fae is treated as humankind's enemy not only because its constructs threaten people's physical safety, but because the power is a source of moral and spiritual corruption. The Church on Erna rejects fae on the same basis that Christianity rejects the occult, i.e., the belief in magic is a transgression of the Second Commandment "Thou shalt have no other gods" and usurpation of God's authority, since occultism is based on moral relativism and instructs people that they can manipulate natural forces to obtain their private goals. In this context, the Church on Erna is right to equate fae with occultism. People with inborn skills to control fae often use the alien power to fulfill their own desires, whereas others are attracted to "godlings" constructed from fae, who offer immediate satisfaction of human needs. In both cases, people need not put their trust in an immaterial God or strive for moral perfection. The Patriarch, who claims that "the more we expose it [fae] to humankind's greed, the more it stinks of our excesses" (*BSR* 26), believes that succumbing to any temptation, also that posed by the possibility of wielding divine-like power, is an inherent part of human nature. Thus, the Church argues that fae should be avoided in every possible way, so that humankind may build a civilization founded on their trust in the One God, not on their reliance on an insentient power that grants instant satisfaction of one's needs. The Patriarch's perception of human nature is a clear echo of Augustine of Hippo's conviction that people are born weak and blemished by original sin, and their only path to redemption is through faith in God, not through their personal achievements (McGrath 150).

However, on closer inspection the similarities between fae and occultism might seem rather superficial, and probably because of that a faction of Friedman's Church acknowledges the power's usefulness. Damien claims that fae is not a type of "alien magic" (*BSR* 28), because the former is a natural part of Erna's ecosystem and the latter was never able to freely interact with human consciousness. Rather than by occult powers, Friedman's concept of fae was inspired by Isaac Asimov's essay "Why I Do Not Believe in Magic" in which the author claims that if magic existed, it would be conditioned by the same physical laws which apply to any natural force ("The Coldfire Trilogy: Author's Notes," n.p.). It should be added that the characters' ability to wield fae is not a result of some magic practices or the act of trading one's soul for occult powers, but the natural consequence of evolution: to survive, the colonists had to adapt to the new environment and coexist with the alien force. And even though some people obsess over fae and fall into its temptation (Senzei, a secondary character, dies in a foolish attempt to obtain more power), others (e.g., Damien and the Patriarch who, ironically, possess inborn skills to "Work" fae) refuse to use the power for personal gain. It is also worth noticing that at no point is fae presented as an omnipotent entity; on the contrary, it is said that the One God's inexplicable complexity cannot be reproduced by the insentient force. Yet despite its clearly inferior position, in the end fae is almost entirely suppressed and, according to the Patriarch's mystical vision, this will lead to humankind's prosperity—as if Friedman were arguing that only by relinquishing external powers and following the One God can people achieve greatness. Thus, *Coldfire* ends with the undisputed triumph of the Church.

It is important to note that a link between Christianity and the Church on Erna exists also in the colonists' consciousness, because they acknowledge the fact that their Church is rooted in a tradition that originated on Earth and that their "One God" is but another name for the God that was worshipped on Earth. When Damien prays, he addresses the One God of Erna as the "God of Earth" (*WTNF* 52) or says: "This is the way of the Lord the One God, who created Earth and Erna, who led us to the stars, whose faith is the salvation of humankind" (*WTNF* 132)—his words not only commemorate the home-planet, but also affirm that it was God's will that people should explore the universe. What is more, Earth has become one of the symbols of the Church on Erna: people possess the so-called "earth-disks" which represent both a person's faith in the One God and their original planet. These disks can be carried (*BSR* 108), but Gerald wears his own in an old-fashioned way on a chain around his neck, as if the disk were a holy chaplet (similar to the chaplets worn by Christians).

However, the lack of celibacy within the Church on Erna again indicates that *Coldfire*'s religious body is a reconstruction of Christianity, not simply its continuation. The Prophet of the Church on Erna taught that it is destructive to perceive natural urges as impure (*WTNF* 147); that is why, Damien— a consecrated priest—is never condemned or even rebuked for having lovers, and at times he thinks that it would be good to have children (though it is never explicitly said whether any of Erna's priests of the One God has a family). This absence of celibacy in *Coldfire*'s reconstruction of Christianity is a controversial issue, despite the Christian practice of clerical marriage. In Protestantism and Anglicanism a member of the clergy is allowed to marry and raise a family. The Eastern Orthodox Church excludes clerical marriage, but does ordain men who are already married (though only widowers and priests who swore celibacy can be chosen for bishops). The Roman Catholic Church excludes clerical marriage and instead insists on clerical celibacy. Given this variety within Christian denominations, Damien's behavior would not be that controversial if he fulfilled his sexual needs within the bonds of marriage, but since he never settles down with any of his lovers, his behavior might be treated as sexual promiscuity unbecoming a priest.

Celibacy is not the only "inconvenient" concept which Erna's Prophet (who himself had a wife and three children) wished to eradicate from the revised doctrine. It is revealed that while the Prophet was designing the Church on Erna, he intended to omit the belief in Hell, because he saw it as "excess philosophical baggage" (*WTNF* 101). The idea of eternal punishment was eventually restored, because the colonists did not accept such a radical change. This suggests that they possessed some degree of knowledge about the original Christian doctrine and were determined to preserve it—or at least some parts of it. If the issues of female empowerment, fae-using priests, lack of celibacy, and the Prophet's machinations are all taken into consideration, it is clear that though the structure and tenets of Erna's Church of Human Unification are strongly embedded in Christianity, it is perhaps better to talk about a reconstruction rather than a mere preservation of tradition.

Biblical References and Christian Morality in the Portrayal of the Protagonists

The teachings of the Church on Erna are reflected in the choices and actions of *Coldfire*'s major characters who are all, in one way or another, bound with the institution: Gerald is its founding-father and ex–Prophet, Damien—its consecrated priest, and the Patriarch—its supreme leader. Consequently, *Coldfire*, more than any of the series discussed in this book, explores the dimensions of human faith and invests a lot of time in the spiritual development of its protagonists. Without belittling the entertaining aspect of the trilogy's fantastic adventures, it can be argued that Friedman uses them as a background on which she examines various human attitudes toward faith and attempts at acting according to its dictates (or according to one's personal interpretations of religious dictates). In Friedman's own words, she makes her characters "explore that uncomfortable realm within ourselves where there is no black or white, only gray" ("The Coldfire Trilogy: Author's Notes," n.p.). Thus, the characters' opinions, choices, and actions become the author's dialogue with Christian morality and a frame for her reworking of several biblical motifs.

Gerald Tarrant, the ex-Prophet, is a charismatic and arrogant man whose immense faith in the One God resulted in his wholehearted devotion to the shaping of Erna's Church. Paradoxically, his devotion was so great that to observe the development of the institution, Gerald established a compact with the malicious Unnamed One, which turned him into the Hunter—a semi-immortal man feeding on blood and fear, who is weak against fire and sunlight. Gerald still remembers himself prior to the transformation:

> He remembered a man of faith riding to war in the name of his God, the banner of the one true Church whipping in the wind overhead. So idealistic, that man. So pure in motive. So dedicated to everything that was moral and just. No longer. The memory sank to the bottom of his soul and was lost again. If I had not loved God so much, there would have been no power in betraying Him [*Dominion*, n.p.].

Tarrant betrayed not only his God, but also his family whom he killed in a bloody ritual to invoke the evil being. His act can be recognized as a form of apostasy. Apostasy, from Greek *apostasia* which means "revolt" or "defection," is a complete rejection of Christianity by a baptized person. It is also defined as "a gradual and self-willed movement away from God," which might take the form of a rebellion against God or turning one's heart away from Him (Ryken et al. 38–39). Though Gerald never publicly rejects his faith, he consciously severs his relationship with the One God and forsakes the Church's ideals in order to fulfill his private ambitions. Christianity teaches that refusing the gift of a personal relationship with the benevolent God is the ultimate sin (Jonas 252), and that is exactly what Gerald Tarrant commits to satiate his desires.

What is more, Gerald is the epitome of a fallen man, Erna's heir to Adam and Eve who yielded to temptation because they wished to obtain knowledge offered by the forbidden fruit and, consequently, lost their inborn innocence. Gerald also wished to obtain knowledge—knowledge of what would happen to "his" Church—and that overpowering ambition led him to commit the sins that marred his entire existence. Adam, Eve, and Gerald transgress divine law, for which they are severely punished. The pair is banished from Eden, which deprives them of life in God's light and presence, and Gerald is also symbolically deprived of God's light—as the Hunter, he is forced to live in darkness, because sunrays can literally destroy his transformed (or, in another sense, corrupted) body.

Paradoxically, Gerald's Fall was precipitated by his fear of eternal damnation in Hell. The man believed that after his expulsion from the Church, people's animosity toward him might have made a lasting impression on fae and turned it against him (*BSR* 7). Tormented by the vision of future suffering, Gerald uses "the primal pattern of Erna" (*BSR* 7), i.e., a sacrifice, to gather enough power to fulfill his desire. By killing his family and sacrificing his own humanity, he bargains with the evil Unnamed One[4] whom he then must serve to retain immortality. Still, Gerald claims that what he traded in that bargain was his body and service, never his soul (*BSR* 314), and that as long as he can maintain the integrity of his identity, he will not become a mindless demon (*BSR* 214). This claim is significant for several reasons. First, it proves Gerald is more cunning than Goethe's Faust who quickly signed away his soul and whose fate Friedman seems to be reworking in the figure of the ex–Prophet. Second, in Christian tradition the human soul is the entity over which Satan battles with God, intending to corrupt it with sin in order to separate a person from the Creator. Finally, it suggests that Gerald, despite all the atrocities which he commits as a servant of evil, is still not beyond the possibility of atonement and redemption.

Gerald's attitude toward religion and relationship with the Church are ambiguously complex. Though the man was expelled from the Church and turned into a servant of evil, in his black fortress[5] he has a chapel dedicated to the One God. Also, even long after his metamorphosis, he still considers himself the creator of Erna's Church and actively observes its development.[6] On the one hand, he rejoices at the power and moral freedom he has gained through the bargain with evil (*BSR* 437), and on the other, he still fears damnation in Hell and despairs that he may not encounter God or experience his divine presence. Exposed to Damien's ardent faith and strict morality (at one point, Gerald announces that he does not intend to help Damien any longer and instead wants to "[w]ash his soul clean with killing, until the taint of his contact with humankind was nothing more than an unpleasant memory" (*BSR* 482), which sounds like a mockery of Christian baptism with water), he gradually changes his prerogatives, rejects a tempting offer of true immortality, and eventually makes a conscious decision to protect the Church from destruction at the expense of his own life. This self-sacrifice is a milestone in his path to redemption.

While the figure of the ex–Prophet allows Friedman to develop the motifs of sin, fall, and atonement, the character of Damien Vryce, the Warrior Priest, allows her to explore other dimensions of a person's dedication to religion. Damien is initially an idealist who became a priest because he believed that the One God and the Church are humankind's only hope and because he felt that dedicating his life to religious service somehow justified his existence (*WTNF* 367–368). Damien is a truly devout man who frequently thinks about God and prays when he is in need of consolation. At times, he even behaves as a zealot who will not compromise with his faith regardless of the circumstances; at the beginning of the first volume he proudly declares: "We all have our temptations. But our ability to rise above them—to serve an ideal, rather than the dictates of selfish instinct—is what defines us as a species" (*BSR* 27). To observe how the man's idealism is shaken and how he must reevaluate his identity is one of the most absorbing parts of the trilogy.

Step by step, Gerald's company forces Damien to choose the lesser evils and justify the bad means which allow him to achieve good goals. Gerald believed in utilitarianism even when he was still the Prophet and so he wrote: "*Evil is what you make of it* [...]. *Bind it to a higher Purpose, and you will have altered its nature.* [...] *We use what tools we must*" (*BSR* 137; italics in the original). Morally acceptable solutions are for him those which are the most beneficial in a particular situation. Thus, when the protagonists discover a boy whose soul has been devoured by evil creatures, Gerald decides that killing the insentient body will be an act of mercy both for the boy and his parents (*BSR* 121–122). Damien objects by voicing the belief of his Church that any human life is sacred and of the utmost value. Gerald, in turn, is convinced that not life itself but the quality of life is what matters. The issue hidden in their dispute is the problem of euthanasia: Gerald embodies modern opinions that people should be given the right to decide about their own or a close relative's death, whereas Damien represents Christianity which adamantly rejects the so-called "mercy killing." To stop Gerald from killing the boy, Damien would have to directly confront his power, which, for the time being, he is unable to do, so he passively witnesses the murder. He is unwilling to oppose Gerald also because he fears that his protest would endanger their mission. Thus, on the one hand, Damien unconsciously emulates Gerald's utilitarian attitude, because his Church would rather have him forsake the mission and kill such a vile creature as the Hunter. Damien's doubts are also artificially amplified by Gerald who confesses that he deliberately behaves in a way which forces Damien to negotiate between the moral demands of his Church and the practical demands of their journey (*BSR* 315). On the other hand, the priest's sense of morality has not been entirely numbed since later he does fearfully wonder whether he became accustomed to the presence of evil (*BSR* 274), and he truly regrets his temporary refusal to recognize the value of human life (*BSR* 355).

The first true moment of crisis comes when Damien learns that the beloved Prophet of his faith and the Hunter are one and the same person. He is devastated, because the Prophet was the Church's role-model, yet he betrayed its ideals and damned his soul (*BSR* 203). It is ironic that Damien, the priest of a merciful God, speaks of eternal damnation—later events will force him to reevaluate his judgment and learn about the true meaning of mercy. Despite the horrid revelation, Damien continues the journey and even feeds Gerald with his fear and blood to sustain his existence. Though the priest is loath to do so and afraid of the Church's punishment, he rises above his personal fears for the sake of Ciani, the woman whom he and Gerald intend to save. Paradoxically, the actions for which the Church could condemn the priest are also a measure of his compassion and ability to sacrifice himself for others. This is one of the many examples illustrating how Friedman skillfully creates a clash between rigid institutional rules and the requirements of a person's conscience in order to force her readers to think what is actually good and wrong.

There are three crucial moments in *Coldfire* when Damien could have abandoned Gerald to suffering and death, but chose otherwise, though for vastly different reasons. In the first case, when Gerald is captured by his enemy, Damien initially declares: "I would sooner walk through the gates of hell [...] than loose that man on the world again" (*BSR* 402), yet he eventually does save him. The ex-Prophet is kept in volcanic fire; his body is burned and regenerated in an unending cycle of torture. This is undoubtedly a Christianity-inspired form of torment: an image of a sinner burning in Hell. In the Old Testament, fire symbolizes God's anger, and burning in fire functions as the means to deliver divine judgment (Ryken et al. 377); the New Testament also states that one of the unrelenting torments awaiting sinners in Hell is suffering in fire (Ryken et al. 377). In addition, the New Testament introduces fire as the symbol of God's presence in the Holy Spirit (Steffler 5). Gerald's weakness against this particular element might suggest that he is weak against it not because of the heat, but because he cannot bear anything that symbolizes God's presence. The man is freed from his ersatz Hell only thanks to Damien's compassion and determination.

In the second case, Gerald is dragged to his personalized Hell after the evil Unnamed One decides that the man has transgressed their compact. Knowing that only the ex-Prophet can save the planet, Damien is ready to bargain with Evil to rescue his companion, even if that endangers his priesthood. Paradoxically, his decision does not stem from moral demise, but from spiritual growth since Damien asks himself: "*Which do you value more, this avocation you've grown so accustomed to, or the chance to do something to help save your world? Is one man's comfort such a great sacrifice for God to require, in order that His people might be defended?*" (*COS* 173; italics in the original). Thus, the priest embarks on a spiritual journey during which he crosses a land of fire and volcanoes, and a land filled with semi-dead female bodies—Tarrant's victims. The scenery of Gerald's Hell again corresponds to Christian imagery: the landscape of fire and brimstone is complemented by a myriad of tortured bodies, which are customarily associated with hellish torment. In this particular scene of damnation—fully deserved, given Gerald's innumerable crimes—Friedman begins to transform the man into *Coldfire*'s Christ figure. This reversal of roles is indicated by the form of Gerald's imprisonment in Hell. The man is bound "cruciform, his arms stretched out tautly to the sides, his legs separated just far enough to make room for the bonds of his ankles" (*COS* 225). Of course, at this point in the story, it is only his position, which mirrors Christ spread on the cross, that establishes Gerald as a Christ figure, because the protagonist is justly suffering for his own crimes. It is Damien's intervention that rescues the man from Hell and gives him another month of life.

The priest rescues Gerald for the third time when the ex-Prophet—now mortal since his compact with evil was broken—is dying because of a weak heart. Endangering his own life, Damien heals his companion, because he believes that Gerald deserves a chance to atone for his sins and make peace with God (*COS* 445). Damien's utterly selfless decision implies that he finally grasped his Church's belief in a merciful God and in the grace of redemption. Ironically, the growth of Damien's understanding of his religion is paired with his willing withdrawal from priesthood. The Patriarch, who initially condemns the priest for his leniency with Gerald, eventually concludes that even if at times people might be forced to do terrible things in the name of faith, their actions should not be associated with the Church (*COS* 253). Given freedom to reevaluate his conduct, Damien first of all sincerely prays to God:

> "*I have loved You and served You all my life. Your Law gave meaning to my existence. Your Dream gave me purpose. In Your service I grew to manhood, measuring myself against Your eternal ideals, striving to set standards for myself that would please You. I live and breathe and struggle and Work—and accept the inevitability of my own death—all in Your Name, Lord God of Earth and Erna. Only and always in Your Name*" [*COS* 282; italics in the original].

Though the prayer is a whole-hearted affirmation of faith, the man decides to leave the Church not to tarnish its reputation. Up until that moment, withdrawal from priesthood was the subject of Damien's nightmares, because religious vocation was the core of his identity. Though his choice transforms him into a fallen priest and threatens his integrity, it is simultaneously the greatest proof of his faith in God and his love for the Church.

Coldfire *and the Motif of (Self-)Sacrifice*

Damien's decision is only one of the many sacrifices which appear in *Coldfire*. In fact, the motif of (self-)sacrifice functions as the trilogy's narrative axis and marks the most prominent events in the plot: the colonists' arrival on Erna, Gerald's transformation into the Hunter and then his victory over evil, and the Patriarch's redemption of the faithful. The sacrifices described by Friedman are clearly inspired by biblical tradition, though the author does significantly reconstruct the motif.

When Gerald calls sacrifice "the primal pattern of Erna" (*BSR* 7), he refers to an event from the period of colonization—the First Sacrifice offered by Ian Casca. Inspired by the Old and the New Testament episodes of sacrifice, Casca concluded that sacrificial offering, the most powerful of humankind's rituals, will be the only key to establishing "communication" with the planet and being accepted by its alien ecosystem (*WTNF* 19). Yet instead of sacrificing human life, Casca made an offering of the colonists' heritage: he detonated their spaceship with its entire equipment and knowledge. Though in consequence of his actions people gained control over fae, they lost their identity and history.

Centuries later, Gerald abuses the pattern established by Casca for personal gains: he sacrifices his family and humanity in an act of brutal murder, and the power evoked through that act transforms him into the evil Hunter. Even so, at the end of the third volume (after months spent in Damien's company) Gerald, standing on a volcano named Mount Shaitan—most probably derived from "Satan," decides to sacrifice his own life and accept his due punishment in Hell in order to thwart Calesta's plans (*COS* 414). Gerald's willing self-sacrifice to protect Erna, its people, and its Church, as well as his subsequent miraculous resurrection, complement his image of Erna's Christ figure. After his rebirth as a free man, Gerald sacrifices his identity and power as the ex–Prophet and Hunter to complete his transformation. Thus, he returns to a state in which a relationship with God—his atonement—is again possible, because the man is no longer deprived of the light (literally and symbolically). According to the *Dictionary of Biblical Imagery*,

> The English word *atonement* is derived from the two words "at onement" and denotes a state of togetherness and agreement between two people. Atonement presupposes two parties that are estranged, with the act of atonement being the reconciliation of them into a state of harmony. The theological meaning is the reconciliation between God and his fallen creation, especially between God and sinful human beings [Ryken et al. 54].

Because of his sacrifice, Gerald Tarrant—*Coldfire*'s epitome of a fallen creation—is freed from his vampiric existence and reunited with the Creator, though it is open to speculation whether he will again strive to become an influential figure within the Church's hierarchy.

Lastly, one more sacrifice is performed by the Patriarch who wishes to redeem his people from sin. In the third volume, the elderly leader is tempted by Gerald, who leaves him a blue crystal that will awaken the Patriarch's consciousness and inborn skills to manipulate fae. Gerald clearly plays the role of the biblical serpent whose offer of the forbidden fruit brings knowledge and power, but in return takes away innocence—the Patriarch must accept his affinity with the loathsome fae, though he still refuses to use it for personal gains. Instead, he decides to wage a holy war against the Hunter and his Forest.

Despite his newly awakened power and his religious authority, the leader feels helpless and vulnerable. His feelings are reflected by his prayer: "*Take this trial from me, Lord. I'm not strong enough to handle it. Give it to someone who won't fail you*" (*COS* 294; italics in the original). His words are clearly an echo of those spoken by Jesus at the garden of Gethsemane before his crucifixion: "Abba, Father, all things are possible to thee; remove this cup from me" (Mk. 14:36).

After the victory over the Hunter, the Patriarch is distressed about his people's capacity for violence even if it is performed in the name of a holy cause. Determined to save them from spiritual corruption, he steps into a river and delivers a passionate speech in which he begs God to forgive people for their sins, to restore their spirits, and to judge him alone for the violence that he had caused (*COS* 493). Afterward, he offers his blood as sacrifice and the gathered people use the blood-stained water to baptize themselves. In a mystical vision, the man sees that his sacrifice dispels the threat of ongoing wars and instead secures Erna's future prosperity. To strengthen the possibility of that future, the Patriarch takes his own life. His actions correspond both to the Old and the New Testament images. According to the Old Testament, "without the shedding of blood there is no forgiveness" (Heb. 9:22). Thus, the Patriarch offers his own blood and life to expiate for his sin-inducing violence and to plead to God for forgiveness. On another level, his sacrifice is reminiscent of the New Testament episode of Christ's baptism in the waters of Jordan, as well as of Christ's crucifixion which was performed to cleanse people of sin and secure their eternal salvation. The Patriarch is, therefore, the second Christ figure of *Coldfire*, whose dedication to the One God and devotion to the Church's congregation are culminated in his willing sacrifice—an act of selfless love.

The magnitude of the sacrifices performed by *Coldfire*'s two Christ figures affects the entire planet and alters the pattern established by Casca: the key to communicate with Erna and to control fae is no longer a sacrifice, but a self-sacrifice. Since only a few people will be desperate or determined enough to use fae at such a price, the alien power will eventually cease to interact with human consciousness and, consequently, will no longer hinder the development of human civilization on Erna.

Though the motif of sacrifice is significantly reworked, it retains many of its Christian connotations. First and foremost, the shift between the sacrifices described by Friedman mirrors the transition which the motif of sacrifice undergoes between the Old and the New Testament. In the Old Testament, the Israelites brunt offerings (lambs, bulls, turtledoves) to express their gratitude to God or to atone for a sin. Human sacrifice was not practiced, and God's order for Moses to sacrifice his son Isaac was only a test of faith. Then in the New Testament Christ's death on the cross surpassed all other sacrifices, because it was the ultimate one—a self-sacrifice of the Son of God—which became the key to humankind's salvation. In a similar order, *Coldfire* begins with the Old Testament type of sacrifice: the burning of the colonists' ship resembles the Israelites' offerings of animals to placate an angry God, whereas Gerald's sacrifice of his family is a postponed fulfillment and a hideous mimicry of the order given to Moses. However, in the third volume Friedman shifts to the New Testament version of sacrifice—the self-sacrifice performed by Gerald and the Patriarch for the sake of others—which saves the denizens of Erna from death.

Divine Grace and Salvation Through Faith

The Patriarch's mystical vision of the planet's future prosperity is a grace offered to a dying man so that he may know that his deed was not meaningless. The motif of divine grace reappears in several moments of *Coldfire*, though readers are not always certain who or what is the source of that grace—the One God, the Mother of Iezu, or fae. In the second volume, for instance, Gerald intends to forcefully extract information from the mind of Jenseny, a young girl rescued during their journey. Enraged, Damien protects the child and earnestly prays to God to give him strength to oppose the all-powerful Hunter. The answer to Damien's prayer is a divine manifestation which he experiences as a blissful "power born of faith" (*WTNF* 350), but which is painful and horrifying for Gerald. Their reactions represent the two sides of human experience of the numinous—humble awe and utter terror. Both men are awed, because neither really expected a direct intervention of the divine into their conflict. Even Damien is surprised, because though he prays to God in times of need, he does not expect Him to actually answer: the priest perceives the deity as a distant entity not involved in earthly problems (*BSR* 467). Thus, for Damien, this unexpected manifestation is something comforting—a visible sign of divine protection. For Gerald, it is a nightmare come true. The ex–Prophet confesses that before his transformation, he believed that people's collective efforts would either reach God or create a God of Erna (*WTNF* 351). Yet he was never entirely sure about the fruit of his efforts and about the identity of the divine being to whom the colonists sent their pleas. When his doubts about the existence of something divine are dispelled, the man is still deeply troubled, though for a different reason—because of the compact with evil, Gerald cannot endure the presence of God: "This is the fruit of my labors, Reverend Vryce. That I can never gaze upon the result of all my labor. I sold my soul for knowledge of the future, only to have that very pact render me forever ignorant" (*WTNF* 352). Though the nature of the manifested force escapes the protagonists' understanding, Gerald believes that his inability to endure its presence is a proof of his damnation and future banishment to Hell. Friedman never clarifies whether the men are faced with the majesty of the One God or the Mother of Iezu. The female entity is later given a few paragraphs in which she voices her hopes and worries, but she never recalls this intervention, which suggests that it could have been the One God that responded to Damien's pleas for protection.

A similarly ambiguous experience of divine grace is given to Jenseny when she fights with the malicious Undying Prince. The Prince prolongs his existence by transferring his consciousness to a new body every few decades, and Jenseny is his latest victim. The Prince does not suspect, however, that the girl offers herself as a host with the intention of killing both of them. When the Prince's soul almost escapes from the trap, an inexplicable force appears in response to Jenseny's pleading for help, and binds the Prince to her body until they both die. Again, nothing is revealed about the nature or motivation of this manifestation. It can only be inferred that since it responds to a person in grave need of help, a person who is acting in a good cause, the force is a benevolent and caring entity.

In addition to the motif of divine grace, *Coldfire* incorporates the idea of salvation through faith, not works. The concept of salvation through works is based on the belief that people may earn their salvation by avoiding sin and atoning for the sins already committed. In contrast, the idea of salvation through faith instructs that salvation can never be earned by good deeds, but is given by the merciful God to his fallen children. Gerald's salvation is clearly an example of the latter. The ex-Prophet never intends for his sacrifice on Mount Shaitan to be a form of compensation for his past crimes nor does he hope for salvation through it. On the contrary, he believes that after his death he will suffer damnation in Hell. His decision to nonetheless forsake his life is perhaps the greatest proof of his dedication to the Church and to the One God. Miraculously, the sacrifice becomes the threshold to redemption which the protagonist may gain in his newly restored human life.

Nevertheless, Gerald's salvation is ambiguous, because it is administered not by the One God, but by the Mother of Iezu who revives the man after his sacrificial death. The Mother of Iezu is an element which distorts the trilogy's Christian context. Readers may only wonder whether she is the being to whom Gerald referred when he said that even before the times of colonization there might have been a god of Erna. Readers might also speculate whether she is actually the One God worshipped by the Church. On the one hand, there are certain similarities between the Mother and the Christian God: both are Creators of life, who bestow on their children free will and a set of rules to follow, and who may punish their children or even destroy them in an instant if such is their will. On the other, it is never said that the Mother is the Supreme Creator of any world (be it Earth or Erna) or humankind. In fact, she cannot create *ex nihilo* (the creation attributed to the Christian God), because she needs to find a "mate" to produce offspring (*COS* 284). The concept of creation *ex nihilo* is immensely significant for Christianity, because it indicates that since God is the source of material creation, then everything coming from Him is inherently good (Lovin 27). *Coldfire*'s treatment of its antagonists seems to emphasize this distinction between the fictional Mother and the One God. The Mother of Iezu may create beings like Calesta, who is purely evil, and the protagonists never even consider the idea of his potential redemption. Yet Gerald—a child of God—is offered a second chance, because despite all his sins, as the creation of a benevolent God he is not entirely evil in nature. Perhaps Friedman's wish to bestow females with religious authority (the Matriarch and the Matria) in what is predominantly a patriarchal religion affected also her representation of divinity, and that is why she created a Heavenly Mother, who appears instead of an Almighty Heavenly Father.

Nonetheless, *Coldfire*'s secondary religion is, without a doubt, strongly rooted in the Christian tradition. References to Christianity are present in the structure of Erna's Church of Human Unification (the Patriarch, the priests, the orders) and in the Church's doctrines (belief in a merciful One God, fear of Hell and damnation, the concept of salvation through faith). Also the contents of the Church's holy scriptures and prayers reflects Christian beliefs and model of worship. What is more, Friedman provides fantastic reconstructions of images and motifs appearing in the Bible: man's Fall into the temptation of knowledge and power, his sin against God, the possibility of damnation in Hell, and redemption through the restorative power of sacrifice and baptism. Though the One God does not make a direct appearance in the story, He is present throughout the narrative in the protagonists' struggle to abide by the rules of their faith, in their prayers, and in the unearned grace that is offered to them in times of greatest need. The protagonists' attitude to religion and relationship with the Church on Erna is the background on which Friedman develops their quest to save the world from the evil Calesta. Though Gerald is eventually freed from the power of the Unnamed One, this supreme evil force is not destroyed. Destruction of the ultimate evil is something only God can do, and Friedman's heroes are never concerned with such a goal; it is enough that that they triumph over a minor incarnation of evil and their own weaknesses.

Damien's, Gerald's, and the Patriarch's moral and religious choices not only determine the stages of their adventures, but, most importantly, condition their psychological development. Developing the protagonists' quests, Friedman invites her readers to wonder whether bad means justify good ends, how much a person can sacrifice for his faith, what it truly means to believe in a merciful God, and whether there is a moment when one's sins are so great that redemption is no longer possible. The final message of the story is one full of hope. The Church on Erna is victorious and will most probably play a significant role in the attainment of Erna's future prosperity. Gerald Tarrant, the malicious Hunter whom almost everyone condemned, is offered a chance to redeem his sins in a moment when everyone was least expecting redemption to come. What is more, it is clear that Gerald's sacrifice was indispensable to ensure Erna's prosperity and that without it, the Patriarch's own sacrifice would not have been that successful. Thus, readers are told that good can be derived from even the greatest evil and it is never too late for salvation. These truths and the final promise of Erna's prosperity—prosperity ensured by the Church on Erna in the name of the One God—can be easily reconciled with Christian beliefs.

Yet other images present in *Coldfire* might be disturbing from a Christian perspective, either because they implicitly criticize some aspects of Christianity or perpetuate ideas which Christianity would reject or even condemn. By introducing female church-leaders, Friedman indirectly questions the Catholic hierarchy in which women are excluded from religious service and authority (a Catholic prioress may have authority over nuns, but Friedman's Holy Mother has authority over both men and women, and even the Patriarch respects her decisions). Damien is a controversial figure, because not only does he eventually become a fallen priest, but from the start he is a priest-sorcerer and does not live in celibacy. His sorcery might create unsettling comparisons with occultism, whereas his love life might be treated as criticism of clerical celibacy in particular Christian denominations. Finally, Erna's Church is mostly presented as an institution unable to adapt to new surroundings and desperately upholding old, perhaps outdated, norms. This is visible in the Church's struggle against fae—a force it cannot comprehend, but which it intends to tame anyway. Still, the fictional Church is eventually shown as victorious. Religious criticism is not the main objective of *Coldfire*; it seems to have its source in Friedman's speculation over the new form of Christianity were it to be transplanted into a completely alien setting, rather than in the author's deliberate attempts at discrediting Christianity.

Celia S. Friedman and the Religious Dimensions of The Coldfire Trilogy

In an online discussion with her fans, Friedman revealed her intentions behind the trilogy's religious dimensions: she deliberately designed *Coldfire*'s secondary religion from elements shared by Judaism and Christianity, because she wished to "speak to the spiritual side of the human soul in terms that would transcend any one religious tradition" ("Ask Your Questions...," n.p.).

Coldfire's references to Judaism are visible, for instance, in the trilogy's greater reliance on the Old Testament rather than the New Testament which Judaism does not acknowledge and, therefore, does not profess faith in Christ the Savior. Likewise, the Church on Erna explicitly names its deity "the One God"; thus, the concepts of the Holy Trinity, the figures of Virgin Mary and Jesus Christ, the events of Christ's crucifixion and resurrection, or even the symbol of the cross never appear in the doctrines of the fantastic Church. Moreover, when one of the heroes is told to participate in the services of the One God, he is told to attend them every sabbath (*COS* 129). In a Jewish week the Sabbath is the day of worship and rest, which commemorates the last day of divine creation when God's work was completed (*Britannica...* 952–3). Also the form of Erna's Church art, which operates with symbols and seldom depicts human subjects—even the Prophet has no recognizable face (*COS* 143)—might have been inspired by Judaism. Following the Second Commandment "You shall not make yourself a graven image, or any likeness of anything," Judaism does not create images of Yahweh, and avoids full-face depiction of people in fear of the sin of idolatry.

Nevertheless, in spite of these parallels to Judaism, the phenomenological analysis of *Coldfire*'s religious dimension proves that references to Christian Scriptures, ethics, and theology abundantly appear in the structure of Friedman's secondary religion, in the portrayal of the protagonists, and in the values promoted by the trilogy. After all, Friedman presents a *Church* on Erna led by a papal figure and priests, not a synagogue with rabbis. Though the New Testament is never explicitly mentioned, some of the original colonists could have been Christians because they do refer to Jesus Christ (*WTNF* 10, 13). Yet most importantly, Friedman gives *Coldfire* its two Christ figures, who might be likened to the Old Testament prophets, but who, nevertheless, reenact the self-sacrifice of Jesus Christ.

All in all, *Coldfire* offers a vision of Christianity embedded in a new, extraterrestrial setting. During the online discussion, Friedman directly addressed the notion of the continuity of religions: "Outside of having a new messiah pop up now and then, religion doesn't really change all that much. The big ones a thousand years ago are still pretty much the big ones today, and even the new ones often harken back to something old" ("Ask Your Questions…," n.p.). *Coldfire*'s secondary religion also "harkens back to something old," i.e., the Judeo-Christian heritage. Yet given the changes introduced by Friedman, it is not enough to perceive Erna's faith in the One God simply as a continuation of Christianity. Rather than preserve Christian beliefs in their unadulterated form, Friedman offers her readers an alternative version of Christianity which has evolved on a distant planet. The *Coldfire Trilogy* is, therefore, an exercise in religious speculation which a fantasist should be entitled to perform. Also, Friedman's creation should not be regarded as a de-evolution or devaluation of Christianity, because the author does not prophesize a decline of faith in the One God. On the contrary, true faith becomes the source of humankind's triumph and prosperity.

The Coldfire Trilogy is an example of a fantasy narrative in which multilayered references to Christianity remain at the core of the story and allow the author to explore both the strengths and weaknesses of monotheistic religion. Though some of Friedman's reconstructions of Christian imagery and motifs might seem disturbing, the overall message of her trilogy—the victory of faith and people's salvation through faith—can be easily reconciled with Christian beliefs. Donaldson created a world in which his Christian upbringing and his later dissatisfaction with institutional religion resurface on various levels of the narrative. Kay conceived of a world in which Christianity is but one component of an intricate sphere of imaginary sacred that supposedly is the matrix for the religious pluralism of the protagonists' modern world. Friedman presents a world in which Christianity, even when sent to outer space, retains its core values, so that humanity may triumph in the name of the One God.

5

The Alternative Vision of Salvation Through Christ in Brandon Sanderson's *Mistborn* Series

Introduction to the Mistborn *Series*

Brandon Sanderson's (b. 1975) status as one of America's bestselling contemporary fantasists is due to two factors. Firstly, since his debut with the novel *Elantris* (2005), Sanderson has been recognized as a writer with an immense talent for world-building, i.e., his novels are set in compelling and intricate secondary worlds which showcase fantastic cultures and magical powers (now treated by readers as the hallmarks of his writing). Secondly, his career was propelled when he was chosen to finish the final part of the multivolume fantasy series, *The Wheel of Time*, according to the notes left by its author, Robert Jordan, who passed away in 2007. At the time of Jordan's death, *The Wheel of Time*, whose first volume was published in 1990, had fans around the globe who were mourning the death of their favorite author and wondering whether the saga would be ever completed. This meant that by accepting the offer of Jordan's publishers, Sanderson assumed the risky task of fulfilling everyone's expectations. Yet it also meant that he would have a chance to reach thousands of new readers and promote his own talent. Today, Sanderson is among the most popular American fantasists, though he has been criticized for the rather simplistic style and language of some of his newest books, which might result from the pace of his work—for most of his literary career, Sanderson has published at least one book per year. The writer is working on continuations to his still open series, e.g., *Wax and Wayne* and *The Stormlight Archive*.

The original *Mistborn* series, Sanderson's second major work, consists of three volumes: *The Final Empire* (2006), *The Well of Ascension* (2007), and *The*

Hero of Ages (2008). The main trilogy follows the adventures of Vin, a young street urchin living in a world in which the nobility enjoys a life of prosperity, whereas the vast majority of the population, called the skaa, are either slaves or outcasts. Vin is recruited by Kelsier, an ingenious thief, who plans to rob and eventually overthrow the tyrannous Lord Ruler. The Lord Ruler was once a mortal man who miraculously obtained divine powers which allowed him to secure his oppressive reign. In the first volume, Vin helps Kelsier in organizing a political coup d'état and also discovers her powers as an Allomancer.

In the world of *Mistborn*, Allomancy, Feruchemy, and Hemalurgy are the so-called three Metallic Arts. In the case of Allomancy, a person's organism is able to burn ingested metals—this innate ability, later referred to as Investiture (*TBOM* 67), grants the person extraordinary powers which vary from gaining extra strength and speed to seeing someone's future movements or affecting the flow of time. A Misting is able to burn only one type of metal, while a Mistborn is able to burn all of them. It is later revealed that on a different plane of existence, metals and people's souls glow with the same light (*SH* loc. No. 97), which implies that there is some transcendental connection between these entities or a shared origin. In contrast to Allomancy, Feruchemy allows a person to use metals as containers of extra skills and powers, provided that the person fills the metal with power drained from his/her own body. Thus, a Feruchemist might heal quickly, but only if s/he spends a number of days sick and stores his/her own health in an appropriate metal. While both Allomancy and Feruchemy are hereditary powers, Hemalurgy might be performed by anyone. In Hemalurgy, spikes made of different metals are driven through the flesh of living people, which steals their inborn powers. The spikes are then driven into the body of another person, who acquires the stolen powers. Hemalurgy is, therefore, a dark and cruel art.

Though both Kelsier and Vin are Mistborns aided by many Mistings, the downfall of the tyrant is achieved only at the cost of Kelsier's death. In the second volume, Vin and Kelsier's allies work to establish a government which will protect their city, Luthadel, from the chaos that arises after the Lord Ruler's demise. At the same time, Vin tries to understand some ancient prophecies about the approaching apocalypse and the mythic Hero of Ages who may save everyone. Believing she is the prophesied savior, Vin struggles with her new identity, only to be tricked into releasing a malicious god of destruction, Ruin. In the third volume, the heroes eventually manage to defeat the god and establish a new society.[1]

In 2011, Sanderson published *The Alloy of Law*, a sequel to the *Mistborn* series, set more than three hundred years after the events of the main trilogy. It follows the adventures of Waxillium Ladrian, a lawkeeper, who solves a series of mysterious crimes. Due to technological progress, Wax's world is much different from that of the *Mistborn* trilogy, so references to the original series are rather scarce. In fact, after its publication, Sanderson decided to expand the standalone novella into a separate cycle loosely connected to *Mistborn*. The second volume, *Shadows of Self*, was published in 2015 and the third, *The Bands of Mourning*, in 2016. The fourth installment, *The Lost Metal*, is still in the making. Since the *Wax and Wayne* series, as the volumes are collectively known, accounts for the development of religions which originated in *Mistborn*, it is included in the analysis conducted in this chapter. In 2016, Sanderson also published *Mistborn: Secret History*, an additional story to the original *Mistborn* trilogy, which is also taken into consideration.[2]

Mistborn's approach to secondary religions is a synthesis of the themes present in Kay's *Fionavar* and Friedman's *Coldfire*. While the former introduced a whole pantheon of major and minor deities who freely interact with humankind, the latter focused on the protagonists' individual attitudes toward faith, institutional religion, and the impersonal fae. *Mistborn* offers a combination of these two approaches. On the one hand, the trilogy presents an intricate image of the fictional numinous, because Sanderson reformulates the concept of divinity and demonstrates how it can be acquired by his mortal protagonists. Consequently, by the end of the third volume, readers encounter around five deities (or people who underwent deification), and are also told that many others might exist in different parts of the fictional universe. On the other hand, Sanderson examines how his characters' attitudes to religion change because of their active participation in a conflict between divine entities. Their experiences of and responses to the numinous of their world are further complicated by the existence of Allomancy and other powers, which—like Friedman's fae—grant the users god-like abilities. In addition to these themes, the *Mistborn* trilogy accounts for the gradual development of completely new cults, which later evolve into full-fledged religions in the *Wax and Wayne* series (thus, religious history also plays a part in Sanderson's fictional universe). Taking everything into consideration, the phenomenological analysis of *Mistborn* investigates the series' portrayals of the numinous (the secondary deities and their attributes, the process of deification, other numinous powers, the motifs of creation and apocalypse), its religious institutions and practices (including the newly formed cults), and the society's approach to the numinous, including their prophecies and mythological/religious knowledge. This analysis is then followed by detailed examination of the series' Christian references (biblical motifs and symbols reworked by Sanderson) and juxtaposition of the trilogy's spiritual values against Christian morality.

Images of the Numinous

For most of *Mistborn*, inhabitants of Scadrial (the fictional planet on which Sanderson set the events of the trilogy) possess hardly any knowledge about their gods: the few secondary myths surrounding the Lord Ruler's ascension and divine power are meant to legitimize his tyrannical reign over humanity rather than offer religious enlightenment, whereas the gods Preservation and Ruin remain unknown for most of the narrative and it is only with painstaking effort that the protagonists eventually learn something about their existence and attributes. Apart from the few individuals who have retained some fragmentary knowledge about Scadrial's religions and religious history, Sanderson's heroes generally cannot freely debate about topics such as the nature of the numinous or the shape of theological doctrines—not only because they lack sufficient knowledge (of which they were deliberately deprived), but also because they are more preoccupied with their daily struggle to survive rather than with dissecting the nuances of divine existence. Thus, their experience of the numinous is founded not on reason and comprehension, but on emotions evoked by the presence and actions of the Lord Ruler (direct exposure to the divine).

Unfortunately, the inhabitants of Scadrial experience the numinous chiefly in its negative aspects, as something lethally dangerous, malevolent, and indifferent to human suffering. The divine Lord Ruler is not a benevolent deity, the god Ruin has been scheming how to corrupt humankind and destroy the world for millennia, and the misunderstood power of Allomancy instills fear; the only caring god, Preservation, was long ago reduced to remnants of insentient power and cannot intercede in order to protect his creation. As a result, *Mistborn*'s depiction of the relationship between people and the divine particularly emphasizes the terror and abasement, which Otto ascribed to the human experience of the numinous. The numinous in Sanderson's series is a terrifying mystery (*mysterium tremendum*), whose unfathomable nature, superior potency, and overwhelming magnitude (*majestas*) is the object of fearful awe and demands humble submission. The aspect of worshipful fascination (*fascinas*) with the subject of the numinous is reduced to a minimum, replaced chiefly by dread, and appears mostly in the heroes' attitude toward the power of Allomancy—which offers elevation from mortality to a divine-like omnipotence—rather than in their attitude toward divine entities. It is not until two new deities appear, the Survivor and Harmony, that inhabitants of Scadrial are introduced to a new dimension of the numinous: a more intimate relationship with a caring and benevolent god to whom they can entrust their lives and find comfort in his presence. Until that happens, the people's awe of the grand mystery of the numinous is pervaded by dread, and their dominant response is fearful obedience (*augustum*) to the Holy, whose majesty and disregard for human suffering forces them to resign themselves to the belief in their own insignificance and nothingness (Otto's notion of creature-consciousness).

What is more, Sanderson's depiction of the divine corresponds also to other aspects of Otto's definition of the numinous. Otto argued that the numinous is a concept *a priori*, which escapes logical categorization and is independent of culture, history, and institutionalized religion; he also perceived it as an amoral force. In Sanderson's world, the autonomy of the numinous from institutional worship is quite literal, because the deities themselves are hardly interested in being the object of religious worship. The gods Preservation and Ruin are never mentioned in the context of temples, prayers, and ceremonies, and the religious institution focused on the Lord Ruler is more of an administrative body preoccupied with regulating the socio-political aspects of the society's existence rather than an institution devoted to perpetuating the belief in salvation through faith. Until the Survivor and Harmony make an appearance, most of *Mistborn*'s characters are a-religious—not by choice, but because they have had no benevolent deity with whom they could feel bonded and to whom they could send their pleas for divine protection. It is only in *The Alloy of Law* and subsequent volumes that some religious practices are developed in the name of the new gods, the Survivor and Harmony. Even so, the latter deity insists that the best form of worship is to dedicate oneself to doing something good for the world. Thus, in the original *Mistborn* trilogy a religious institution's role as the bedrock of faith is almost non-existent.

As far as the issue of amorality is concerned, Otto illustrates it by recalling the Old Testament episode in which God tests Abraham's faith by ordering him to kill his son, Isaac. Though God eventually stops the patriarch from fulfilling His order, the image is highly disturbing and escapes human rationalization of what is morally (un)acceptable. In a similar fashion, *Mistborn* heroes' knowledge, morality, and reason constantly prove insufficient for a proper evaluation of the deities' true identities and intents; for instance, what they see as the Lord Ruler's tyranny is, in reality, divine protection from even greater harm (similarly, Wax from the sequel series to *Mistborn* finds it difficult to accept that the benevolent Harmony does not refrain from contributing to his suffering if that is what it takes to save the world from a bigger threat). The deities of *Mistborn* are amoral, because they act in ways which defy or escape humanity's ethical norms and judgments.

Contrary to Otto's description of the numinous, Sanderson presents a world in which mortal people may undergo the process of deification, acquire divine nature and powers, and even comprehend the nature of divinity. For Otto, divinity is something unattainable both in cognitive and physical terms: people cannot map out the numinous with their logic nor can they obtain an transcendent state of being. In *Mistborn*, all of the deities were once mortal people who, at some point, acquired transcendental power that bestowed on them divine attributes. Even the deities who created the planet Scadrial and its inhabitants—Preservation and Ruin—had once been human beings whom a supreme divine force transformed into immaterial entities (*THOA* 125). Even so, Preservation and Ruin did not become entirely immortal: when their human consciousness is annihilated, the divine power is dispersed and two male corpses materialize out of nowhere.

By the end of the trilogy, Sanderson reveals that originally, the key to Preservation and Ruin's mutual existence was Balance: neither deity was mightier than the other and they complemented each other's powers. Alone, the benevolent Preservation could only "preserve," not create, so Ruin, whose goal was total destruction, was also indispensable for the proper existence of the world (*THOA* 405). The limits in the deities' powers enforced cooperation which prevented either from achieving their ultimate goals (*THOA* 472–473). The Balance between the gods was eventually disrupted by the appearance of humankind created by Preservation, who infused them with a part of his own soul. As a result, the benevolent god, now weakened, had something that belonged more to him than to Ruin, but in exchange, Ruin was promised ultimate destruction of all creation (*THOA* 483–484). In order to protect the world and his creation from such a fate, Preservation breached their pact, sacrificed his own consciousness, and imprisoned Ruin in a place known as the Well of Ascension:

> *This event left their powers again nearly balanced—Ruin imprisoned, only a trace of himself capable of leaking out. Preservation reduced to a mere wisp of what he once was, barely capable of thought and action.*
>
> *These two minds were, of course, independent of the raw force of their powers. Actually, I am uncertain of how thoughts and personalities came to be attached to the powers in the first place—but I believe they were not there originally* [*THOA* 490; italics in the original].

These and other fragments of *Mistborn*'s secondary myths reveal that neither Preservation nor Ruin is a self-sufficient, omnipotent, and omniscient deity, since both are limited in their cognition and abilities, and dependent upon the other (a state which might be somehow connected to their original life as mortals). Moreover, it is implied that there does exist a superior entity which is the original source of Preservation's and Ruin's powers—powers which do not disappear after the ruling human consciousness is gone, but which can be reabsorbed by another being. Yet since this supreme entity never makes a direct appearance or intervenes in the affairs of Scadrial, it can be assumed that *Mistborn*'s cosmological vision is founded on the idea of divine dichotomy—a perennial struggle between Preservation and Ruin, two equally powerful, but contrasting divine beings, who are both responsible for the creation of the material reality and intend to extend their rule over it for their own purposes.

Mistborn's three Metallic Arts play a prominent role in the trilogy's cosmological vision, because they serve as an earthly extension of the deities' powers and are, therefore, an extension of the numinous. Allomancy began after the demise of Preservation; his concentrated power took the form of metal-like beads which, when ingested, turned people into first Allomancers. The power became the last gift of protection—a divine grace—offered by the benevolent deity to his children, and their last vestige of defense against Ruin. To counter it, Ruin established Hemalurgy, a bloody art that steals life and skill from other people. It is said that a Hemalurgic spike driven into a person's body steals Preservation's power (the source of human sentience) from a person's soul (*THOA* 336). In other words, Hemalurgy deprives a person of their free will and turns him/her into the servant of the evil god, who can easily manipulate and corrupt those that carry the spikes. It was thanks to Hemalurgy that the Lord Ruler could later turn people into powerful yet gruesome beings (the Inquisitors, koloss, and kandra) whom he could manipulate according to his will and who became, therefore, an evidence of his twisted nature. Feruchemy, situated between the other two Arts, is a power of balance which predates both Allomancy and Hemalurgy (*THOA* 303). The status of Feruchemy supports the claim that a balance between positive/good and negative/evil aspects is what lies at the core of divine creation in *Mistborn*'s cosmology.

Feruchemy is a hereditary skill among the Terris people, an ancient nation that worshipped a god called Terr—a name which meant "to preserve." The holy texts of the Terris religion describe the conflict between Preservation and Ruin, elevate the notion of creation over destruction, and claim that a savior figure known as the Hero of Ages will be the successor to Preservation's power. Unfortunately, after the Lord Ruler claimed that divine power for himself, he strove to eliminate all of Scadrial's religions. Thus, though the Terris people once possessed their own rituals, traditions (e.g., the lore of Anticipation which described the prophesied Hero), religious leaders (e.g., the keepers of knowledge known as Worldbringers), and codes of conduct (*THOA* 653), none of that is described in the trilogy. Also, since the Terris religion was the only one that accounted for the existence of Preservation and Ruin and their divine conflict, due to the Lord Ruler's anti-religious campaign the people of Scadrial became ignorant of the origins and nature of their world.

The true identity and motivation of the Lord Ruler—a mortal man who seized divine power and became a god—remain obscure for most of the trilogy. According to the official religious-political doctrine of the theocratic Empire, he was the prophesied Hero of Ages who saved the world from the evil Deepness[3]; the power that he acquired at the sacred Well of Ascension supposedly legitimized his reign. In reality, Rashek, as he was originally known, was never the prophesied savior, though he did save the world. Afterward, he reluctantly became a deity, the Lord Ruler, to protect the world from future threats. That is why he later strove to erase the Terris religion. Originally, the Terris prophecies claimed that the Hero of Ages may use Preservation's power to save the world, but should not release it, because that would free Ruin. The malicious god began to subtly alter the prophecies, until they claimed the opposite: that only by releasing divine power would the Hero save the world. Thus, Sanderson presents religion as something subject to external manipulation and corruption.

What is more, Sanderson uses the figure of Rashek to demonstrate the negative effects of a person's transition from human morality into divine amorality: Rashek's reign is a period of religious tyranny which corrupts the entire world. The setting of *Mistborn* is a post-apocalyptic world with a blood-red sun, ash falling from the sky, and landscapes blackened by its fall—evidence of the man's inability to fully comprehend and wield divine power. While the descendants of Rashek's original supporters lead a life of prosperity, the descendants of his rivals, the skaa, are treated as cattle and deprived of any rights whatsoever. Neither group dares to oppose the Lord Ruler's religious and political supremacy. Though they are aware of his past mortality, they fearfully perceive him as an unconquerable divinity: "The Lord Ruler was a force, like the winds or the mists. One did not kill such things. They didn't live, really. They simply *were*" (*TFE* 83). Some philosophical texts describe him as "unique, unplanned, uncreated" (*THOA* 286); he is also called the Ascended Avatar of God (*TFE* 164), and one of the heroes says: "the Lord Ruler is only a *piece* of God. He is the Sliver of infinity—not omniscient or omnipresent, but an independent section of a consciousness that *is*" (*TFE* 191). These comments again imply that there is a supreme entity which exceeds all the lesser deities of whom they are but fragments. Nonetheless, the people of Scadrial hardly ever wonder about this supreme authority. Some vague allusions to its existence appear, perhaps, when the heroes talk about external providence which—they hope—will save their world from destruction.

Religious Institutions and the Process of Religious Reformation

The Lord Ruler is a deity who is physically present among his people (he resides in a palace called Kredik Shaw) and who constantly controls all spheres of their socio-political life. His church—the Steel Ministry, which consists of the Cantons of Finance, Resource, Orthodoxy, and Inquisition—not only perpetuates the official religious doctrine, but also regulates politics, economy, and trade. The Ministry's priests-administrators, called the obligators, have to witness and acknowledge every transaction, contract or union for it to be considered legal and binding. As a result, the institution's authority reaches far beyond matters of faith. The most significant unit of the Ministry is the Canton of Inquisition, because it is operated by Steel Inquisitors—people enhanced with Hemalurgic spikes—who are the Lord Ruler's supreme tool of social oppression. Surprisingly, the Steel Ministry neither forces people to worship the Lord Ruler nor develops any religious practices that would confirm and reinforce his godhood; instead, it aims at maintaining and controlling the country's economic stability through a complex *"bureaucratic mercantile system"* (*THOA* 221; italics in the original). That is why the protagonists plan to undermine the deity by destabilizing his financial position—paradoxically, in Sanderson's world a god might fall not because he lacks worshipful adoration from his followers, but because he lacks the resources to support his reign.

There is a significant difference in how separate social groups perceive religion. Only the nobility are familiarized with the doctrines of the Steel Ministry, because religion is a privilege of which the slaves, the skaa, are deprived as of everything else. Even so, the privileged group itself is not particularly encouraged to religious worship. Elend Venture, a nobleman, observes: "There was something proprietary about the Ministry, an air that implied they would take care of religious things—that we didn't need to worry ourselves" (*TWOA* 161). Consequently, there are no buildings meant for religious gatherings, ceremonies, holy days, or words of prayer. The Lord Ruler's divine status and victory over the undefined malevolent Deepness are commemorated only by artistic representations: statues (*TFE* 21) and elaborate stained-glass windows in the houses of the nobility (*TFE* 222). This lack of religious life confirms the claim that the Steel Ministry is an administrative body which is hardly interested in establishing true faith. The Lord Ruler himself also does not inspire any desire for heartfelt worship. On the contrary, his mere presence makes everyone around him feel numb inside and lack the will to oppose him in any way (*TFE* 433–434).

As for the skaa, given that the only religion which they know is the cult established by the tyrant, it is highly unlikely that they would be interested in worship even if they received proper instructions. Though they acknowledge the Lord Ruler as an incarnation of the divine and even invoke his name as a curse or expression of surprise, they hold no personal relationship with him. This attitude is best expressed by Vin:

> He was ... well, he was the *Lord*. He ruled all of the world. He was the creator, protector, and punisher of mankind. He had saved them from the Deepness, then had brought the ash and the mists as a punishment for the people's lack of faith. Vin wasn't particularly religious—intelligent thieves knew to avoid the Steel Ministry—but even she knew the legends [*TFE* 112].

Religious prohibitions and the skaa's emotional indifference to their deity (stemming from their social abasement and daily struggles) deprive them not only of belief in divine protection, but also of other forms of consolation present in faith (*TWOA* 141). Only the rebellious heroes dare to question the Lord Ruler's authority and call him a pseudo-deity (*TFE* 127). If all of these aspects of the Lord Ruler's reign are taken into consideration, it is clear that Rashek's rise to godhood was a mistake that produced a theocratic empire in which the numinous is the source of terror and oppression. Yet since Rashek absorbed only one type of creative power (Preservation, without Ruin), his failure might not be due to his personal shortcomings, but rather a tangible result of the distortion in the cosmic Balance.

While the Lord Ruler's case exemplifies deification by divine power, Kelsier, one of *Mistborn*'s protagonists, becomes integrated into the structures of the secondary numinous by undergoing the process of social deification, i.e., the people's collective wish to follow in his steps and adhere to his teachings transforms him into a divine figure known as the Survivor. At the beginning, Kelsier—a Mistborn and former thief—is reverently called "the Survivor" because he escaped from the Pits of Hathsin (the Lord Ruler's prison). Though the nickname marks him as a person of great power, it has no religious connotations. After his escape, Kelsier wanders between villages and spreads words of hope and dreams of freedom in order to motivate the skaa to rebellion. This, as well as his semi-divine position as "the Survivor," likens him to a prophet foreshadowing social and religious upheaval—a role he is not entirely comfortable with (*TFE* 351). Yet though his ideas of rebellion may seem divinely inspired, Kelsier is no saint on a holy mission. He is a man motivated by social injustice, not by faith or religious visions, and does not hesitate to kill his opponents—at one point he arrogantly claims that "any night that ended with a group of dead noblemen was a successful one" (*TFE* 103). Despite his occasional cruelty, he is also capable of self-sacrifice: he plans his own martyrdom to initiate the rebellion. In order to turn his death into a revolutionary event, Kelsier surrounds himself with a façade of otherworldliness and mysticism: he offers public displays of Allomancy and spreads rumors about his own powers. At the same time, he forms a bond with the oppressed people, visits them, listens to their problems, and offers them words of consolation. Yet though he is among them, he is clearly not one of them, and the skaa treat the man with respect becoming a person of superior status. Vin observes that Kelsier's relationship with the skaa is "*more like the love of a parent for a child than it is like the love of a man for his equals*" (*TFE* 539; italics in the original). The protagonist eventually challenges the Lord Ruler, but fails to defeat him. Before he is killed, he defiantly declares that he represents one thing the tyrant will never be able to destroy: "I am hope" (*TFE* 573).

Though Kelsier can hardly be called a religious person, his self-sacrifice is grounded in his knowledge of the mechanisms that inspire religious worship. Whenever he asked Sazed, a Terrisman who preserved knowledge of various denominations, how any religion exerts influence over individuals and the society, he was told that a religion is powerful, because its followers strongly believe in something or someone (*TFE* 582). Consequently, Kelsier assumed that in order to rebel, the skaa needed an incentive in the form of a new god (*TFE* 583), so he offered himself. To strengthen the impact of his martyrdom, Kelsier ordered one of the kandra to recreate his physical body, and then show itself among the people. The skaa, angered by the bloodshed, but reassured by Kelsier's "resurrection" and words of encouragement, finally overthrow the divine tyrant.

The death of the Lord Ruler initiates Scadrial's period of religious reformation: as the world again moves toward the apocalypse, some people begin to question the validity of their previous beliefs and seek consolation in faith. Sazed, who collected the beliefs of around five hundred denominations and sects, hopes that people might wish to retrieve one of these old traditions. He is Scadrial's equivalent of a phenomenologist of religion: an impartial scholar who believes that all religions are equally important, yet he is never tempted to convert. His attitude might even be called utilitarian when he states: "The right belief is like a good cloak, I think. If it fits you well, it keeps you warm and safe. The wrong fit, however, can suffocate" (*TFE* 165). Consequently, throughout the trilogy Sazed freely uses—even appropriates—rites and prayers from various religions according to his intuitive assumption which seem more relevant to a given situation. It is through him that Sanderson mentions several of the forgotten fantastic religions of Scadrial: in Trelagism, named after the god Trell, the faithful emphasized the beauty of darkness and claimed that the stars were the Thousand Eyes of Trell; Jaism was founded by a man murdered by a king for bringing social discord (*TFE* 199); Cazzi instructed its followers that the spirits of the dead leave their bodies and return to a mountain of souls; the Astalsi believed that every person had a finite amount of bad luck, and it diminished with every unlucky occurrence, so life constantly got better (*TFE* 485); the Bennet people claimed that knowledge and discovery contributed to understanding the world, which in turn resulted in peace and harmony (*TFE* 494); other people turned to Duis— the god that protected travelers (*TWOA* 215); finally, a land called Khlennium possessed cathedrals adorned with stained-glass windows (*TFE* 532)—the religious stained-glass windows in the castles of the present nobility seem to be a continuation of the old Khlenni tradition.

Yet to Sazed's disappointment, people are not interested in these old religions. On the one hand, they are either still indifferent to religion altogether (*TWOA* 39) or, ironically, pray to the fallen tyrant (*TWOA* 97). On the other hand, once the late Kelsier becomes part of Scadrial's numinous as the god Survivor, a growing number of people embrace the new cult. Vin is shocked to learn that her friend—once, a mortal man—has become a religious authority (*TFE* 580). Throughout the second and the third volume, the unofficial worship is organized into the Church of the Survivor, whose members venerate Kelsier as "The Lord of the Mists" and "progenitor—the father of everyone who is free in this land" (*TWOA* 366); Vin is recognized as his Lady Heir. The faithful wear pendants in the form of a spear—the weapon that killed both Kelsier and the Lord Ruler. The Church's priests publicly teach about Kelsier's deification and try to establish an official doctrine (because the man left none). The main tenets of the new religion are hope and survival—two concepts which defined Kelsier's existence. Nonetheless, at this very early stage, the Church of the Survivor exists rather as a joint name for people revering a certain figure than as a religious institution regulated by rules and rites. Yet this is exactly what the skaa need, since they lack experience with willing worship and religious dedication (*TWOA* 436–437). For the skaa, the Church of the Survivor, despite its lack of rites, becomes a chance to substitute the experience of numinous terror with a comforting belief in a caring deity. The Survivor is a god with whom, in contrast to the Lord Ruler, they might identify and establish a personal relationship.

Deification

While the late Kelsier undergoes the process of social deification, Vin becomes part of the conflict between Preservation and Ruin, and experiences her own ascension to godhood. Manipulated by Ruin, she discovers the sacred Well of Ascension—a gleaming pool filled with Preservation's power. When the girl steps into the pool, she experiences apotheosis (*TWOA* 753). Despite her seemingly divine omnipotence and omnipresence, Vin understands that she lacks experience in wielding such immense force, so she decides to do what seems to be the only right thing to do: to release it. Yet by doing so, she frees Ruin. The girl is eventually able to defeat the malevolent deity when she retrieves the divine power and decides to sacrifice her life. Her ascension to godhood is only a brief episode and Vin is never officially worshiped as a deity. Though her suicidal attack on the god is an act of a spontaneous self-sacrifice, it is inscribed in *Mistborn*'s cosmological vision. The god Preservation knew that due to the constraints on his power, he alone would never destroy Ruin, so he put trust into his ultimate creation—humankind, whose sentience originates from his soul (*THOA* 539). Thus, *Mistborn* does not present humanity as a fallen creation that must strive to be united with their creator, but as the creator's hope for the world.

Vin's and Ruin's corpses are found by Sazed who, at that time, is undergoing a crisis of faith. In the face of a personal loss, Sazed, who has never questioned the truths of "his" religions, suddenly realizes that none of them can appease his grief. What is more, he becomes aware of numerous discrepancies between the various systems of belief, wonders if they contain any truths at all, and questions the existence of divine mercy and providence (*THOA* 558). Thus, Sazed is no longer an impartial scholar, but an embittered and disillusioned man who seeks consolation in religion, and apparently can find none. In the past, he advised people to trust in providence (*TWOA* 503). Now, when his friend tells him to do the same, the prevailing confusion does not allow Sazed to partake of this simple truth (*THOA* 507). He concludes that rather than believe in a god that has failed to protect humankind, it is better not to believe at all. Grief-stricken and angered, he desperately addresses a nondescript divine entity:

> "Why leave me like this? I studied everything about you. I learned the religions of *five hundred* different peoples and sects. I taught about you when other men had given up a thousand years before.
> "Why leave *me* without hope, when others can have faith? Why leave *me* to wonder?" [*THOA* 559–560].

As if in answer to his desperate plea, Sazed miraculously discovers that the Terris religion, his people's heritage, has been preserved despite the Lord Ruler's attempts to annihilate it. He also learns the ultimate religious truth (which echoes Otto's analysis of the numinous): there will never be a religion entirely compatible with logic, because logic is not the same as faith, and it is the latter, not the former, that constitutes the core of any religious belief. It is Sazed's, as it is anyone's, free choice to decide whether he wishes to believe under such conditions or not. Though at the time he finds Vin's and Ruin's corpses, his dilemma is still not resolved, Sazed accepts the role of a savior, reabsorbs their divine powers, and manages to control both (*THOA* 715). Mediating between the contradictory forces of preservation and destruction, Sazed becomes Harmony—a god who reinstitutes divine Balance and restores the material world of Scadrial after its apocalypse.[4]

Religious Pluralism in the Wax and Wayne *Series*

Due to Sazed's ascension to godhood, the world of *Mistborn*'s sequel series, the *Wax and Wayne* series, is an entirely different place: denizens of Scadrial might choose from a variety of religions, form very personal relationships with their gods, and actively experience the sacred of their world by participating in diverse religious practices. A handful of names and events from the original trilogy appear as part of the new series' secondary mythology: people use the names of Preservation and Ruin as curses or exclamations ("Rust and Ruin," "Ruination" or "Preservation's Wings"), and they talk about the Great Catacendre (the destruction and remaking of the world), the Final Ascension (Sazed's transformation into Harmony), the Ascendant Warrior (Vin), the Counselor of Gods (Breeze), and the World of Ash. These references create a sense of continuity between Scadrial's past and present, and point to the internal evolution of *Mistborn*'s religious traditions.

The Church of the Survivor is one of the major denominations. Since Kelsier was a thief and rebel, his cult evolved into one that neglects traditional morality in favor of survival, independence, and resourcefulness. Consequently, the faithful are people from all walks of life: "Anyone who survived on his own—or who fought for himself—was someone who followed the Survivor, whether he knew it or not" (*TAOL* 268). Because in *The Alloy of Law* Sanderson provides little information about the rites and doctrines of the Church, being a Survivorist initially seems to denote a pragmatic attitude to life rather than religious worship of Kelsier as a deity. Fortunately, the details scattered throughout the following volumes give the Church more substance. The doctrine of the Church is one that emphasizes both the necessity of perseverance and the fact of human fallibility; it also contains soteriological elements: it is stated that the Survivor transcended death and is bound to return when people will need him the most (*TBOM* 194).

The Church's internal hierarchy consists of priests and conventicalists, i.e., men and women who work in the churches (*SOS* 202). The worship of the deity includes reverence for the mists (an attribute associated with Kelsier because of his identity as the Mistborn): one of the ceremonies described is called "the mistdown sermon" (*SOS* 203), and during a wedding the mists are symbolically represented by smoke produced by braziers (*TBOM* 47). Yet though the Survivorists revere the mists, they also regard it with some anxiety (as Wax observes more than once), which corresponds to the dual attitude of admiration and fear that Otto identified in people's reaction to the Holy. The main symbol of the Church is the spear—the weapon with which Kelsier was killed by the Lord Ruler. For instance, the sign of the spear appears on graves (*TBOM* 201), and when Wayne enters a pub, he dips his finger in beer and then anoints his forehead and navel with "the mark of the spear" (*SOS* 213). The priests' clothing also alludes to their god: the men (no female priests have been mentioned so far) wear a garment which resembles a mistcloak (typically worn by the Mistborn) and robes whose sleeves are marked with stitches that represent Kelsier's scars (*TBOM* 430). When they are emotionally agitated, many people invoke the deity's name with phrases such as "*by the Survivor's scars*" (*TAOL* 120; italics in the original), "By the Survivor's spear" (*TAOL* 139), and "*What in the Survivor's Deadly Name*" (*TAOL* 227; italics in the original).

The other major denomination is the religion of the Path, in which the Pathians venerate the god Harmony. As a god, Sazed-Harmony is very specific about what his followers should do: "don't waste time worshipping Harmony. Doing good *was* the worship" (*TAOL* 74). The rules of the Path are inspired by Sazed's own experience with religion. Thus, he instructs his followers to do something meaningful in his name, to study the various religions and philosophies which he collected as a Keeper, to respect different truths, and to pray and mediate. During prayer, a person needs to wear a special earring with ten interlocking rings which symbolize the Path (the earring should be worn also on occasions when the person is doing something of great importance),[5] listen to his/her own thoughts, and reflect on his/her life. No particular gestures, postures, or formulas are required, only honesty and genuine emotional and intellectual involvement (such simple demands might be the most difficult to fulfill). Even the Pathian sanctuaries reflect this simplicity of worship. The small sanctuaries resemble old Terris huts and contain only two chairs: one for the person visiting and another—symbolically—for the deity (*SOS* 228). The Pathian clergy may offer help and advice, but they do not lead any formal worship (*SOS* 229). Also, the sanctuaries are open to the mists, which the Pathians (like the Survivorists) regard as part of the divine. According to the script of the Words of Founding, written by the deity himself,[6] Vin melded with the mists after her death, and Wax believes he can sometimes see her shape (*SOS* 178). All in all, the Path is a religion based on introspection, moral reflection, and mutual respect, not on external instructions or mechanical repetition of set formulas. Though the novels do not state that directly, the Path is probably favored more by the Terris people, since the god Harmony was originally one of them. While during the reign of the Lord Ruler the Terris people were persecuted, in the second trilogy they live peacefully, preserve their customs, and regard their legendary homeland, Old Terris (a land of snow), as a sort of mythic paradise (*SOS* 96). Thus, some Terris fundamentalists are said to live in the mountains (*SOS* 294).

Because Wax, the protagonist of the series, is half–Terris and a Pathian, readers witness one of his prayers—a casual conversation rather than a formula-directed address to a god: "*How are things up there in the mists?* […] *Life's good, I assume? What with you being God, and all?*" (*TAOL* 73; italics in the original). In response to his meditation, the man usually senses some spiritual encouragement, but occasionally he receives more precise answers. For instance, when Wax asks for divine help in a conflict with his enemy, Harmony responds that his help is limited, because he cannot upset the Balance. As a god, Sazed-Harmony intends to remain neutral and respond to different choices, thus sustaining human freedom and accounting for both Preservation's and Ruin's contribution to the creation of Scadrial's humankind (as favoring only Preservation would disrupt the Balance). Ironically, Wax reacts by asking the same questions that Sazed asked so long ago: how can god witness cruelty and crime and do nothing? Harmony answers that he sent Wax to help the people in need.

Despite his policy of limited interference, Sazed-Harmony is an active god and his followers have tangible evidence of his existence and care: it is said that he was the one to design Elendel, Scadrial's greatest city (*TAOL* 28), and to establish the rules of university education (*TAOL* 219). He affirms that he is omnipresent (*SOS* 130), though he is not omniscient and omnipotent since apparently another holder of divine powers may challenge his knowledge and reign—as proven by the case of his own rebellious servant (*SOS* 132). Harmony does acknowledge his own fallibility and admits that his leniency with humankind might have made them lazy (*SOS* 134–135). The faithful invoke his name with phrases such as "may he rest with the Hero" (*TAOL* 51), and "Harmony's forearms" (*TAOL* 77). His direct servants are the kandra, known to people as the "hands of Harmony" and "the Faceless Immortals" (*TAOL* 74). While some people perceive the kandra as demigods, the kandra MeLaan sent by Harmony to aid the protagonists admits that she has never read her god's scriptures (*SOS* 237), and often acts in ways which contradict any claims to divinity. In general, both the deity and his servants occasionally exhibit features of character more easily associated with humanity than with divinity.

Surprisingly, the belief in the tyrannical Lord Ruler is still present, preserved by the descendants of one of the original obligators (priests of the Steel Ministry). Over the centuries, the belief has evolved into a religion called Sliverism, because the Lord Ruler was known as the Sliver of Infinity; it also includes a figure known as Ironeyes (or Death), who is the last of the Lord Ruler's demonic Inquisitors. Sliverism is called a terrible religion, but no details have yet been revealed about its doctrines or practices, and it has not influenced the narrative in any significant way. The protagonists only learn that the Lord Ruler might have somehow evaded death, since one of the new characters claims that the deity—now known as the Sovereign—also saved some nations from apocalyptic destruction and hid his instruments of power (the Bands of Mourning) in a secret temple (*TBOM* 327). It is worth mentioning that both Marasi and Wax briefly use these Bands, and they bestow on them divine attributes and powers—their own experience of a temporary ascension to godhood. Sanderson might describe the fate of the Sovereign in the final volume of the *Wax and Wayne* series.

Though the plot of the second series also heavily relies on religious themes, for the present moment, it is mostly defined by the tensions in and between the Path and Survivorism. Like in the first trilogy, the secondary world is plagued by social injustice: while Kelsier fought to free the slaves, the technologically advanced world created by Harmony is still one in which manual laborers are oppressed by the affluent nobility. And like Kelsier, who intended to transform society and politics through a coup, one of the antagonists of the *Wax and Wayne* series—the rebellious kandra—plans to undermine religion and Harmony's reign to free people from social and political oppression. To achieve that goal, the kandra Bleeder incites hatred between the Pathians and Survivorists. Her machinations reveal the already uneasy relations between the two religions: some Survivorists express their distrust of a religion that lacks clear rules and ceremonies (*SOS* 203), and one of the main heroes, Marasi, states that the Survivor—the one who fought and transcended death—seems to be a more dependable god (*TBOM* 320). Such a freedom of choice and expression would have been unavailable in the theocratic empire of the Lord Ruler. Still, this freedom does not mean that Sanderson's characters are no longer plagued by religious doubts and worries. On the contrary, Wax's difficult relationship with his god is one of the major themes of the series, and the protagonist's attitude to religion undergoes a serious revolution. First, the man's lukewarm belief in the deity's existence is shaken by a direct contact with the Holy. Then, his faith and loyalty are gradually undermined by the tasks Harmony has him perform. Traumatized, Wax begins to hate his god. Only later is he able to recognize the necessity of Harmony's actions and accept his own role as "Harmony's Ruin," i.e., the one who can perform what god himself cannot (*SOS* 327).

In addition to the Church of the Survivor, the Path, and Sliverism, Wayne, of the *Wax and Wayne* series, refers to "the God Beyond" (*TAOL* 177), though it is not clear which god he has in mind—one from the major denominations or the supreme entity that was the original source of Preservation's and Ruin's powers. Another character, Miles, explains that his intrigue was inspired by the rebellious actions of the Survivor and the tenets of Trellism (one of the religions preserved by Sazed-Harmony in the Words of Founding); the narrative does suggest that an unknown god might be responsible for the current turmoil on Scadrial. All of these themes will undoubtedly be explored in the series' next volume, and Sanderson's vision of Scadrial's fictional numinous and religions will then acquire even more depth.

All in all, the phenomenological analysis of *Mistborn* reveals that Sanderson's work is strongly focused on the concept of divinity: its aspects, transformations, social roles, and reception by people. Sanderson initially creates a theocratic yet irreligious empire on the verge of an Apocalypse, whose inhabitants coexist with gods, but know very little about true faith. On the background of this conflict between dichotomous forces (Preservation against Ruin), the plot focuses on the theme of one's ascension to godhood, be it through social deification (Kelsier) or through the act of appropriating divine powers (the Lord Ruler, Vin, Sazed, and Kelsier[7]). The trilogy also examines the position of faith in human life—several of its characters (Kelsier, Vin,

Sazed, Wax) begin to question the nature of religious worship, and then struggle to reestablish their relationship with the divine. Their religion-oriented endeavors delineate both their personal development and the development of the plot. Moreover, Sanderson focuses on the transformations of the religions which accompany the transformation of the numinous—the (dis)appearance of particular deities/divine powers entails corresponding changes in people's perception of the Holy. As a result, though *Mistborn* initially depicts an irreligious society, *The Alloy of Law* showcases religious diversity. Though Sanderson initially forces his characters to live in a corrupted theocracy, he eventually allows them to save both their world and their religiousness—despite the Lord Ruler's religious tyranny, the heroes do not discard religion altogether, but manage to found a society which appreciates religious pluralism and freedom. Thus, even if *Mistborn*'s vision of a society tormented by a cruel god might appear as a severe critique of (organized) religion, its final vision of a world in which faith is reinstated and its significance reaffirmed, is a highly positive one. The *Mistborn* books, on the one hand, do what is expected of good fantasy fiction: they present believable characters in a compelling fantasy world with an original system of magical powers. On the other, by posing serious questions about the nature of religious worship and the social functions of religions, they become a thought-provoking example of how fantasy fiction may participate in the discourse about human spirituality.

Christian Elements in the Portrayal of the Fictional Numinous

The fictional gods and religions of *Mistborn* are both reconcilable and irreconcilable with Christianity. The parallels between Christian beliefs and Sanderson's creation are present in the series' reconstruction of the motifs of creation and temptation, in its Christ figure (Kelsier) and Christian-like religion that develops around him (the Church of the Survivor), in its affirmation of divine protection and the necessity of faith, in several fragmentary references to biblical tradition, and, finally, in Sanderson's reworking of the Mormon concept of human ascension to godhood. At the same time, *Mistborn* contains elements which point to traditions other than Christianity. For instance, the series' plurality of deities contradicts the Christian belief in the One God, its cosmic conflict between Preservation and Ruin resembles the Manichean clash between light and darkness, and the imagery surrounding the mysterious supreme deity seems indebted to the Jewish Kabbalists. Also, the emphasis on the concept of Balance and the god Harmony—who requires his followers to meditate, who combines opposite forces: good and evil, light and dark, male and female (*SOS* 237), and whose religion is called the Path, which is a direct reference to Taoism since "Tao" means "the way"—visibly corresponds to Eastern spirituality.

As far as divine creation is concerned, *Mistborn*'s secondary mythology explains that humankind was created by the combined efforts of two opposing deities, Preservation and Ruin. Yet it is also emphasized that human sentience and free will have their source in a benevolent god, and that it was Preservation, not Ruin, who insisted on creating humanity in the first place. After the original deities are annihilated, their supremacy over the material world is claimed by the god Harmony whose reign reinstitutes a Balance of divine powers. Consequently, *Mistborn*'s model of creation does not resemble the biblical one and the relationship between divine powers does not correspond to Christianity. In Christianity, the Lord God is the sole creator of life and the world, everything created by Him is inherently good, and the Devil/Satan, who intends to usurp authority over the creation, is vanquished so that the heavenly Kingdom of God can become reality. *Mistborn*'s vision of two competing but equally limited divine forces, whose union in the form of the god Harmony restores a much needed Balance, hardly corresponds to Christian beliefs.

Nonetheless, the trilogy's assumption that people are the creation of a caring deity implies that, despite their often violent or destructive behavior, they ultimately are, or at least have the potential to be, good. After all, the evil god can manipulate people only through deception, and even the tragic Lord Ruler believes that he is saving humankind from destruction. Sanderson's belief in humanity's inborn goodness does have its reflection in Christian theology. In contrast to Augustine of Hippo, who firmly claimed that Adam and Eve's disobedience to God trapped people in sin from which they might be redeemed only by God's merciful grace (McGrath 136), Thomas Aquinas, who also acknowledged the necessity of God's grace, believed that the human soul is not entirely corrupted by sin and that even after the Fall people were still capable of discerning God and recognizing evil (Woodhead 27). Also the Christian belief in creation *ex nihilo* implies humankind's inborn goodness, because it assumes that everything that has its source in God has to be in some way good (Lovin 27). It is significant that though *Mistborn*'s world does not account for such concepts as Eden, the Fall, and the original sin, the author considers it necessary to point out that his imaginary people are the cherished creation of a good god who is the source of their sentience and free will, which allows them to overcome evil. Thus, the most basic premises of *Mistborn*'s divine genesis do correspond to Christian theology.

The motif of temptation, which is immensely significant for the Bible and which defines much of the relationship between *Mistborn*'s protagonists and the numinous of their world, constitutes another parallel between Sanderson's trilogy and Christian tradition. According to the *Dictionary of Biblical Imagery*, the many biblical episodes of temptation can be divided into the following stages:

> a process of manipulation by which the tempter allures the victim to do a forbidden or wrong thing, the process by which the victim deals with the allurement (usually first resisting but then gradually succumbing) and final closure, in which the intended victim either thwarts the tempter or assents to the forbidden action. Most temptation stories end in victory for the tempter, but this is not the only possibility [Ryken et al. 851–852].

Temptation to eat the forbidden fruit is what caused Adam and Eve's Fall and exile from Eden. Other biblical stories of temptation revolve around a person's desires to obtain power, wealth, and sexual favors. Temptation might be posed by external agents or come from within, in the form of personal ambitions and yearnings. The Devil/Satan is the figure of the ultimate tempter. As the Old Testament serpent, he lures Eve to take the apple. In the New Testament, he wishes to convince Jesus, who is fasting in the wilderness, to manifest his divinity and sovereignty over the world. In general, the Christian tradition portrays Satan as the one who tempts people to sin, so that they will distort their relationship with God. Successful resistance to temptation is simultaneously a resistance to sin.

Sanderson both subverts and retains the Christian significance of temptation. In the trilogy, the greatest source of temptation is the divine power accumulated in the Well of Ascension. The heroes are told that, according to prophecies, only by releasing the power from the Well can they save their world from destruction. Thus, to resist the desire of greedily keeping power to oneself is supposedly the proof of greatest virtue. In reality, the evil Ruin—who is restrained by the power of the Well—has for centuries tampered with the prophecies so that one day he could be liberated from his prison. The malevolent god is *Mistborn*'s equivalent of Satan—the master of subtle deception, lies, and temptation. In consequence of his manipulation, Vin assumes that by releasing this divine power she is courageously resisting the temptation of a divine status, while, in fact, she is fulfilling Ruin's plan. The result of her actions is similar to the biblical Fall. Like Eve tempted by the serpent to take the apple, the manipulated Vin reaches for the forbidden fruit, the power of the Well; both females are falsely convinced that their transgression is performed for the benefit of humankind. In the Bible, Adam and Eve manage to obtain the knowledge of good and evil, but lose their life in Eden and become exposed to corruption and death. In *Mistborn*, thanks to Vin's actions, the heroes eventually learn the truth behind the divine conflict between Preservation and Ruin (knowledge that was previously forbidden to them), but in exchange, their world is threatened by apocalyptic destruction and death.

The fatal Well of Ascension, which holds divine power in the form of a silvery liquid, also pertains to Christian tradition. In the Bible, a well is shown as the source of a community's physical existence, but it is also a metaphor for spiritual sustenance and transformation associated with baptism and eternal life (Steffler 128). The most significant scene of biblical baptism—Christ's immersion in the waters of Jordan—proclaimed Christ's status as the Son of God and symbolized his fate, i.e., the "burial" under the water and subsequent reappearance represented his up-coming death and resurrection (Ward et al. 117). Sanderson's Well of Ascension blends this Christian imagery of baptism, proclamation of divine identity, and the well as the source of life. Vin's full immersion in the Well's silvery liquid—the essence of Preservation's divine powers—transforms her mortal nature, expands her cognition (until it encompasses the entire planet), and bestows on her god-like powers. Thus, in Sanderson's reconstruction of the biblical motif, immersion in water is not only a symbolic representation of a person's spiritual transformation and elevation, but it becomes the means to a literal transformation of mortality into divinity.

The Christ Figure and the Fictional Church

Mistborn's most conspicuous and complex parallels with Christianity are present in its Christ figure, Kelsier, and his cult, the Church of the Survivor, which resembles the early Christian Church and later develops into an institution whose practices mirror Christian ones. In contrast to other fantastic Christ figures identified in previous chapters, Kelsier's likeness to Jesus Christ is not based solely on his self-sacrifice for the community he intends to protect. On the contrary, Kelsier's affinity to Christ is developed on several levels, which correspond to the complexity of Jesus' identity in the New Testament. Analyzing the numerous roles of Jesus, the *Dictionary of Biblical Imagery* accounts for, among others, the images of Jesus as a prophet and leader, as a stranger and scorned one who wanders between various friendly and hostile communities to spread his teaching, as a friend of sinners who does not turn away from or abandon anyone in need, as a controversialist who contests people's opinions and actions, as a savior who delivers people from sin and eternal death, as a liberator of slaves who frees people from the bondage of sin, and as a suffering servant who sacrifices himself for humankind (Ryken et al. 438–451).

All of these images are reflected in Sanderson's construction of the hero Kelsier. The man is initially presented as an itinerant prophet who wanders between villages and dares the oppressed skaa to think about rebellion against their tyrant. Though he is also half-skaa, he is clearly a stranger among them, both feared and scorned for his revolutionary ideas. Yet his sense of mission does not allow him to surrender even if his endeavors to question the existing socio-political order are a threat to his own safety. Gradually, from an intrusive prophet Kelsier becomes a spiritual leader whom others follow because they believe in his promises of a better life and in his power to refashion the world.

Jesus was very critical toward the corrupted religious elites and benevolent toward the poor and the outcasts (Woodhead 10). Kelsier similarly condemns the sinful elite and sides with the most abased people of the Empire. Though he does not instruct them about religious morality and faith like Christ did, he listens to their problems, consoles them, and offers hope. Eventually, he becomes the liberator who frees the skaa from slavery, and the savior who delivers them from the hands of a cruel deity. What is more, he consciously adopts the role of a "suffering servant" who, despite his extraordinary powers as a Mistborn, willingly sacrifices his own life for the benefit of the community. Even though Sanderson does not reconstruct the motifs of crucifixion, since Kelsier is killed with a spear, the man's death is similar to Christ's in that both are slain by the adversary establishment: Jesus was persecuted by Jewish religious leaders and sentenced by Pilate, whereas Kelsier is killed by the Lord Ruler. It is also worth mentioning that a spear features prominently in the Christian tradition as well: the Spear of Longinus, also known as the Holy Lance, was wielded by a soldier to stab the crucified Jesus. Thus, its choice as the weapon used to murder Kelsier also consitutes a minor parallel with Christianity. Though Kelsier's sacrifice is followed by a staged resurrection (he is imitated by a shape-changing kandra), the effect it has on people corresponds to the revelation of the New Testament sacrifice: the skaa's faith and fate are transformed and restored, thus giving rise to a new religion—the Church of the Survivor.

The development and form of the Church of the Survivor are reminiscent of the early Christian Church and, therefore, constitute another parallel between *Mistborn* and Christianity. First of all, it is significant that Sanderson chose to name the new religion the *Church* of the Survivor, which is an explicit reference to Christian institutions. Secondly, similarly to the early Christian Church, the Church of the Survivor is established by people inspired by the teachings of a single leader and the extent of the sacrifice performed in the name of their salvation. Thirdly, it is these people that are vastly responsible for fashioning the doctrines of the new faith. After Christ's death it was the task of the Apostles and other people who knew his teachings to establish the doctrines of the Christian Church (Woodhead 6). Likewise, since Kelsier leaves no specific religious instruction for his followers (probably because he never planned to become a deity worshipped by an organized religion), his followers must establish the unified doctrine and religious practices of the new Church on their own. Moreover, the identity of Kelsier as a deity is another point of comparison. The official Christian doctrine ascertains that

Jesus was both the Son of Man and the Son of God, i.e., a mortal man born of Virgin Mary and simultaneously God made manifest in human flesh. Jesus' claim to divine status was what outraged the Jewish leaders, and what modern people—driven by reason—might find difficult to comprehend. In a similar manner, some of *Mistborn*'s heroes who knew Kelsier as a man find it difficult to acknowledge his divine status. For instance, Vin confronts Captain Demoux about his belief in Kelsier, arguing that both of them knew Kelsier as a mortal man. Undaunted by Vin's dismay, Demoux recalls an experience when Kelsier used the power of Allomancy to aid him: "I felt him use me, making me more than I was. I think I can still feel him, sometimes. Strengthening my arm, guiding my blade" (*TWOA* 439). It is easy to imagine a similar discussion taking place after Jesus' death on the cross and his subsequent resurrection, when people—including those who did not witness the events, but who remembered him as a man made of flesh—had to decide whether to believe in his divinity and promise of salvation. The disputes which surround Kelsier's deification and his position within the fantastic Church are, therefore, a likely reflection of the disputes pertaining to Jesus' nature as the Son of Man and the Son of God.

Finally, the manner in which the Church of the Survivor chooses it official symbols also mirrors the Christian tradition. To commemorate their deity, some members of the new Church wear pendants in the form of a spear—the tool which the Lord Ruler used to kill Kelsier and which was later used by Vin to kill the tyrant. The spear is, therefore, an object associated with violence and death. That is why Vin cannot comprehend why the new Church should choose it as its symbol. A similar question could have been asked about the Christian cross. Crucifixion was a death sentence reserved for criminals, which entailed extreme suffering and humiliation. Yet because of Christ's resurrection, the cross became recognized by Christians as a revolutionary symbol of victory over death, salvation, and eternal life in Christ, though it was not until the 4th century CE that the cross acquired its present meaning (Ward et al. 251). Likewise, it can be assumed that by adopting the spear as their symbol, members of the Church of the Survivor intended to commemorate their founder's victory over evil, gift of hope, and promise of protection. The Survivor's spear functions like a Christian cross also in other contexts: the sign of the spear appears on graves and is performed as a religious gesture.

As far as other parallels are concerned, they are present in the rites and tradition of the fictional Church. The priests of the Church of the Survivor are called "Fathers." A Survivorist wedding is similar to a Christian one in that the bride and groom wear white, the union is symbolized by wedding pendants, the ceremony is conducted by the priest and in front of gathered guests, and the bride and groom are preceded by the "ash girl" who sprinkles ash under their feet (*TBOM* 42–47). In addition, at least one member of Kelsier's crew wrote a testimony—the Testimony of Hammond (*TBOM* 56)—which might resemble the Gospels written by the Apostles (though Sanderson does not specify the contents of the testimony). Finally, the belief in the Survivor's return when people will need him the most is a distant reflection of the belief in Christ's Second Coming. Perhaps in the continuation of the series Sanderson will provide more information about the Church of the Survivor, which will allow us to determine whether its correspondences to Christianity appear also on other levels.

Though *Mistborn*'s extensive reconstruction of certain religious motifs (e.g., its model of creation) might question their relevance to Christianity, the trilogy's affirmation of divine providence and necessity of faith corresponds to Christian theology. Despite the reign of a cruel deity and lack of religious gatherings, Sanderson's heroes still find emotional consolation in the belief that some higher force will protect their world from harm. Faith in divine providence allows them to continue their struggle against the malevolent Ruin in spite of ubiquitous evidence that their world is dying. For instance, when one of the heroes, Alendi, observes a beautiful sunrise, he believes that he senses a greater, benevolent power watching over him and the world, and that sensation offers him hope against all odds (*TFE* 633). Though *Mistborn*'s heroes might lack knowledge of the deity to whom they send their pleas and though the deity might greatly differ from the Christian image of God, the characters' words—"[f]aith [...] means that it doesn't matter what happens. You can trust that somebody is watching. Trust that somebody will make it all right. [...] It means that there will always be a way" (*THOA* 507)—express humble submission to the will of God and a belief in his benevolence, which is similar to Christian practice.

What is more, the figure of Sazed—an impartial scholar of religion who desperately seeks spiritual consolation after the loss of a beloved person—allows Sanderson to examine a dilemma experienced by many modern Christians. Faced with a personal tragedy, Sazed examines different religions in hope of finding logical evidence which would support his waning belief in divine protection and the existence of an afterlife. His desperate accusations that he has been abandoned by god, as well as his pleas for spiritual guidance, faintly recall the laments of the biblical Job whose faith was tested by undeserved suffering. Eventually, Sazed learns that religious faith is a matter of a person's free choice, not uncontested evidence. His quest for a religion grounded in logic mirrors the conundrum of modern people who, immersed in technology and reason, find it extremely difficult to believe in something not supported by scientific evidence. The answer obtained by Sazed—that the true power of faith does not depend on logic, but on unconditional belief (as Otto claimed, emotions and intuition over logic and reason)—should be acknowledged also by modern Christians who hesitate between faith and reason, and are therefore unable to put their trust in God.

In addition to its reconstruction of the motifs of creation and temptation, its Christ figure and Christian-like religion, and its affirmation of divine protection and necessity of faith, *Mistborn* contains a handful of other, fragmentary references to Christian history and biblical tradition. For one thing, Sanderson names a particular group of characters "the Inquisitors," and their brutality and blind obedience to the Lord Ruler vaguely recall the image of the medieval Inquisitors and their ill-perceived service to God. Second, the heroes occasionally mention hell and devil, as in "bloody hell" (*TFE* 528), "what the hell" (*TWOA* 522) and "I had a devil of a time" (*THOA* 615). Since *Mistborn*'s secondary mythology does not account for the existence of a devil or hell, such expressions are either remnants of one of Scadrial's long-forgotten religions which imprinted on people's language or evidence of the influence of the author's own speech on the characters' vocabulary. In the case of the latter, such references should be eliminated from the imaginary world for the sake of its integrity. Finally, the text briefly mentions Khlenni *cathedrals* with stained-glass windows, which might have belonged to a forgotten Christian-like religion.

Christianity and Ascension to Godhood

One more element of the trilogy's imaginary numinous which should be examined within the context of the Christian tradition is the concept of ascension to godhood. In fact, ascension to godhood is a motif which appears not only in *Mistborn*, but also in Sanderson's other works, which are set in the imaginary universe of the Cosmere. According to Sanderson's secondary cosmology, the Cosmere was originally created and supervised by the ultimate divine power called Adonalsium.[8] It has been revealed that Adonalsium, who created the first humans (*SH* loc. No. 982), was killed by sixteen people (*SH* loc. No. 976) who shattered the supreme being into sixteen parts called the Shards, which they then absorbed. As a result, these people ascended to godhood and acquired divine powers, which allowed them to create new races (Preservation and Ruin created people on the planet Scadrial) or move between worlds. Despite their divine powers, these "Shardholders" (as fans of Sanderson's works call them) are not completely immortal, their personalities are heavily influenced by the Intent of the Shard which they control (an Intent is a specific action or ideal connected with the Shard's part in the power of creation; that is why the holders have such specific names as Preservation or Ruin), and they can be annihilated. The Shards, however, are not destroyed and can be reabsorbed (thus, Sazed became Harmony). Since

Sanderson has, so far, not revealed much about the true nature of the Cosmere and Adonalsium, the subject is still open to readers' speculation. Thus, the figure of Adonalsium can be regarded as indebted not only to Christianity, but also to the Jewish Kabbalah. The sixteen Shards with their very specific Intents are similar to Kabbalistic Sephirot. The Sephirot are ten divine attributes or vessels for divine essence through which En Sof ("Without End"— the Infinite/Limitless divine entity) manifests himself and performs creation; the *Zohar* introduces the Sephirot as "Keter (Crown), Hokhamah (Wisdom), Binah (Sagacity), Chesed (Grace), Gevurah (Power), Tif'eret (Glory), Netsach (Longevity), Hod (Magisterial Dignity), Yesod (Foundation), and Malkhut (Kingdom)" (*Britannica*... 895). According to *Britannica*, "These names may seem rather arbitrary, and the internal logic upon which they are based is never made clear in any known text" (*Britannica*... 895). These entities and names could have well served as inspiration for Sanderson's Shards.

On the other hand, the motif of ascension to godhood as well as some other minor elements of the *Mistborn* series can be recognized as firmly rooted in the Latter Day Saint tradition. The Latter Day Saint movement, whose major faction today is the Church of Jesus Christ of Latter-Day Saints (in short, the LDS Church, known also as the Mormon Church), originated in the 19th century United States after Joseph Smith, inspired by the Angel Moroni, discovered some golden plates with an ancient scripture, which he translated and then published as the *Book of Mormon*. While Latter-Day Saints wholeheartedly declare themselves as Christians and profess a belief in Jesus Christ as the Savior of humankind, they are not acknowledged as such by other Christian denominations (Mills loc. 125). One point of dissent is the Mormon concept of Apostasy and restoration, i.e., the belief that after the death of the Apostles the early Church lost priesthood authority, gradually became corrupted, and needed restoration—restoration which was eventually delivered through the Prophet John Smith and the emergence of the LDS Church (Ouellette 129–131; Mills loc. 2586).

Another point of dissent is the *Book of Mormon*. Though the existence of the golden plates was confirmed only by Smith and his witnesses—for, according to Mormon tradition, Smith had to return the plates to the Angel— the belief in their authenticity is an essential part of the Mormon faith (also, the *Book of Mormon* refers to other metal plates that recorded significant religious and historical events, and thus establishes an entire tradition of engraving text in metal). While Latter-Day Saints generally accept the Christian Bible, they also claim that it is the *Book of Mormon* that presents the entire truth about the doctrine of salvation in Christ. Because of the additional scriptures and their different theological claims in comparison to Catholic and Protestant dogmas, members of the LDS Church are not accepted by other members of the Christian world. The theological doctrines which are the source of disagreement are, for instance, Mormon beliefs in man's ascension to godhood and eternal life (exaltation), living prophets, and separate personas of the Holy Trinity (*Britannica*... 750), as well as certain ordinances such as baptism for the dead (Mills loc. 891). While Latter-Day Saints elevate their *Book of Mormon*, they believe that other religions might voice some truth about man's relation to God, so they do not discredit other faiths.

As far as the *Mistborn* series is concerned, the Mormon belief in man's ascension to godhood is what underlies Sanderson's vision of the imaginary divine. By absorbing one of the Shards of the supreme force, Adonalsium, *Mistborn*'s characters experience a form of exaltation and become akin to gods: they partake of divine nature and are worshipped by other people, though apparently they are never made entirely omniscient or immortal. Of course, because the Mormon concept of exaltation is tied with certain ordinances (sacred rites such as baptism) and a life in faith, it is difficult to argue that the ascension to godhood experienced by *Mistborn*'s characters mirrors all of the nuances of Mormon religious practices. Thus, it is perhaps better to see the series' imagery of deification as a loose reworking of a specific tenet of the LDS Church. Another parallel between the Mormon tradition and *Mistborn* is the belief frequently voiced by Sazed that all religions and philosophies contain some religious truth. In the *Wax and Wayne* series, Sanderson ultimately transforms this belief into a plurality of fictional faiths and the simultaneous existence of the Church of the Survivor, Sliverism, and the Path—which explicitly advises its followers to study dozens of other denominations. Still, since in the world of *Mistborn*, and in the universe of Cosmere in general, all divine powers seem to have their origin in Adonalsium, it is not inappropriate for the series to claim that all religions addressing these minor divine forces somehow touch upon the ultimate divine truth. *Mistborn* also honors the Mormon tradition of texts engraved on plates. At one point in the story, the heroes discover ancient records engraved into steel, and later learn that the malicious Ruin might confuse their thoughts and manipulate the written word unless it is secured on metal. Afterward, they use metal as the medium for conveying information, so that their knowledge will not be falsified. Even in the second series the heroes still have their legal credentials put on small steel sheets (*SOS* 232). Thus, words engraved on metal are presented as the undisputed source of truth, to which, interestingly, only some characters have access. It can be inferred that in the original trilogy, apart from the protagonists, the masses of Scadrial's inhabitants have no clue about the true nature of their world and the origins of the divine—which becomes quite a strong religious statement if it is read in the context of the Latter-Day Saint tradition, the *Book of Mormon*, and other religions of the real world.

Brandon Sanderson and the Religious Dimensions of the Mistborn Series

While discussing one of his other works, Sanderson touched upon the topic of creativity and argued that "creativity is really the recombination of things you've seen before. We as human beings, by our very nature, can't imagine something we've never seen. What we can do is take different things we've seen and combine them in new ways" ("Brandon Sanderson Answers...," n.p.). In other words, Sanderson is apparently a writer who is well aware of the mechanisms of fantastic world-building, and consciously interweaves certain elements, including religious motifs and figures, from various existing cultures in order to create the alien settings of his imaginary realms. Still, the abundance and prominence of *Mistborn*'s Christian references stems not only from the writer's conscious attempt at reconstructing Christianity, but also from his private beliefs. Sanderson is a member of the Church of Jesus Christ of Latter-Day Saints, served as a missionary in Seoul, Korea, between 1995 and 1997 ("About Brandon"), and in 2005 graduated from Brigham Young University, which is owned and operated by the LDS Church.[9] When in an interview for *Mormon Artist* Nathan Morris asked Sanderson about the influence of faith on his writing, Sanderson replied that though, as a writer, he wishes to create gripping stories rather than to preach, faith is also a prominent factor at work (Morris n.p.). He declares that:

> With the *Mistborn* books, I wasn't ever trying to be overtly LDS. Yet my values shape who I am and what I determine to be important. I then end up having characters who deal with these same things, and I think there are a lot of LDS things going on. But of course I think there are a lot of Buddhist things going on as well. I served my mission in Korea and have a lot of respect for the Buddhist religion [Morris n.p.].

In the same interview, Sanderson also states that he does not wish to predetermine the theme and message of his books. This does not mean, however, that he is a writer who remains (blissfully or ignorantly) oblivious to the statements made by his works. On the contrary, he is deeply concerned with the messages delivered by his books, and he even runs a website on which he provides extensive annotations to every novel (or even to every chapter of a given novel) to clarify its meaning. For instance, annotations to chapter eighty of *The Hero of Ages*, in which an entire social group commits mass suicide, offer both a warning against similar actions and some spiritual advice: "The thing you can try is what Sazed did, actively using his religion and calling upon a higher power to bring him help. This is one of the core tenets of many religions—that we, as humans, cannot do all things on our own and need the help of others" ("Annotations"). Yet though Sanderson is concerned with the psychological and spiritual impact of *Mistborn* (and his other works), he—true to his claims—does not use the narrative as a means for preaching. While Mormon ideas are quite prominent in the series (for it is only natural, one might argue, that the author's background resurfaces in his writing—which is certainly the case for Stephen Donaldson and his *Chronicles of Thomas Covenant*), the series does not extol the merits of Mormonism, and Sanderson does not seem to proselytize his readers. Instead, the characters of *Mistborn* talk about religion in general and try to discover, for instance, why faith is important to them and what it really means to believe in a supreme divine entity.[10]

To conclude, Brandon Sanderson's *Mistborn* is another inspiring example of how a fantasist may use the genre's potential to acknowledge his own beliefs and to discuss issues related to religion in general. It presents yet another way in which a fantasist may rework Christian motifs to make them an integral part of his/her imaginary world and still retain their original significance. Like Donaldson in *The Chronicles of Thomas Covenant*, Sanderson designed the gods and religions of his world largely as a reflection of his private beliefs—though in the case of Sanderson, who is a proclaimed believer, inclusion of references to Mormonism, or Christianity in general, were probably a more deliberate choice than it was for Donaldson who has diverged from the religious upbringing he received in his childhood. Like Kay in *Fionavar Tapestry*, Sanderson combined several traditions—including Mormonism, elements of Kabbalah and Buddhism—to create the diversified spheres of secondary numinous and sacred appearing in his imaginary world. Yet in contrast to Kay's *Fionavar*, in which Christianity seemed but one component among many others of equal importance, Sanderson's *Mistborn* is strongly embedded in the Christian tradition. Sanderson also demands that his heroes ponder the nature and existential significance of faith—something which Kay's heroes hardly ever do. Moreover, like Friedman who explored the shared background between Judaism and Christianity, Sanderson draws inspiration from the shared themes of Mormonism and other Christian denominations: the figure of Christ, the motif of temptation, and belief in divine providence, to mention but a few. Yet while Friedman's trilogy ends with the unquestionable triumph of faith in the One God, Sanderson's *Mistborn* is but a fragment of the unknown history of the divine Adonalsium. Finally, Sanderson's imaginary numinous and religions are different from the achievement of the other writers in that he presents an alternative, fantastic version of the life of Christ and the beginning of Christianity: Kelsier and the Church of the Survivor. This creation is—like Friedman's transformation of the Judeo-Christian tradition into the extraterrestrial Church of Human Unification on Erna—an exercise in fantastic speculation over a well-established religion. Undoubtedly, readers with various religious backgrounds may enjoy *Mistborn* in spite of the ubiquity of its religious (Christian) themes, because Sanderson does not intend to proselytize to his readers and addresses issues that pertain to people of different denominations (e.g., the significance of faith). Nevertheless, readers with a Christian background or knowledge of Christianity may find the work more accessible and meaningful, due to its religious connotations. All in all, once Sanderson is done with his Cosmere cycle,[11] it might be worthwhile examining his complete vision of the divine Adonalsium and the overall religious premises of his imaginary universe.

Conclusion

The phenomenological analysis of the selected novels by Stephen R. Donaldson, Guy Gavriel Kay, Celia S. Friedman, and Brandon Sanderson has unequivocally demonstrated, firstly, that complex secondary religions are a prominent element of fantastic world-building; secondly, that the structure of the secondary numinous and sacred is permeated with references to biblical tradition, Christian ethics, and Christian theology; thirdly, that fantasists use the genre to enter into a dialogue with Christianity and to deliver their private views on religion and faith. In this respect, the investigated novels fit Alister E. McGrath's classification of "Christian literature," in which he distinguishes texts that serve the needs of Christian congregations and institutions (sermons, prayers); texts, written by both Christians and non–Christians, which "are not specific to the Christian faith, but which have been shaped or influenced by Christian ideas, values, images, and narratives," and texts which "involve interaction with Christian ideas, individuals, schools of thought, or institutions, often written by those who would regard themselves as observers or critics of Christianity" (338–339).

In Donaldson's *Chronicles of Thomas Covenant, the Unbeliever*, Christian elements have been identified in the name and portrayal of the main hero, in the structure of the imaginary realm's cosmology (the supremacy of the Creator versus the destructive intents of Lord Foul the Despiser, the pseudo-angelic beings), in the reconstructions of certain motifs and symbols (freedom of will, self-sacrifice, baptism through water and fire, the plagues), and in the author's language which is infused with allusions to the Scriptures. What is more, the moral premises of Donaldson's imaginary world are embedded in Christian morality (humble service to others, rejection of arrogant pride, resistance to temptation). Yet despite these numerous parallels with Christianity, the series paints an unfavorable picture of institutional religion, which is a reflection of Donaldson's personal views.

Guy Gavriel Kay's *The Fionavar Tapestry* is a combination of several distinct traditions, among which the position of Christianity becomes ambiguous. On the one hand, the biblical tradition is treated like any other ancient source whose figures, motifs, and symbols might be freely reconstructed for the sake of creating a fantastic reality. Thus, references to the Old and the New Testament appear in the portrayal of the fictional gods, in the nature of divine beings, and in the roles adopted by the protagonists, and they are then interwoven with elements of various mythologies and Eastern spirituality. On the other hand, not only is Fionavar's morality rooted in Christian ethics, but Kay's development of such themes as the freedom of human will, sin, redemption, divine grace, and salvation all pertain to Christian theology. As a result, *The Fionavar Tapestry* is an example of a work which neither explicitly promotes nor criticizes Christianity, but which freely draws inspiration from Christian history and beliefs.

The phenomenological analysis of Celia S. Friedman's *The Coldfire Trilogy* has revealed that numerous aspects of her fictional Church are based on the Judeo-Christian tradition: its worship of the One God and the attributes ascribed to him, its internal structure (priests supervised by the Patriarch), doctrines (salvation and damnation), practices (masses), sacred places (cathedrals and churches), and values (humble obedience to the One God, belief in divine providence and salvation through faith, the value of self-sacrifice). Moreover, Friedman reconstructs several images and motifs appearing in the Bible: man's Fall into the temptation of knowledge and power, his sin against God, the possibility of damnation in Hell, and redemption through the restorative power of baptism and sacrifice. The Christian dimension of the trilogy is strengthened also by the figures of the protagonists: a priest who decides to withdraw from priesthood not to tarnish the reputation of his Church, and the Church's ex–Prophet who eventually becomes a Christ figure and is redeemed from sin. Friedman's *The Coldfire Trilogy* offers a fantastic reconstruction of Christianity in an extraterrestrial environment.

Brandon Sanderson's *Mistborn* series is based both on beliefs shared by major Christian denominations and on tenets specific to Mormonism. Elements of the former are particularly visible in the series' development of an alternative story of Christ's life, death and worship, as well as in a handful of fragmentary references to biblical tradition. The latter is represented by the Mormon belief in the possibility of man's ascension to godhood, and by reconstructed elements of Mormon traditions. Both threads are grounded in the author's private beliefs. Even though *Mistborn*'s vision of a society tormented by a cruel god might seem a severe critique of (organized) religion, its final vision of a world in which faith is reinstated and reaffirmed, is a highly positive one.

Interestingly, multiple references to Christianity are only one of the aspects shared by all four series as far as their construction of the imaginary numinous and fictional religions is concerned. Firstly, what the works also share is their insistence on the fact that their imaginary worlds were created by benevolent and caring deities, and were later stealthily corrupted or jeopardized by malevolent antagonists. Consequently, one can assume that everything in them is inherently good and can be, therefore, redeemed and restored to greatness. Secondly, the novels intensely focus on the portrayal of the numinous: its attributes, shapes, transformations, social roles, and relationship with people. The issue of relationship is particularly significant, because on the background of a cosmic conflict between divine forces, the heroes struggle to rediscover their spirituality. Their efforts are inhibited by the transformations or ruptures within the fantastic numinous, which need to be dealt with if the relationship with the Holy is to be established or restored (and their quests completed). Thirdly, all of the novels, in one way or another, contrast the profane and secular life with religious life engulfed by the sacred.

This complex relationship between the fantasy genre and Christianity—and religion in general—is a phenomenon indicative of transformations within the culture and religiousness of the postmodern world. As Bronislaw Szerszynski explains, "in contemporary society the discourses and practices of the sacred have been set free from their long incarceration in institutionalized monotheism, and have become generally available as a cultural resource" (27). One aspect of these postmodern transformations is addressed by Emily McAvan in *The Postmodern Sacred* (2012), in which the author investigates the emergence of popular culture spirituality grounded, among others, in "the postmodernist collapse of the scientific meta-narratives that made atheism so powerful" (1). Focusing mostly on movies and TV series, e.g., *The Matrix*, *Harry Potter*, *The Lord of the Rings*, *Buffy the Vampire Slayer*, and *The X-Files*, McAvan argues that their shared features include "a virtualization of the sacred, a foregrounding of the virtual as a legitimate form of experience, a pastiche of multiple traditions and generic tropes [...] and lastly a consumptive approach to that sacred" (6). She is particularly concerned with the consumptive dimension of the postmodern sacred, because, as she argues, the "secondhand experience of transcendence and belief" (19) offered by it:

> displaces the need for belief or real-world practice into a textual world, requiring little of its consumers. While they seem to suggest a desire for a magical world outside of capitalism, the wonder produced by these texts, however, is only temporary; eventually the consumer must return again to purchase another text [19].

In this respect, the sacred becomes a commodity that can be bought at will, a type of pseudo-spiritual sustenance for the postmodern man, which, like any other form of mass entertainment, does not require a lasting commitment. As far as the structure of this commoditized postmodern sacred is concerned, McAvan observes that though it reconstructs several traditions, its relationship with Christianity is particularly significant:

the postmodern sacred remains highly indebted toward Christianity as its primary symbolic source, even as it looks elsewhere for an ontological foundation for its textual universes. It is thus best understood as *post*-Christian; even when it defines itself against religious institutions it remains fixated on such typically Christian themes of sacrifice and redemption, as well as Christian symbols like the Cross or holy water [61].

Though McAvan is critical of the nature of the postmodern sacred, suggesting that the satisfaction offered by popular culture spirituality is only temporary and not transformed into a search for the sacred in real life (which is perhaps true of the texts she chose for analysis), her research confirms what has been demonstrated also by this work: that Christianity has been embraced by popular culture as a source of inspiration and that postmodern people are therefore offered new paths to spirituality. These new paths are not necessarily as illusory as McAvan suggests. In *The Re-Enchantment of the West* (2005), Christopher Partridge, who examines the ways in which the contemporary Western world rediscovers its spirituality, argues that "just because beliefs are transmitted through popular culture does not mean that they are, therefore, trivialized" (1). Though Partridge focuses in his work on the growing interest in Eastern practices (yoga, meditation), healing practices, cyberspirituality, and sacralization of the extraterrestrial, the fantasy genre—with its evocation of complex religious dimensions—also represents the Western "confluence of secularization and sacralization" (2) identified by the scholar, which may expand postmodern people's perception of spirituality.

This is perhaps what Karen Armstrong has in mind when she writes in *Short History of Myth* (2005) that the category of myth must be redeemed (135), and that "unless there is some kind of spiritual revolution that is able to keep abreast of our technological genius, we will not save our planet" (137). Armstrong believes that this spiritual revolution might be conducted by artists and writers who salvage our mythological heritage (2005, 138), and she points to the works of Angela Carter, Italo Calvino, and Jorge Luis Borges as cases in point. The works of Donaldson, Kay, Friedman, and Sanderson, as well as of other prominent fantasists, could also be added to Armstrong's list, because they fulfill similar roles:

> If it is written and read with serious attention, a novel, like a myth or any great work of art, can become an initiation that helps us to make a painful rite of passage from one phase of life, one state of mind, to another. A novel, like a myth, teaches us to see the world differently; it shows us how to look into our own hearts and to see our world from a perspective that goes beyond our own self-interest. If professional religious leaders cannot instruct us in mythical lore, our artists and creative writers can perhaps step into this priestly role and bring fresh insight to our lost and damaged world [Armstrong 2005, 148–149].

What Armstrong postulates is, therefore, similar to Marek Oziewicz's claims that mythopoeic fantasy literature can contribute to the shaping of a new mythology for the unified humanity. Though Bogdan Trocha and Brian Attebery are right in their concerns about the genre's exploitation and appropriation of myth, by showing a life immersed in the sacred, fantasy literature might participate in the contemporary reconfiguration of religion and contribute to the re-mythologizing of the de-mythologized postmodern world.

Fantasy literature, as a whole, should not be perceived as an adversary of Christianity. Inarguably, there are fantasy novels whose dubious morality and inappropriate portrayals of magic and the occult might rightly raise the concern of religious-conscious readers. There are also fantasy novels, e.g., Pullman's *His Dark Materials*, whose aim is to object against or discredit Christianity. But "collective responsibility" should not become the argument for disqualifying the entire genre, because accomplished fantasy fiction can become a medium of expression which Christianity can embrace, as it did in the case of Lewis's *The Chronicles of Narnia* and Tolkien's *The Lord of the Rings*. In fact, as Matthew Dickerson and David O'Hara assert, "fantasy literature should have an ally in Christianity, in that both affirm the existence of the supernatural and of moral freedom, both affirm the importance of our choices, both encourage escape from materialist determinism, and both find a materialistic worldview to be insufficient" (53–54). Elise Brooke believes that since "we cannot speak of God or of any divine activity save by means of analogy, it is clear that any form of imaginative writing stands at least as good a chance of success as any purely dogmatic statement" (Brooke 76). And Jack Zipes goes as far as to claim that "the Bible and certain fantasy literature are sacred texts: unlike reality, they open the mysteries of life and reveal ways in which we can maintain our integrity. They compensate for the constant violation of the sacred and the everyday violence in our lives" (in Aichele and Pippin 1998, ix).

The ways in which the fantasy genre addresses and reconstructs Christianity discussed in this work represent only a fragment of the complex relationship between fantasy and religion. I believe that further research on the genre—also with the help of the phenomenology of religion—may reveal other examples of how and why fantasists evoke the numinous with a Christian worldview, design secondary religions based on Christianity, and address issues pertaining to the history and future of Christianity (or any other religion).[1] Such research will most probably confirm my belief that the genre should be recognized as a prominent voice in the discourse on the shifting postmodern sacred and the nature of postmodern spirituality—a discourse which the fantasy genre, given its intricate secondary religions and reconstructions of various religious traditions, is entitled to join and enrich.

Chapter Notes

Chapter 1

1. See John H. Timmerman's *Other Worlds* (1983), Lisa Tuttle's *Writing Fantasy and Science Fiction* (2005), and Farah Mendlesohn's *Rhetorics of Fantasy* (2008).
2. For more information about the historical development of American fantasy fiction see Brian Attebery's *The Fantasy Tradition in American Literature: From Irving to Le Guin* (1980) and Paul Kincaid's chapter in *The Cambridge Companion to Fantasy Literature* (2012, edited by Edward James and Farah Mendlesohn).
3. Paradoxically, Kay's internationally successful *Fionavar Tapestry* was greatly influenced by Tolkien's Middle-earth. Kay's trilogy is both derivative and original in that it simultaneously emulates and reworks patterns set by Tolkien. This puts Kay in one line with American fantasists of the 1960s and 1970s, who tried either to imitate Tolkien's conception of a fantasy world or diverge from it.
4. For more details on the historical development of Canadian speculative fiction see David Ketterer's *Canadian Science Fiction and Fantasy* (1992), Douglas Ivison's *Canadian Fantasy and Science-Fiction Writers: Dictionary of Literary Biography* (2002), and *The Canadian Fantastic in Focus: New Perspectives* (2015, edited by Allan Weiss).
5. Trocha's theory proved useful for my analysis of how fantasists reconstruct the images of mythic creatures such as unicorns and werewolves. See "The Reinvention of Lycanthropy in Modern Fantasy Literature" (*Basic Categories of Fantastic Literature Revisited* edited by Andrzej Wicher, Piotr Spyra, and Joanna Matyjaszczyk, 2014, pp. 91–203) and "Peter S. Beagle's Transformations of the Mythic Unicorn" (*Mythlore* 33.1, 2014, pp. 53–65).
6. Even the subtitle of one of Campbell's books—*Myths to Live By*—explicitly supports this claim: "How we re-create ancient legends in our daily lives to release human potential."
7. For a detailed definition of mythopoeic fantasy see Oziewicz pp. 83–90.
8. Another translation of *phantasia* is "making visible" (Gates et al. 2).
9. Carlos Ruiz Zafón (b. 1964) is a Spanish novelist whose most famous works are *The Shadow of the Wind* (2001), *The Angel's Game* (2008), and *The Prisoner of Heaven* (2011). These novels can be categorized as representative of magical realism, because something undoubtedly supernatural exists on the borders of Zafón's fictional Barcelona, yet it never reveals its true nature or form.
10. For a juxtaposition of phenomenology of religion and philosophical phenomenology attributed to Edmund Husserl see Cox, pp. 24–47.
11. Originally published in 1917 as *Das Heilige—Über das Irrationale in der Idee des Göttlichen und sein Verhältnis zum Rationalen*.
12. Originally published in 1933 as *Phänomenologie der Religion*.
13. This claim is repeated by James L. Cox in his *Introduction to the Phenomenology of*

Religion (2010). Cox argues that the object of any religious studies is a given community with its approaches to divinity. Those involved in religious studies examine people's behavior and "make no comment on alleged divine interventions in the human condition" (ix).

14. Originally published in 1949 as *Traité d'histoire des religions*.
15. Originally published in 1957 as *Le sacré et le profane*.
16. Originally published in 1952 as *Images et symboles*.
17. Eliade himself wrote over twenty stories which include elements of the fantastic (Kleiner 13), e.g., *The Snake* (1937), *With the Gypsies* (1959), "The Cloak" (1975).
18. I have first discussed the applicability of the phenomenological method to the study of fantasy fiction in the article "Phenomenology of Religion and the Study of Modern Fantasy Literature" (*Acta Neophilologica*, XVI (1), 2014, pp. 179-189). This chapter is an extended discussion of some arguments first presented therein.
19. The essay "On Fairy-Stories" was first delivered as a lecture at the University of St Andrews. The poem "Mythopoeia" was inspired by Tolkien's discussion with C.S. Lewis on the nature of Christianity.
20. Arthur also published *Walking with Frodo* (2003), *Walking through the Wardrobe* (2005).
21. Dalton also makes an interesting point by claiming that not all Christ imagery placed in a text has to be intentional, and that by producing stories about saviors and sacrifices writers might be tapping into "the deep truths that are bred in our bones" (140).
22. Pullman provides an alternative story of Jesus Christ's life in a controversial book *The Good Man Jesus and the Scoundrel Christ* (2010), in which the figure of Jesus Christ is divided between two brothers—Jesus and Christ—with very different personalities.
23. Arguments presented in this paragraph first appeared in my article "Finding God(s) in Fantasylands: Religious Ideas in Fantasy Literature" (*Crossroads: A Journal of English Studies*, 1/2013, pp. 24-36).
24. A detailed analysis of these works appears in my essay "The Anti-Christian Dimensions of Fantasy Literature" (in *The Light of Life: Essays in Honour of Professor Barbara Kowalik*, edited by Maria Błaszkiewicz and Łukasz Neubauer, Kraków: Libron 2017, pp. 203-216).

Chapter 2

1. Donaldson was most probably able to create a convincing portrait of a leper because of his personal experiences: during his childhood he lived in India where his father, an orthopaedic surgeon, worked with lepers.
2. For instance, in the art of suru-pa-maerl, Stonedownors use Earthpower to create sculptures from fused stones, whereas in the art known as *anundivian yajña* (marrowmeld) the Ramen work with fused bones.
3. The Masters, like the Lords and the Clave before them, dwell in Revelstone, an enormous city-fortress built by the Giants. Though Revelstone does not possess its own power, its masterful stonework and rich history bestow authority on subsequent leaders, and legitimate their reign. In the first trilogy a counterpart of Revelstone is Revelwood—a giant tree inhabited by people studying lore in service of the Land. However, while Revelstone remains a central place through the entire *Chronicles*, Revelwood is destroyed in the first series and never returns to its original splendor.
4. They came to Earth by crossing a rainbow bridge linking heaven and Earth. Though the rainbow has Christian connotations, the motif of a rainbow bridge appears also in Scandinavian mythology: a rainbow bridge called Bifrost links Asgard, the land of gods, with Midgard, the land of mortals (Cotterell 181).
5. Other features of the *Elohim* make them equally similar to elves and fairies from traditional folktales: both groups dwell in dazzling realms inaccessible to mortals without their inhabitants' consent; both are playful, capricious, and aloof creatures that act according to their own wishes; and both are condescending towards people whom they perceive as inferior.
6. There might be but one example of the Creator's direct intervention in the Land.

When Covenant and his companions are doomed to die, the leper uses the Seven Words as a prayer for help and suddenly the mythic Fire-Lions come to their rescue. Since the Lions are creatures of Earthpower, and Earthpower is linked to the Creator, the succor of the beasts might be treated as the god's act of grace.

7. This victory seems inspired by a quotation from Mark Twain who wrote in *The Mysterious Stranger Manuscripts*: "Against the assault of laughter nothing can stand."

8. Another reference to redemption through sacrifice is present in the story of how Kelenbhrabanal, the Father of the Horses, allowed himself to be killed so that the herd could be spared (*The Chronicles...* 753). This imagery is similar to the biblical concept of the innocent lamb (Christ) whose blood is spilt for the redemption of others. What is more, the Ranyhyn's commemoration of the sacrifice performed for their sake is a distant echo of the Eucharist: while the faithful of the church partake of the Holy Communion to be united in and with Christ, the horses drink from a tarn and unite their minds to share their sorrow and rage.

9. The disambiguation of the main protagonist's name revealed several biblical connotations. The names of other characters also possess them. "Dr. Johnson" and "Matthew Logan" allude to the two authors of New Testament gospels, John and Mathew. Linden's son is named after Jeremiah—an Old Testament prophet, whom Donaldson calls a prophet of woe (*The Runes...* 68). Though Linden Avery's name has less religious connotations, it is not altogether meaningless. The linden tree is a symbol of love and peace, and it is Linden's destiny in the Land to find love and restore peace. Her surname, Avery, is similar to the word "every," and might denote that Linden is the Everyman (or Everywoman) that surpasses his/her shortcomings and limitations. Some of the other names appearing in *The Chronicles* are inspired by foreign languages. The names of the demonic Ravers—*moksha* Jehannum, *samadhi* Sheol and *turiya* Herem—are a combination of Sanskrit and Hebrew. In Sanskrit, *moksha* means "liberation," *samādhi* describes a transcendental state of mind, and *turiya* stands for an experience of consciousness. In Hebrew, *Sheol* means "the abode of the dead," *Gehinnom* is the Valley of the Son of Hinnom were children were sacrificed in fire and which came to mean Hell (in Arabic *Jahannam* also means Hell), and *herem* stands for "destruction." Thus, the names are an inherent part of characterization.

Chapter 3

1. For the sake of brevity, titles of individual volumes will be shortened to acronyms: *The Summer Tree*—TST, *The Wandering Fire*—TWF, and *The Darkest Road*—TDR.

2. My first attempt at analyzing the trilogy's religious dimension appeared in the article "Phenomenology of Religion and the Study of Modern Fantasy Literature" (in *Acta Neophilologica*, XVI (1), 2014, pp. 183-189). This chapter develops ideas and arguments which were first mentioned therein. Also, a brief analysis of the trilogy's motif of sacrifice appeared in the chapter "Reinterpretacja chrześcijańskiego motywu ofiary i odrodzenia w cyklu *Fionavarski Gobelin* Guya Gavriela Kaya i *Trylogii Zimnego Ognia* Celii S. Friedman" (in *Motywy religijne we współczesnej fantastyce* edited by Mariusz M. Leś and Piotr Stasiewicz, Białystok: Wydawnictwo Uniwersytetu w Białymstoku, 2014, pp. 215-226). This chapter is an extended discussion of some arguments first presented therein.

3. A full moon appears outside the natural lunar cycle to mark Dana's presence, while a red moon is treated as her declaration of war against Rakoth.

4. My first attempt at analyzing Fionavar's beasts appeared in the article "Benevolent and Malevolent Creatures in Guy Gavriel Kay's *Fionavar Tapestry*" (in *Imaginary Creatures in Medieval and Modern Fantasy Literature* edited by Łukasz Neubauer, Kraków: Libron, 2016, pp. 69-83). This chapter develops ideas and arguments which were first signaled therein.

5. It seems that Kay's *Fionavar Tapestry* was inspired not only by Tolkien's Middle-earth, but also by Donaldson's *Chronicles*: the Paraiko's kanior resembles the Giants' *caamora*, and both realms include a sentient forest that hates people.

6. As far as instruments of power are concerned, though none of these objects are directly linked to evil, the power evoked by them can be used for both good and evil purposes. Thus, these instruments reaffirm the claim that Fionavar's numinous is ambiguous and escapes moral categorization. Among the most powerful items there is the Cauldron of Khath Meigol which can resurrect the dead; Lökdal, a cursed knife that will destroy anyone who kills with it without love in his heart; Owein's Horn which summons the Wild Hunt; the ring Baelrath (the Warstone) linked to the war-goddesses; and the Circlet of Lisen whose Light can repel the Dark. When they are wielding these items, the protagonists acquire divine-like powers, but the consequences are as often tragic, as they are positive, and the protagonists learn that divine power is better left to the gods.

7. To offer her soul as a gift, the previous Seer not only has to kill herself, but also renounce her life after death: "Once given, the soul is gone. [...] There can be no passage beyond the walls of Night to find light at the Weaver's side" (*TST* 202). This implies that there is some kind of afterlife for the Weaver's human children, yet this idea is never explored.

8. Many of the names used by Kay are also derived from Celtic myths and languages, e.g., Connla, Cader Sedat, Gwen Ystrat.

9. Similarly, Kay uses the number three to symbolize the Fionavarian divine. The heroes often say that the Goddess works by threes (i.e. performs three miracles or interventions), and the High Priestess says that "three times touches destiny" (*TST* 129).

10. Trying to find Kay's comments on Christianity, Fionavar's religious background, or religion in general, I have read more than twenty interviews with the writer. Everything I was able to find was included in this chapter.

11. Kay continues to mention Fionavar as a legendary land of origin and gods in his other works (as Finavir, Finvair, Fionavrre, etc.). This perpetuates the idea that Fionavar and its numinous are the matrix which all the other fictional worlds, more or less distortedly, reflect.

Chapter 4

1. In citation, titles of individual volumes are shortened to *BSR* (*Black Sun Rising*), *WTNF* (*When True Night Falls*), and *COS* (*Crown of Shadows*). A brief analysis of the trilogy's motif of sacrifice appeared in the chapter "Reinterpretacja chrześcijańskiego motywu ofiary i odrodzenia w cyklu *Fionavarski Gobelin* Guya Gavriela Kaya i *Trylogii Zimnego Ognia* Celii S. Friedman" (in *Motywy religijne we współczesnej fantastyce* edited by Mariusz M. Leś and Piotr Stasiewicz, Białystok: Wydawnictwo Uniwersytetu w Białymstoku, 2014, pp. 215–226). This chapter develops ideas and arguments which were first mentioned therein.

2. Earth fae, the primary type, is produced by the planet's core and changes according to its seismic activity. Dark fae, considered evil, is strongest during a True Night—a phenomenon occurring when Erna's sun, moons, and stars are all hidden, thus basking the planet in complete darkness. Tidal fae depends on the pattern of tides (Erna has three moons), whereas solar fae is generated by the sun and stars (and can neutralize Dark fae).

3. It might seem strange that the Patriarch—a morally conscious man—can rely on Tarrant's teachings without worrying about the Prophet's later fall. This lack of doubt supports the claim that the Church somehow decided that the Prophet's "madness" did not contest the authenticity of his earlier works.

4. When he is inside a cathedral, Damien sees "a jeweled mural of the Prophet binding the Evil One to darkness—one of the few representations which the Church permitted" (*BSR* 22). Has the Prophet actually defeated the evil Unnamed One before his transformation? Is that the reason why the Unnamed One is particularly interested in having him succumb to its temptation? Or is the mural just a symbolic representation of Gerald's role as the founding-father of the Church? These issues are never explored in the trilogy.

5. The fortress is situated in a Forest which is inhabited by fae-born monsters. Here Friedman deliberately or not emulates a motif from early American literature: the Puritans

perceived the forest as the abode of the devil and witches, which threatened the pious Christian communities. *Coldfire*'s Forest is literally an abode of monsters and their devilish master.

    6. The prequel to the trilogy, *Dominion*, describes the events which have probably led to the Church's Holy War against the Hunter. Having captured a female soldier, Gerald releases her so that she can deliver his message to the Church, which "will be a test of their faith.... If they have the courage to challenge me here, in this place, then I will know my creation was worthy of me" (*Dominion*, n.p.). The Church did try to challenge the Hunter, but was defeated.

Chapter 5

    1. It is worth praising the structure of *Mistborn*'s plot, which Sanderson based on deception and hidden truths. By sparsely revealing crucial tidbits of information, Sanderson forces his readers to constantly reevaluate and update their knowledge about the true nature of characters and events; readers achieve a full understanding of the trilogy only at the end of the third volume. Thus, reading *Mistborn* is like solving a riddle, and readers who have had enough of formulaic and easily predictable fantasy books will find this series quite appealing.

    2. In citation, titles of individual volumes are shortened to *TFE* (*The Final Empire*), *TWOA* (*The Well of Ascension*), *THOA* (*The Hero of Ages*), *TAOL* (*The Alloy of Law*), *SOS* (*Shadows of Self*), *TBOM* (*The Bands of Mourning*), and *SH* (*Secret History*).

    3. The Deepness is only vaguely described as "a thing of destruction, madness, and corruption. It would destroy this world not out of spite or out of animosity, but simply because that is what it does" (*TFE* 457). If destruction is the core of this entity's identity, then "Deepness" might be simply another name for the god Ruin.

    4. In the final scene he promises to watch over humankind and reassures his friends that he had talked with Vin and Kelsier—an indirect confirmation that human souls survive the death of the body. Sanderson returns to this episode in *Mistborn: Secret History*, in which readers get a glimpse of the heroes on their way to afterlife which is presented as a mysterious dimension simply called "the Beyond."

    5. The Pathian earrings are, in fact, tiny Hemalurgic spikes through which the deity can communicate with the people wearing them. Preservation's ability was to hear people, and Ruin's to speak to them. Harmony, as the mediator between their powers, possesses both abilities (*SOS* 133).

    6. Other "holy texts" were composed by the Originators, i.e., people who survived the apocalypse and remaking of the world (*SOS* 306).

    7. In *Mistborn: Secret History*, Sanderson describes how after his death Kelsier refused to move to the afterlife, and instead remained in an in-between dimension of shadows and mists (where he briefly held Preservation's power), which also allowed him to ascend to divinity. This idea might be explored in the *Wax and Wayne* series.

    8. The name which appears in my copy of *The Hero of Ages*, when Sazed writes about "*a fractured presence, something spanning the void*," is "Adonasium" (344; italics in the original). It is either a misprint or a deliberate mistake which emphasizes the incompleteness of the characters' knowledge about the supreme divine.

    9. During his studies, Sanderson attended a science fiction/fantasy writing class which was initiated in honor of Orson Scott Card, who is also a member of the LDS Church and a prominent American writer of science fiction and fantasy literature (The Geek's Guide...). Card's religious beliefs have also had a significant influence on his writing. A case in point is his saga *The Tales of Alvin Maker* (1987–2003).

    10. Sanderson does not rule out the possibility that one day he will write an urban fantasy novel in which he will deal more explicitly with Mormonism and Mormon characters. He also claims that his readers who are not members of the LDS Church only occasionally object to him being a member of the LDS, and usually appreciate his books (Morris n.p.).

11. At the time of writing this chapter, Sanderson has already published almost two dozen books related to the Cosmere and still plans to have several more.

Conclusion

1. A different aspect of the relationship between fantasy and religion has been studied, e.g., by William Sims Bainbridge in *eGods: Faith Versus Fantasy in Computer Gaming* (2013). Bainbridge analyzes the backgrounds of gaming worlds which are rich in religious elements, figures, and symbols, and argues that such games offer implicit commentary on religion, require their players to make moral and religious choices, allow them to interact with various forms of religion, and show them how religion is tied to history and economy. In his work, Bainbridge examines issues such as the shape of divinity, immortality of soul, function of priests, portrayal of sacred places, and the meaning of death, whose presence in games should be perceived not as "the erosion of religious faith" but as "a form of cultural progress that liberates the playful human imagination" (24). Bainbridge also claims that Christian gamers might have problems with the non–Christian and magic-based contents of some games. A similar problem has been identified in the case of fantasy fiction and Christian readers.

Works Cited

Primary Sources

Donaldson, Stephen R. 1983. *The One Tree. The Second Chronicles of Thomas Covenant.* New York: Ballantine Books. Print.
_____. 1983. *White Gold Wielder. The Second Chronicles of Thomas Covenant.* Glasgow: Fontana/Collins. Print.
_____. 1985. *The Wounded Land. The Second Chronicles of Thomas Covenant.* Glasgow: Fontana/Collins. Print.
_____. 1996. *The Chronicles of Thomas Covenant, The Unbeliever* (*Lord Foul's Bane, The Illearth War, Power That Preserves*). London: *Voyager*, imprint of HarperCollins Publishers. Print.
_____. 2005. *The Runes of the Earth. The Last Chronicles of Thomas Covenant.* London: Gollancz. Print.
_____. 2007. *Fatal Revenant. The Last Chronicles of Thomas Covenant.* London: Gollancz. Print.
_____. 2010. *Against All Things Ending. The Last Chronicles of Thomas Covenant.* London: Gollancz. Print.
_____. 2013. *The Last Dark. The Last Chronicles of Thomas Covenant.* New York: Putnam Adult. Kindle file.
Friedman, C.S. 1991. *Black Sun Rising.* New York: DAW Books. Print.
_____. 1994. *When True Night Falls.* New York: DAW Books. Print.
_____. 1996. *Crown of Shadows.* New York: DAW Books. Print.
_____. 2011. *Dominion. A Coldfire Saga.* Electronic file.
Kay, Guy Gavriel. 2001. *The Summer Tree.* New York: Roc Trade. Print.
_____. 2001. *The Wandering Fire.* New York: Roc Trade. Print.
_____. 2001. *The Darkest Road.* New York: Roc Trade. Print.
Sanderson, Brandon. 2009. *Mistborn: The Final Empire.* London: Gollancz. Print.
_____. 2009. *The Well of Ascension. Book Two of Mistborn.* London: Gollancz. Print.
_____. 2010. *The Hero of Ages. Book Three of Mistborn.* London: Gollancz. Print.
_____. 2011. *The Alloy of Law: A Mistborn Novel.* London: Gollancz. Print.
_____. 2015. *Shadows of Self: A Mistborn Novel.* New York: Tor Books. Kindle file.
_____. 2016. *Mistborn: Secret History.* London: Gollancz. Kindle file.
_____. 2016. *The Bands of Mourning: A Mistborn Novel.* London: Gollancz. Print.
Zafón, Carlos Ruiz. 2010. *The Angel's Game.* London: Orion Publishing Group. Print.

Secondary Sources

Abanes, Richard. 2002. *Fantasy and Your Family: Exploring The Lord of the Rings, Harry Potter and Modern Magick.* Camp Hill: Christian Publications. Print.

"About Brandon." 2014. Brandonsanderson.com. Dragonsteel Entertainment. Site by Blumountain Media. Web. Retrieved: 22 Jan. 2018.
Aichele, George. 2006. *The Phantom Messiah: Postmodern Fantasy and the Gospel of Mark*. New York: T&T Clark International. Print.
Aichele, George, and Tina Pippin, eds. 1992. *Semeia 60: Fantasy and the Bible*. Atlanta: The Society of Biblical Literature. Print.
_____. 1997. *The Monstrous and the Unspeakable: The Bible as Fantastic Literature*. Sheffield: Sheffield Academic Press. Print.
_____. 1998. *Violence, Utopia, and the Kingdom of God: Fantasy and Ideology in the Bible*. London and New York: Routledge. Print.
"Annotations." 2014. Brandonsanderson.com. Dragonsteel Entertainment. Site by Blumountain Media. Web. Retrieved: 22 Jan. 2018.
"Ask Your Questions Here for C.S. Friedman." 2013. Fantasy Bookclub at Reddit.com. Site by Reddit Inc. Web. Retrieved: 22 Jan. 2018.
Armstrong, Karen. 2001. *The Battle for God*. New York: The Random House Publishing Group. Print.
_____. 2005. *A Short History of Myth*. Edinburgh: Canongate. Print.
Arthur, Sarah. 2005. *Walking with Bilbo: A Devotional Adventure Through The Hobbit*. Wheaton: Tyndale House Publishers. Print.
Attebery, Brian. 1980. *The Fantasy Tradition in American Literature: From Irving to Le Guin*. Bloomington: Indiana University Press. Print.
_____. 1992. *Strategies of Fantasy*. Bloomington: Indiana University Press. Print.
_____. 2007. "Exploding the Monomyth: Myth and Fantasy in a Postmodern World." In *Considering Fantasy: Ethical, Didactic and Therapeutic Aspects of Fantasy in Literature and Film*. Eds. Justyna Deszcz-Tryhubczak and Marek Oziewicz. Wrocław: Oficyna Wydawnicza ATUT, 207–220. Print.
_____. 2014. *Stories About Stories: Fantasy and the Remaking of Myth*. New York: Oxford University Press. Print.
Bainbridge, William Sims. 2013. *eGods: Faith Versus Fantasy in Computer Gaming*. Oxford: Oxford University Press. Print.
Barkley, Christine. 2009. *Stephen R. Donaldson and the Modern Epic Vision: A Critical Study of the "Chronicles of Thomas Covenant" Novels*. Critical Explorations in Science Fiction and Fantasy, vol. 17. Series editors: Donald E. Palumbo and C.W. Sullivan III. Jefferson, NC: McFarland. Print.
Batto, Bernard F. 1992. *Slaying the Dragon: Mythmaking in the Biblical Tradition*. Lousiville: Westminster/John Knox Press. Print.
Beal, Timothy K. 2002. *Religion and Its Monsters*. New York: Routledge. Print.
Boym, Svetlana. 2001. *The Future of Nostalgia*. New York: Basic Books. Print.
"Brandon Sanderson Answers Your Questions About *The Way of Kings*." 2014. Tor.com. 10 June. Site by Macmillan. Web. Retrieved: 22 Jan. 2018.
Brawley, Chris. 2014. *Nature and the Numinous in Mythopoeic Fantasy Literature*. Critical Explorations in Science Fiction and Fantasy, vol. 46. Series editors: Donald E. Palumbo and C.W. Sullivan III. Jefferson, NC: McFarland. Kindle file.
Brekus, Catherine A., and W. Clark Gilpin. 2011. *American Christianities: A History of Dominance and Diversity*. Chapel Hill: University of North Carolina Press. Print.
Brooke, Elise. 1977. *Theology and Fantasy*. Butler: Clergy Book Service. Print.
Bruner, Kurt, and Jim Ware. 2001. *Finding God in The Lord of the Rings*. Wheaton: Tyndale House Publishers. Print.
_____. 2007. *Shedding Light on His Dark Materials*. Wheaton: SaltRiver, imprint of Tyndale House Publishers. Print.
Buswell, Robert E., Jr., ed. 2003. *Encyclopedia of Buddhism*. 2 vols. New York: Gale. Print.
Campbell, Joseph. 1991. *The Power of Myth with Bill Moyers*. Ed. Betty Sue Flowers. New York: Anchor Books. Print.
_____. 2004. *The Hero with a Thousand Faces*. Princeton: Princeton University Press. Print.

Carpenter, Humphrey. 1995. *J.R.R. Tolkien: A Biography*. London: HarperCollinsPublishers. Print.
Chidester, David. 2000. *Christianity: A Global History*. New York: HarperOne. Print.
Clute, John, and John Grant, eds. 1997. *The Encyclopedia of Fantasy*. London: Orbit. Print.
Cotterell, Arthur. 2006. *The Encyclopedia of Mythology: Norse, Classical, Celtic*. London: Hermes House. Print.
Cox, James L. 2010. *An Introduction to the Phenomenology of Religion*. London: Continuum. Print.
Dalton, Russell W. 2003. *Faith Journey Through Fantasy Lands: A Christian Dialogue with Harry Potter, Star Wars, and The Lord of the Rings*. Minneapolis: Augsburg Books. Print.
Daly, Kathleen N., and Marian Rengel. 2010. *Norse Mythology A to Z*. 3d edition. New York: Chelsea House. Print.
Detweiler, Robert and David Jasper, eds. 2000. *Religion and Literature: A Reader*. Louisville: Westminster/John Knox Press. Print.
Dickerson, Matthew and David O'Hara. 2006. *From Homer to Harry Potter: A Handbook on Myth and Fantasy*. Grand Rapids: BrazosPress. Print.
Doniger, Wendy, ed. 2006. *Britannica: Encyclopedia of World Religions*. Chicago: Encyclopædia Britannica. Print.
Eason, Cassandra. 2008. *Fabulous Creatures, Mythical Monsters, and Animal Power Symbols: A Handbook*. Westport, CT: Greenwood. Print.
Eliade, Mircea. 1959. *The Sacred and the Profane: The Nature of Religion*. Trans. Willard R. Trask. New York: Harcourt, Brace & World. Print.
_____. 1961. *Images and Symbols: Studies in Religious Symbolism*. Trans. Philip Mairet. London: Harvill Press. Print.
_____. 1996. *Patterns in Comparative Religion*. Trans. Rosemary Sheed. Lincoln and London: University of Nebraska Press. Print.
Fedler, Kyle D. 2006. *Exploring Christian Ethics: Biblical Foundations for Morality*. Louisville: Westminster John Knox Press. Print.
Feldt, Laura. 2012. *The Fantastic in Religious Narrative from Exodus to Elisha*. Sheffield: Equinox. Print.
Friedman, C.S. 1995. "The Coldfire Trilogy: Author's Notes." Csfriedman.com. 2 Jan. Web. Retrieved: 22 Jan. 2018.
Frye, Northrop. 1982. *The Great Code: The Bible and Literature*. London: Routledge & Kegan Paul. Print.
Gates, Pamela S., Susan B. Steffel and Francis J. Molson. 2003. *Fantasy Literature for Children and Young Adults*. Lanham, MD: Scarecrow. Print.
The Geek's Guide to the Galaxy. 2013. "Interview: Brandon Sanderson." *Lightspeed Magazine*. April. Web. Retrieved: 22 Jan. 2018.
"Gradual Interview." Stephendonaldson.com. Web. Retrieved: 22 Jan. 2018.
Hawthorne, Nathaniel. 2006. "Preface." *The Marble Faun*. Eldritch Press. Web. Retrieved: 12 July 2016.
Hein, Rolland. 2002. *Christian Mythmakers*. 2d edition. Chicago: Congress Press Chicago. Print.
Hick, John. 1995. *A Christian Theology of Religions: The Rainbow of Faiths*. Louisville: Westminster John Knox Press. Print.
"An Interview with Richard Marcus." 2002. Brightweavings.com. Site by Deborah Meghnagi. Web. Retrieved: 22 Jan. 2018.
"Interview with Solaris." 1995. Jean-Louis Trudel. Brightweavings.com. Site by Deborah Meghnagi. Web. Retrieved: 22 Jan. 2018.
Irwin, W.R. 1976. *The Game of the Impossible: A Rhetoric of Fantasy*. Chicago: University of Illinois Press. Print.
Ivison, Douglas, ed. 2002. *Canadian Fantasy and Science-Fiction Writers: Dictionary of Literary Biography*. Vol. 251. Detroit: A Bruccoli Clark Layman Book. Print.
James, Edward, and Farah Mendlesohn, eds. 2012. *The Cambridge Companion to Fantasy Literature*. Cambridge: Cambridge University Press. Print.

Jenkins, Philip. 2011. *The Next Christendom: The Coming of Global Christianity.* 3d edition New York: Oxford University Press. Print.
Jonas, W. Glenn. 2010. *Christianity: A Biblical, Historical, and Theological Guide for Students.* Macon: Mercer University Press. Print.
Kay, Guy Gavriel. 2003. "The Fionavar Tapestry Afterword." Brightweavings.com. Site by Deborah Meghnagi. Web. Retrieved: 22 Jan. 2018.
Ketterer, David. 1992. *Canadian Science Fiction and Fantasy.* Bloomington: Indiana University Press. Print.
Kleiner, Elaine L. 1994. "Mircea Eliade's Theory of the Fantastic." In *Visions of the Fantastic: Selected Essays from the Fifteenth International Conference on the Fantastic in the Arts.* Ed. Allienne R. Becker. Westport, CT: Greenwood, 13–20. Print.
Łaba, Jolanta. 2010. *Idee religijne w literaturze fantasy: Studium fenomenologiczne* [*Religious Ideas in Fantasy Literature: A Phenomenological Study*]. Gdańsk: Gdański Klub Fantastyki. Print.
Łaszkiewicz, Weronika. 2013. "Finding God(s) in Fantasylands: Religious Ideas in Fantasy Literature." *Crossroads. A Journal of English Studies,* 1, 24–36. E-journal.
_____. 2014. "Phenomenology of Religion and the Study of Modern Fantasy Literature." *Acta Neophilologica,* 1, 179–189. Print.
_____. 2014. "Reinterpretacja chrześcijańskiego motywu ofiary i odrodzenia w cyklu *Fionavarski Gobelin* Guya Gavriela Kaya i *Trylogii Zimnego Ognia* Celii S. Friedman." In *Motywy religijne we współczesnej fantastyce* ["The Reinterpretation of the Christian Motif of Sacrifice and Rebirth in Guy Gavriel Kay's *Fionavar Tapestry* and Celia S. Friedman's *Coldfire Trilogy."* In *Religious Motifs in Contemporary Fantastic Literature*]. Eds. Mariusz M. Leś and Piotr Stasiewicz. Białystok: Wydawnictwo Uniwersytetu w Białymstoku, 215–226. Print.
_____. 2016. "Benevolent and Malevolent Creatures in Guy Gavriel Kay's *Fionavar Tapestry."* In *Imaginary Creatures in Medieval and Modern Fantasy Literature.* Ed. Łukasz Neubauer. Kraków: Libron, 69–83. Print.
Le Guin, Ursula K. 1993. "Why Are Americans Afraid of Dragons?" In *The Language of the Night: Essays on Fantasy and Science Fiction.* Ursula K. Le Guin. New York: HarperPerennial, 34–40. Print.
Lindow, John. 2002. *Norse Mythology: A Guide to the Gods, Heroes, Rituals, and Beliefs.* New York: Oxford University Press. Print.
Lovin, Robert W. 2011. *An Introduction to Christian Ethics: Goals, Duties, and Virtues.* Nashville: Abingdon Press. Print.
Manlove, Colin. 1992. *Christian Fantasy: From 1200 to the Present.* Notre Dame: University of Notre Dame Press. Print.
Mathews, Richard. 2002. *Fantasy: The Liberation of Imagination.* New York: Routledge. Print.
Matson, Gienna, and Jeremy Roberts. 2010. *Celtic Mythology A to Z.* 2nd edition. New York: Chelsea House. Print.
McAvan, Emily. 2012. *The Postmodern Sacred: Popular Culture Spirituality in the Science Fiction, Fantasy and Urban Fantasy Genres.* Jefferson, NC: McFarland. Print.
McGrath, Alister E. 2006. *Christianity: An Introduction.* 2d edition. Malden: Blackwell Publishing. Print.
Mendlesohn, Farah. 2008. *Rhetorics of Fantasy.* Middletown, Connecticut: Wesleyan University Press. Print.
Mills, Christopher. 2009. *The Holy Bible & Mormonism: Understanding the Mormon Faith.* Salt Lake City: Millennial Mind Publishing. Kindle edition.
Monaghan, Patricia. 2004. *The Encyclopedia of Celtic Mythology and Folklore.* New York: Facts on File. Print.
Morris, Nathan. 2009. "Brandon Sanderson." *Mormon Artist.* March. Web. Retrieved: 22 Jan. 2018.
New, W.H. 2003. *A History of Canadian Literature.* 2d edition. Montreal & Kingston: McGill-Queen's University Press. Print.

New World Translation of the Holy Scriptures. 1984. Rendered by the New World Bible Translation Committee. New York: Watchtower Bible and Tract Society of New York, Inc. and International Bible Students Association. Print.
Otto, Rudolf. 1923. *The Idea of the Holy: An Inquiry into the Non-Rational Factor in the Idea of the Divine and Its Relation to the Rational*. Trans. John W. Harvey. London: Oxford University Press. Print.
Ouellette, Richard D. 2002. "*Christianity: A Global History* David Chidester; *A World History of Christianity* Adrian Hastings, ed.; *The Next Christendom: The Coming of Global Christianity* Philip Jenkins." *BYU Studies Quarterly*, vol. 41, no. 4, 129–144. Print.
Oziewicz, Marek. 2008. *One Earth, One People: The Mythopoeic Fantasy Series of Ursula K. Le Guin, Lloyd Alexander, Madeleine L'Engle and Orson Scott Card*. Critical Explorations in Science Fiction and Fantasy, vol. 6. Series editors: Donald E. Palumbo and C.W. Sullivan III. Jefferson, NC: McFarland. Print.
Partridge, Christopher. 2005. *The Re-Enchantment of the West: Alternative Spiritualities, Sacralization, Popular Culture, and Occulture*. Vol. 2. London: T & T Clark. Print.
Pas, Julian F. 2006. *The A to Z of Taoism*. The A to Z Guide Series, No. 13. Lanham: The Scarecrow. Print.
Rabkin, Eric S., ed. 1979. *Fantastic Worlds: Myths, Tales, and Stories*. Oxford: Oxford University Press. Print.
Ryken, Leland, James C. Wilhoit and Tremper Longman III, eds. 1998. *Dictionary of Biblical Imagery*. Downers Grove: IVP Academic. Print.
Senior, W.A. 1990. "The Significance of Names: Mythopoesis in 'The First Chronicles of Thomas Covenant.'" *Extrapolation*, vol. 31, no. 3. Kent: Kent State University Press, 258–269. Print.
_____. 1995. *Variations on The Fantasy Tradition: Stephen R. Donaldson's Chronicles of Thomas Covenant*. Kent: Kent State University Press. Print.
Sill, Gertrude Grace. 1975. *A Handbook of Symbols in Christian Art*. London: Cassell. Print.
Simons, Kate. 2010. *The Leprous Man: A Psychoanalytical Investigation into Stephen Donaldson's Fantasy Novels*. Oxford: Peter Lang. Print.
Stableford, Brian. 2005. *Historical Dictionary of Fantasy Literature*. Lanham: The Scarecrow. Print.
Steffler, Alva William. 2002. *Symbols of the Christian Faith*. Grand Rapids: William B. Eerdmans Publishing Company. Print.
Summit, Margaret. 2007. *Catholic Literature: An Introduction*. Arcadia: Tumblar House. Print.
Szerszynski, Bronislaw. 2005. *Nature, Technology and the Sacred*. Oxford: Blackwell Publishing. Print.
Timmerman, John. H. 1983. *Other Worlds: The Fantasy Genre*. Bowling Green: Bowling Green University Popular Press. Print.
Todorov, Tzvetan. 1980. *The Fantastic: A Structural Approach to a Literary Genre*. Trans. Richard Howard. Ithaca: Cornell University Press. Print.
Tolkien, J.R.R. 1988. *Tree and Leaf*. London: Unwin Hyman. Print.
Traill, Catherine Parr. 2004. *The Backwoods of Canada*. Project Gutenberg, Electronic file.
Trocha, Bogdan. 2009. *Degradacja mitu w literaturze fantasy* [*The Degradation of Myth in Fantasy Literature*]. Zielona Góra: Oficyna Wydawnicza Uniwersytetu Zielonogórskiego. Print.
Tuttle, Lisa. 2005. *Writing Fantasy and Science Fiction*. London: A & C Black. Print.
van der Leeuw, Gerardus. 1967. *Religion in Essence and Manifestation*. Vols. 1 & 2. Trans. J.E. Turner. Gloucester: Peter Smith. Print.
Ward, Kaari, et al., eds. 1991. *Reader's Digest Illustrated Guide to the Bible*. Pleasantville: Reader's Digest Association. Print.
Weiss, Allan, ed. 2015. *The Canadian Fantastic in Focus: New Perspectives*. Jefferson, NC: McFarland. Print.
Wicher, Andrzej. 2013. *Selected Medieval and Religious Themes in the Works of C.S. Lewis and J.R.R. Tolkien*. Łódź: Łódzkie Towarzystwo Naukowe. Print.

Wogaman, J. Philip. 2011. *Christian Ethics: A Historical Introduction.* Louisville: Westminster John Knox Press. Print.

Woodhead, Linda. 2004. *Christianity: A Very Short Introduction.* Oxford: Oxford University Press. Print.

Works Consulted

Bushman, Richard Lyman. 2008. *Mormonism: A Very Short Introduction.* Oxford: Oxford University Press. Print.

D'Ammassa, Don. 2006. *Encyclopedia of Fantasy and Horror Fiction.* New York: Facts On File. Print.

Frye, Northrop. 1976. *The Secular Scripture: A Study of the Structure of Romance.* London: Harvard University Press. Print.

Gorden, Kurt van. 1995. *Mormonism.* Series ed. Alan W. Gomes. Grand Rapids: Zondervan. Print.

Hume, Kathryn. 1984. *Fantasy and Mimesis: Responses to Reality in Western Literature.* New York: Methuen. Print.

Manlove, C.N. 1983. *The Impulse of Fantasy Literature.* London: Macmillan Press. Print.

Oramus, Dominika. 2011. *Imiona Boga: Motywy metafizyczne w fantastyce drugiej połowy XX wieku* [*The Names of God: Metaphysical Motifs in Fantastic Literature of the Second Half of the 20th Century*]. Kraków: Universitas. Print.

Oswalt, John N. 2009. *The Bible Among the Myths: Unique Revelation or Just Ancient Literature?* Grand Rapids: Zondervan. Print.

Reilly, Robert, ed. 1985. *The Transcendent Adventure: Studies of Religion in Science Fiction/Fantasy.* Westport, CT: Greenwood. Print.

Schlobin, Roger C., ed. 1982. *The Aesthetics of Fantasy Literature and Art.* Notre Dame: University of Notre Dame Press. Print.

Shipps, Jan. 1987. *Mormonism: The Story of a New Religious Tradition.* Urbana: University of Illinois Press. Print.

Index

Abanes, Richard 53
Aichele, George 43–44, 45, 54, 198
Alexander, Lloyd 18, 29
Alighieri, Dante 10, 13, 18, 45
American fantasy 15–19
Anderson, Poul 54
Anglicanism 4, 147, 150
animism 105, 139
Anthony, Piers 18
Aquinas, Thomas 182
Armstrong, Karen 30, 197
Arthur, Sarah 49, 50, 200n20
Asimov, Isaac 149
Attebery, Brian 5, 10–11, 14–15, 18, 25, 27–29, 32, 134, 198, 199n2
Atwood, Margaret 22
Augustine of Hippo 100–101, 132, 148, 182

Bael, Timothy K. 40
Bainbridge, William Sims 204n1
Bakker, R. Scott 23
Barker, Clive 54
Barkley, Christine 66
Batto, Bernard F. 30
Baum, L. Frank 15–17; *The Wonderful Wizard of Oz* 19
Beagle, Peter S. 18, 39
Beowulf 18, 45
the Bible 1, 3, 5–7, 30–32, 43–46, 49, 50, 55, 79–80, 83, 90, 91, 93, 99, 100, 102, 129, 130, 146, 160, 182, 189, 195, 198; *see also* the New Testament; the Old Testament
Bird, Isobel 53
Blake, William 43, 45
Borges, Jorge Luis 197
Boym, Svetlana 32
Bradbury, Ray 17
Brawley, Chris 6, 33, 38
Brekus, Catherine A. 7
British fantasy 14–15
Brooke, Elise 46, 198

Brooks, Terry 18
Bruner, Kurt 49, 50, 52, 54
Buddhism 124–125, 146, 191, 192
Bugnet, Georges 22
Bunyan, John 13, 45
Burroughs, Edgar Rice 15, 17
Buswell, Robert E., Jr. 125

Cabell, James Branch 16, 17
Calvino, Italo 197
Campbell, Joseph 5, 25, 27–28, 31–32, 47, 199n6
Canadian fantasy 19–24
Card, Orson Scott 29, 203n9
Carroll, Lewis 14; *Alice's Adventures in Wonderland* 21
Carter, Angela 197
Catholicism 4, 7, 31, 46, 47, 54, 132, 147, 150, 161, 189
Chambers, Robert W. 16
Chesterton, G.K. 13
Chidester, David 7
Christian fantasy 13, 45
Christ (Jesus) 7, 27, 31, 34, 44, 47, 48, 49, 50, 51, 52, 80–82, 84, 90–92, 95–97, 99, 101–102, 105, 128, 132, 147, 154–157, 162, 164, 181, 183, 184–188, 189, 192, 195, 200n21, 200n22, 201n8
The Chronicles of Thomas Covenant 1, 4–6, 54, 57–106, 108, 110–111, 114, 134, 135, 137, 140, 145, 192, 194
The Church of Jesus Christ of Latter-Day Saints 7, 181, 189–190, 191–192, 195
Clute, John 12, 13, 108
The Coldfire Trilogy 1, 4–6, 54, 136–163, 166, 192, 195
Collodi, Carlo 10
Colombo, John Robert 22
Cook, Glen 18
Cotterell, Arthur 91, 126, 200n4
Cox, James L. 33, 40–41, 199n10, 199n13
Crowley, John 10, 13

211

Dalton, Russell W. 8, 50, 128, 200n21
Daly, Kathleen N. 125, 126
de Gaspé, Philippe Ignace François Aubert 22
deism 66
de Lint, Charles 23–24, 54
de Mille, James 22
Derleth, August 17
Detweiler, Robert 43
Dickens, Charles 10
Dickerson, Matthew 8, 31, 45, 52, 53, 137, 198
Dickson, Gordon S. 20
Donaldson, Stephen R. 1, 4, 18, 29, 57–106, 123, 127, 163, 194, 197, 200n1, 201n5; see also *The Chronicles of Thomas Covenant*
Duncan, Dave 23
Dunsany, Lord 11, 14

Eason, Cassandra 91, 126
Eastern Orthodox Church 147, 150
Eddings, David 18
Eddings, Leigh 18
Eliade, Mircea 5–6, 25–26, 36–38, 39, 61, 70, 75, 76, 200n17
The Epic of Gilgamesh 10, 96
epoché 35, 40–42, 55
Erikson, Steven 23
Ewing, Lynne 53

Fedler, Kyle D. 101
Feist, Raymond E. 18
Feldt, Laura 44–45, 54
Findley, Timothy 22
The Fionavar Tapestry 1, 4–6, 22, 54, 107–135, 137, 140, 145, 166, 192, 194–195
Friedman, Celia S. 1, 4, 29, 136–163, 194, 197; see also *The Coldfire Trilogy*
Frye, Northrop 43

Gaiman, Neil 13
García Márquez, Gabriel 10
Gibson, Eva Katharine 15
Gibson, William 20, 22
Gilman, Charlotte Perkins 15
Gilpin, W. Clark 7
Goodkind, Terry 18
Gotlieb, Phyllis 21
Grant, John 12, 13, 108

Haggard, H. Rider 14
Hawthorne, Nathaniel 21, 44
Hébert, Anne 22
Hein, Roland 46
Hick, John 134–135
high/epic fantasy 4, 5, 12–14, 18, 19, 23, 28, 29, 137
Holdstock, Robert 54
Homer 10, 18; *The Odyssey* 11
Hopkinson, Nalo 23
Howard, Robert E. 10, 12, 15–17, 39

Huff, Tanya 23
Husserl, Edmund 42, 199n10
Ingarden, Roman 42

Irwin, W.R. 10
Islam 146
Ivison, Douglas 19–20, 22, 24, 108, 199n4

Jackson, Peter 18
James, Edward 13
James, Henry 15
Jasper, David 43
Jenkins, Philip 7
Jesus see Christ (Jesus)
Johansen, K.V. 23
Jonas, W. Glenn 87, 88, 97, 131, 132, 151
Jordan, Robert 18, 28, 164
Judaism 132, 161–162, 192
Jung, Carl Gustav 10

Kabbalah 181, 189, 192
Kalevala 10, 18
Kant, Immanuel 134
Kay, Guy Gavriel 1, 4, 19, 29, 107–135, 163, 194, 197, 199n3, 202n10, 202n11; see also *The Fionavar Tapestry*
Ketterer, David 20–22, 199n4
Kincaid, Paul 16–17, 199n2
Kingsley, Charles 46

Łaba, Jolanta 6, 33, 38–40
Leacock, Stephen 22
Le Guin, Ursula K. 18, 19, 29, 38, 39; *Earthsea* 5, 28
L'Engle, Madeleine 18, 29
Lewis, C.S. 1, 4, 6, 13, 29, 31, 38–39, 42, 46, 49, 53, 54, 137, 200n19; *The Chronicles of Narnia* 3, 8, 15, 50–51, 198
Lindow, John 125
London, Jack 15
Lovecraft, H.P. 16–17
Lovin, Robert W. 160, 182

Mabinogion 10, 18
MacDonald, George 11, 14, 15, 18, 46
MacEwen, Gwendolyn 22
Manlove, Colin 13, 43–45, 54
Marlowe, Christopher 45
Martin, George R.R. 18, 54
Mathews, Richard 9, 10, 14
Matson, Gienna 125, 126
McAvan, Emily 196–197
McGrath, Alister E. 97, 100–101, 127, 132, 148, 182, 194
McKillip, Patricia 18
Mendlesohn, Farah 12–15, 199n1
Merril, Judith 22
Merritt, A. (Abraham) 16
Meyer, Stephenie 19
Mills, Christopher 189, 190

Milton, John 10, 13, 45, 85
the *Mistborn* series 1, 4–6, 54, 164–193, 195
Monaghan, Patricia 126
monomyth 5, 27–28
the Mormon Church *see* The Church of Jesus Christ of Latter-Day Saints
Morris, Nathan 191, 203n10
Morris, William 11, 14, 18
Morrow, James 13
Moyers, Bill 31
myth 5, 14, 24–32, 37–40, 90–91, 125–126, 134, 197–198
mythopoeic fantasy 29, 38, 197, 199n7

New, W.H. 20
the New Testament 7, 34, 44, 79, 81–82, 89, 91–93, 100, 126, 129, 134, 154, 156–158, 162, 183–185, 195, 201n9
Nibelungenlied 10
Norton, Andre 10, 11, 18, 39

O'Hagan, Howard 22
O'Hara, David 8, 31, 45, 52, 53, 137, 198
the Old Testament 7, 34, 44, 79–82, 89, 91–93, 98, 100, 126–127, 130, 134, 146, 147, 154, 156–158, 162, 168, 183, 195, 201n9
Otto, Rudolf 5, 25–26, 33–35, 37–39, 48, 61, 63–65, 71, 73, 99, 102, 111, 113, 138, 167–168, 176, 177, 187
Oullette, Richard D. 189
Oziewicz, Marek 5, 25, 29, 32, 197

Paolini, Christopher 18
paranormal romance *see* supernatural romance
Partridge, Christopher 197
Pas, Julian F. 124
Pearl 45
Pelagius 101, 132
phenomenology of religion 1, 5–6, 32–42, 61, 108, 137, 166, 198
Pippin, Tina 44–45, 54, 198
Protestantism 4, 7, 147, 150, 189
Pullman, Philip 1, 4, 6, 42, 46, 53–54, 200n22; *His Dark Materials* 3, 8, 51–52, 198

Rabkin, Eric S. 25, 47
religious fantasy 13
Rengel, Marian 125, 126
Roberts, Sir Charles D.G. 22
Roberts, Jeremy 125, 126
Rowling, J.K. 1, 4, 6, 42, 46, 53–54; *Harry Potter* 3, 8, 52–53, 196
Ryken, Leland 80–82, 85–86, 89, 90, 92, 93, 97, 99, 128–130, 151, 154, 156, 183, 184

Sanderson, Brandon 1, 4, 18, 29, 164–193, 194, 197, 203n9; *see also* the *Mistborn* series
Senior, W.A. 58–59, 82

Sill, Gertrude Grace 80, 84, 91, 92, 97, 130
Simons, Kate 85
Sleight, Graham 13
Smith, James Thorne 16
speculative fiction 20, 21, 24
Spenser, Edmund 10, 45
Stableford, Brian 12, 13
Star Wars 8
Steffler, Alva William 84, 92, 93, 129, 130, 154, 184
Stoker, Bram 14
Sturluson, Snorri 45
sub-creation 31, 47
Summitt, Margaret 47
supernatural romance 19
sword and sorcery fantasy 16, 39
Szerszynski, Bronislaw 196

Taoism 124, 182
Tardivel, Jean-Paul 22
Taylor, G.P. 13
Thurber, James 17
Tiernan, Cate 53
Timmerman, John H. 12, 199n1
Todorov, Tzvetan 43–44
Tolkien, J.R.R. 1, 4–6, 11, 29, 31, 38, 39, 42, 46–48, 51, 53–54, 107, 119, 199n3; *The Hobbit* 10, 15, 49; "Leaf by Niggle" 46, 47–48; *The Lord of the Rings* 3, 5, 8, 13, 15, 18, 21, 28, 49–50, 196, 198; "Mythopoeia" 46, 48–49, 200n19; "On Fairy-Stories" 46–47, 200n19; *The Silmarillion* 48–49, 107, 119
Traill, Catharine Parr 21
Trocha, Bogdan 5, 6, 25–27, 29, 32, 33, 38, 198, 199n5
Tuttle, Lisa 12, 13, 14, 199n1
Twain, Mark 201n7

urban fantasy 19, 23, 24

Vance, Jack 54
van der Leeuw, Gerardus 5, 25, 33, 35–38, 61

Ward, Kaari 82–85, 90–92, 97, 127, 128, 184, 186
Ware, Jim 49, 50, 52, 54
weird fiction 16
Weiss, Allan 20, 22, 199n4
White, T.H. 15
Wicher, Andrzej 51
Williams, Charles 46
Williams, Tad 18
Wogaman, J. Philip 100
Wolfe, Gene 13
Woodhead, Linda 182, 185

Zafón, Carlos Ruiz 32, 199n9
Zelazny, Roger 18, 39
Zipes, Jack 44, 198

www.ingramcontent.com/pod-product-compliance
Lightning Source LLC
Chambersburg PA
CBHW032054300426
44116CB00007B/734